PERILOUS PATH

*Surviving Wars, Famines, and Embargos Motivated
by the Power of Faith, Love, and Human Solidarity*

Ari Barzanji

ISBN 978-1-63525-110-4 (Paperback)
ISBN 978-1-68197-866-6 (Hard Cover)
ISBN 978-1-68197-867-3 (Digital)

Photos courtesy of Saman, M.; Ranj, A.; and Frotah, M.

Recitations and quotes are made exclusively from author's memory unless indicated otherwise.

Christian Faith Publishing, Inc.
296 Chestnut Street
Meadville, PA 16335
www.christianfaithpublishing.com

Printed in the United States of America

Contents

Part 2—Coming to America

Acknowledgment

To my American friends I owe my life. I thank you all for supporting and encouraging me to write this book. You changed my life and belief system, and for that I am thankful to you all until eternity.

Foreword

The stories that you are about to read have been told to us many times since we met the author soon after his arrival in the US. Yet, however often his stories are repeated, they never cease to be remarkable. For many years, as his friend, I urged him to write an account of these events but he was hesitant. He doubted that the story was worthy of general interest or that he had the skills necessary to write in English. Now after many requests from hundreds of people whom he has met through his work as a professional speaker and teacher, he has at last documented his life in Iraq and the events that led to his escape to America.

You are about to embark on a remarkable journey. Through the author's eyes, you will see war-torn Iraq firsthand, experience fleeing into the mountains as a refugee, and learn about the culture and religion of the Middle East from the inside. You will imagine the taste of food gratefully devoured after days of starvation. You will be impressed by the beauty and power of a landscape both breathtaking and cruel. You will hear the lilt of foreign tongues expressing emotion and beliefs framed in a culture that stresses politeness to an extreme, while excusing practices that sound barbaric to Western ears. You will learn of the hardship, tragedy, strength, miracles, and quest for truth that define the life of a man thrust unwillingly into situations beyond his control, yet determined and in love with life. You will be both humbled and uplifted.

This book is not ghostwritten, but is the author's own work, told in his own words and style. In spite of my familiarity with the oral version of these stories, I found it to be a fascinating book, with a power of its own. I trust that you will do the same. It is not like any other that you have read. This is a book that you will want to read more than once, and a story that you will never forget.

Stacey

Preface

The mountains of Kurdistan in northern Iraq stand as they have stood since the dawn of history, vast and unchanging. The drama of human civilization has unfolded at their feet. Silent, ancient, unmoving and unmoved, they have witnessed life and death, hope and tragedy, glory and shame. Without alteration, they endure.

I was born in the shadow of those mountains, born into a culture rife with conflict, war, and inconsistency. Yet even as a child, I found no home in my surroundings. My heart yearned for peace and freedom, concepts as elusive to my culture as the wisp of mist playing on the mountaintops. Inexplicably, I dreamed of a different life, but without hope of ever finding it. It was as unthinkable as the movement of a mountain…

This is the story of my journey from despair to hope, from oppression to freedom. It is an impossible story. If I had not lived it, I'm not sure I would believe it myself. I share it so that others might also dare to have faith, for I now truly know that faith can move mountains.

Ari Barzanji
Los Angeles, California

Introduction

Los Angeles, California

It has been many years since I left the region of Iraqi Kurdistan. I now call Los Angeles my home.

It is one of those Southern California weekends, warm and sunny, perfect for a beach walk or perhaps a dip in the waters of the Pacific.

"Hey, you want to go to the beach?" I enthusiastically asked Suha, my niece.

A senior in high school, Suha and her blonde friend Cassi readily agree to a stroll over the light sands of Malibu. We packed some beach towels, Frisbees, a rocket football, and bottles of water and headed out to Malibu and the Santa Monica pier.

Living on the West Coast the past few years has included everything that constitutes a carefree, relaxed life.

The diverse nature of California astonishes me. On one hand, the mountains, the valleys, and the rivers remind me of my birth country. The sequoia trees are as old as the pyramids of Egypt, and the snow is six feet deep in some areas around Lake Mammoth—only a hint of the beauty of nature in this country we call America.

On the other hand, the Pacific holds a special place in my heart thanks to Operation Pacific Haven, signed by Bill Clinton, wherein 3,500 Kurds with their families were relocated to Guam.

An American territory south of Japan, the tiny island of Guam became our makeshift home for the first three months of 1997.

As my car approached Malibu, the blue waters of the Pacific loomed in the distance. Beholding the broken waves against the rocky cliffs of Malibu reminded me of the dusky evening when our plane landed at Anderson Air Force Base in Guam. Suha, only six years old at the time, does not remember many details of our landing. Because of her curious nature however, she has asked me repeatedly over the course of the past few years to tell her the story of our transition to America.

In an attempt to avoid reigniting my feelings of resentment, I have eluded her questions thus far. Now that she has grown up, I feel I have a historic duty to explain what happened in those fateful days. I have written this book to document the events leading to this point, a document she can take in her hands to read for herself and show to her future children. As a result, generations to come might learn to value freedom, contentment, and perseverance. This story is about courage, love, hate, envy, deceit, faith, and miracles.[1]

---

[1] Some names, locations, and circumstances have been slightly changed or modified per requests and/ or to protect individual's privacy.

PART 1

Six Days and Six Nights

724 Days of Peace

The Iran-Iraq War ended on August 8, 1988. For the first time in eight years, the land witnessed peace. During the next two years in Iraq, we experienced tranquility. No more echoes of bombing, no shrieking sirens, no hiding in shelters, and no images of war on TV monitors. At last, Iraqis thought of something other than war and conflict.

Despite that, Saddam Hussein's face continued to monopolize TV screens, major streets, and roundabouts that one happened to drive past. The Baath regime, burdened by the heavy toll of an eight-year war against Iran and extremely low oil prices, reeled under financial pressure. Iraq, a secular socialist country, needed quick reform from socialism to partial capitalism by passing on some business transactions to the private sector. The government began advertising and encouraging private citizens to do commerce across borders, to import and export nonessential items. Meanwhile, they forced merchants to transact their trade in US dollars as the currency of choice. Merchants had to purchase dollars from the government.

Since no stock market existed, at least not officially, this encouraged the formation of the black market and with it an increase in prices and inflation. Every time a socialist government switches partially or totally to the private sector approach or capitalism, it always encourages an establishment of a black market. The black market determined the true value of goods, especially currencies, based on supply and demand.

The stability of the situation and the integrity of the government of Iraq was no exception to this rule. A hulking black market began trading dollars and imports chiefly controlled by Saddam's sons Udday and Qussay. The value of the Iraqi dinar took a nose-dive for the worse. Prices of commodities went up, and inflation was the subject of debate among commoners. People were obsessed with comparing the past to the current circumstances.

"Oh, alas for the long ago days when goods were cheap and easily available," said the shop owner near my apartment. "I do not understand. We are in a time of peace. Why are prices so high? How can a person sustain a family with one income when everything costs four to five times more?"

"It's called inflation and black market," I replied as I rummaged through his display of fruit. "Everything you buy and trade is going to be based on the price of the dollar. If the dollar is up, you have to pay more, and if it's down, you pay less."

"Remember when one Iraqi dinar equaled 3.3 dollars, in the happy old days?" the store owner sighed.

"What is it worth now?" I asked out of curiosity.

"I think it is over four dinars—one dollar is worth four dinars. 'Our homes are ruined,'" said the shopkeeper, quoting an expression of distress in Arabic.

"I am sorry to have to tell you, but it's only going to get worse. The dinar will never recover its value because the country is in such massive debt," I remarked.

"Oh well, Allah is bountiful. He will take care of us," the shopkeeper proclaimed

I bought my one grapefruit, paid him, and headed back to my apartment located in the Mansur quarters of Baghdad.

The end of the war did not just bring inflation and backdoor markets onto the scene. Another phenomenon also started emerging. Kuwaiti men legally crossed the border at Basra, entered Iraq with their fancy cars, and waved and flashed the purchasing power of their money against the Iraqi dinar. At this point, one Kuwaiti dinar was worth more than ten Iraqi dinars. In their white *dishdashas*, a traditional garment for Arabian desert dwellers, Kuwaitis walked around the streets of Baghdad visiting nightclubs and bars. They patronized prostitutes, bought real estate, and practiced temporary marriages with minor Iraqi girls, enticing them with large amounts of money. To them, the cost was only one-tenth, since the exchange rate was imbalanced between the currencies of the two neighboring countries. This mischief continued and grew between 1989 and 1990.

Meanwhile, behind the scenes, another conflict was perking and brewing between the governments of Iraq and Kuwait. The days of peace were in jeopardy.

Invasion of a Neighbor

August 2, 1990, was the 724th day of peace in Iraq. It was summer vacation. I was back in my city of Slemani in the region of Kurdistan, located in the northeastern part of Iraq. I had just graduated from University of Baghdad, College of Agriculture, and my friend Sallam and I had an appointment to meet downtown, just to hang out and catch up on things. He attended the College of Science at the University of Mosul and also just graduated this year. We had not had a chance to see one another during the school year. I missed my friend terribly. He was one friend I could talk to about anything and everything.

Around 10:00 a.m., I jumped out of the city bus that transported me from my brother's house to the downtown area. I was worried that I had been late to see Sallam, but as I was walking toward our meeting place, I saw him coming. The tradition of that culture demands that men hug and kiss the cheeks a few times, back and forth, right cheek and left cheek, and then again. In addition, men have no shame or limitations regarding innocent physical gestures of affection. Holding hands in public, for example, is a friendly gesture. However, if a man should hold a woman's hand in public, it might cost him taunts and derogatory comments from passersby.

"Hey, Ari, I've missed you!" shouted Sallam.

"I've missed you too," I responded.

We hugged and kissed perhaps ten times or more as we stood by a fence near the main street. In front of us was a barbershop. The owner, Mr. Raffeeq, was my barber; and I never trusted my hair to anyone else. As I waved hello to Mr. Raffeeq, he waved back. Soon, submerged in deep conversation, Sallam and I were in our own world. We were inquiring about each other's past few months when, unexpectedly, Mr. Raffeeq cranked up the volume of the radio in his shop so that it broadcasted into the street.

"*There has been a revolution in Kuwait. Brave military officers of the Kuwaiti army overthrew the corrupt leadership of Jabir Ahmad Al-Sabah, the ruler of Kuwait. Details will be broadcast later,*" Iraq's official news agency announced through the radio.

"I can't believe this! Why would Kuwaitis overthrow their government? They have a comfortable and luxurious lifestyle," said Sallam incredulously.

"Unbelievable." I shuddered. "It was Iran for eight years. Now it is Kuwait's turn."

Immediately, we went into Mr. Raffeeq's barbershop to listen to more details. As we made conversation about the breaking news, the announcer came back on.

"*This morning a few brave officers of the Kuwaiti army overthrew the corrupt leadership of Al-Sabah and contacted His Excellency Saddam Hussein, Allah preserve him,*[2] *calling for assistance. The officers asked His Excellency to send Iraqi army forces in an effort to secure the country. His Excellency immediately responded by sending a division of our brave Iraqi army into Kuwait City and successfully secured the capital,*" declared the announcer.

"Oh my god, they just took over Kuwait," said Mr. Raffeeq, laughing as he continued cutting the hair of a young boy, who sat still on the barber chair.

"He needs oil, more oil means more money, and how else is he going to pay for the war?"

"What a joke! Uprising in Kuwait?" I said sarcastically.

---

[2] It was mandatory that all Iraqi media personnel say this after mentioning Saddam's name.

Most people were glued to their radios and television sets that day to find out more about this alleged coup in Kuwait. Very few people in Kurdistan listened to Iraqi radio stations, for there just was not enough trust in the media. They repeated and broadcasted whatever their master Saddam and his regime commanded them. Instead, BBC and Radio Monte Carlo, the Arabic version, were some of the most trusted stations to tune in to among the Kurds.

During the eight-year war with Iran, Saddam's regime did everything it could to block and interfere with these two radio stations. The government feared common, everyday Iraqis hearing the true version of what was happening on the front with Iran, so they blocked BBC radio. During the eight-year war with Iran, Iraqi radio broadcasted that the army was triumphant, blamed Iran for wrongdoings, and consistently described them as losers. However, every peaceful gesture and good intention was credited to Saddam Hussein. The possibility of extracting truth from Iraqi newscasts was next to zero.

Attempts were ongoing to deceive the public and give the illusion that Kuwait was not overrun by Iraqi troops but that they called for help from Saddam and poor Saddam could not resist helping a neighbor. After all he was the "Knight of the Arab nations." By the end of that day, most of us understood and realized the truth: that Kuwait had been conquered by Iraq.

The information minister began a mammoth campaign of deception alleging that these brave Kuwaiti officers overthrew the old regime of Kuwait, asked for help from Saddam, and now were begging to join Iraq as one country. A short while later, Saddam reluctantly accepted the offer and announced that Kuwait was now part of Iraq.

For the next few weeks, the government put forth massive efforts in order to change the face and core of Kuwait and make it look like it belonged to Iraq. Physical addresses were altered to read "Kuwait City, Iraq." Vehicle license plates were removed and replaced with "Governorate of Kuwait, Iraq." Pictures and posters of Saddam arose high in streets and squares of Kuwait City. Every day, Iraqi TV displayed testimonials of supposedly happy Kuwaiti citizens expressing their gratefulness to Saddam their savior. The minister of education began printing forged historic documents providing "proof" that Kuwait had always been part of Iraq. The Iraqi government blamed the British empire and the West for ripping Kuwait from Iraq decades ago, citing the discovery of oil to be the reason. Meanwhile, the United Nations and the United States scrambled to find a solution for the Crisis of the Gulf, as analysts called it.

Saddam, for his part, kept foreign workers from different countries as hostages, claiming they were only guests of Iraq. Negotiators committed to the release of these foreigners poured into Iraq, a few Americans were in that category. I remember the boxer Mohammad Ali came to visit Iraq, and at this time, supposedly, Saddam released a few captives (guests) in his honor. Then came Jesse Jackson and a few other men of renown and notoriety followed suit in an attempt to release more hostages. However, Saddam did keep a substantial number of captives for various purposes. Some of them were even used as human shield as the American threat to bomb Iraq with a massive air assault escalated.

Saddam and his administration began distributing internees throughout the strategic targets, hoping that the Americans would not strike those locations.

Meanwhile, nations of the world met in New York, at the United Nations headquarters, and attempted to find a peaceful solution to the crisis. Peace efforts fell upon deaf ears as Saddam disregarded them and chose not to respond to any suggestions. With a majority of votes, the UN committee approved the creation of a multinational military force comprising thirty-three countries, including Arab nations such as Syria, Egypt, and Algeria, to dispatch troops to the border of Saudi Arabia with Kuwait. Under a banner of unity, the "coalition forces," with American leadership,[3] trod the desert sands of Arabia, half a million strong. As a precautionary step, coalition

[3]   Of the 956,600 troops, 700,000 were Americans, and were led by General H. Norman Schwarzkopf. (There are different figures, but the US is always shown as providing the majority of the troops.)

troops stood between Saddam and any subsequent advancement of his troops toward Saudi Arabia.

Three days after the invasion of Kuwait, the UN imposed a total embargo on Iraq under the term *UN sanctions*, disallowing international transactions with Iraq of any kind until Iraqi troops withdrew from Kuwait.

The sanctions imposed by the UN did not seem to have a bearing on our daily lives—at least not yet. Food and supplies were plentiful, as Iraqi troops had looted every Kuwaiti silo and storage unit. They hauled the looted items back to Iraq, giving the impression that all was well. Top government officials lined their pockets with stolen money from the banks of Kuwait. An estimated six billion dollars in cash were in Kuwaiti banks the day troops ran over the city. Billions of Kuwaiti dinars were stolen as well. However, the prince of Kuwait nullified the use of all Kuwaiti notes from his exile in Saudi Arabia, preventing Iraqis from using them to purchase more dollars. It was a shrewd move, to say the least.

As the months rolled on and December 1990 approached, the coalition forces around the Iraqi-Saudi Arabia border increased in numbers. Heavily armed with modern equipment and technology coming out of NATO and the US war machine, coalition troops, although not outnumbering the Iraqi troops, outbalanced them technologically. Saddam, however, was so arrogant and uninformed of the size and capabilities of these troops that he joked about it on TV.

I remember watching a TV interview by a French woman journalist with Saddam that, of course, was broadcasted over all Iraqi TV stations. She asked him, "How shall your troops deal with the stealth fighter planes? You know radar cannot detect them."

Saddam chuckled and said, "So what if radar can't detect them? A farmer can see the stealth, and that is our advanced warning system."

"Mr. President, aren't you worried a little about the technological advantage of the coalition forces over your army?" asked the journalist with a concerned look on her face.

"We have the fifth largest army in the world," replied Saddam. "I believe we will do well. Besides, we have Allah on our team."

At the end of the interview, the woman thanked Saddam for his time, she wished him luck and wisdom in the way he handled his affairs.

"I want to reiterate to the Iraqi people," said Saddam as he looked into the cameras. "Do not worry. You can place complete confidence in our leadership. We know what we are about and what we are doing. Your future will be filled with milk and honey. We are sitting on the world's largest oil reserve, and Allah blesses you."

The next day Sallam and I talked about the interview.

"I think this is good," I said. "This means he is not backing out of Kuwait and he will be facing the coalition forces. Maybe this will be Saddam's end."

"I know," replied Sallam. "We all should pray that he won't back out or back down. The Americans will take him out. George Bush is quite serious in his threats."

The UN and the coalition forces issued an ultimatum: Saddam Hussein must withdraw his troops by January 15, 1991, or else he would face the consequences. This was the essence of the ultimatum issued by the UN and repeated by George H. W. Bush several times over the course of the month leading to the coalition's attacks on Iraq.

December was a quiet month. However, things began to go from bad to worse, and finally, the effects of the sanctions began to show in our daily lives. Prices of supplies, food, and even local produce tripled overnight. The government began rationing electricity to only a few hours a night, and by the end of the year, we were in full blackout.

I think that deep in his mind, Saddam did not think that the coalition would execute the threats issued by the UN, NATO, and the United States. He was under the impression that the international community was bluffing and that after a few months or years the de facto annexation of Kuwait would be accepted.

Years later, I was informed that Saddam was also led astray because of the meeting he had had with April Glaspie, the US ambassador to Iraq at the time.[4]

As D-day approached, more Iraqi troops headed to the south. However, the most feared branch of service, Saddam's elite presidential guards, remained near to protect him. My town, and almost all of Kurdistan, was empty of Iraqi soldiers aside from a small force that guarded official buildings, military camps, and prisons. No major forces in the area were to be seen.

Behind the scenes, and in an attempt to reestablish the Kurdish revolution in Iraq, Kurdish political leaders geared up for a return. Jalal Talabani, secretary general of the Patriotic Union of Kurdistan (PUK), sent out messages to a select few to prepare for an all-out assault. In case the coalition forces destabilized Iraq, the Kurds were ready to revolt.

We anxiously awaited the deadline, January 15, 1990. Anything could happen, and anything was possible.

Yet nothing happened on January 15. The day came and went without major news. My friend Sallam and I were together most of the day. That evening we went to visit Saman, our mutual friend. We arrived at his house around dinnertime. Saman's mom had cooked dinner, and they invited us to stay. That is the way in our culture. If someone is visiting and it is near dinner or lunchtime, the hosts insist on having you stay and eat with them. It is an insult if one does not

---

4   Glaspie met with Saddam on July 25, 1990. Based on two versions of the transcripts of this event, one available at the George Bush Presidential Library and another at the Margret Thatcher Foundation posted online, Glaspie said a few things that Saddam took as a tacit approval from the US for what he was about to do. Glaspie is quoted as saying, "But we have no opinion on the Arab-Arab conflicts, like your border disagreement with Kuwait." This remark was posted in the *New York Times International*, September 23, 1990.* Saddam had good reason to believe her; after all, the US supported him most of the time during his conflict with Iran, as did France, Germany, and Russia. Saddam was confident that the US was not going to react militarily to the invasion of Kuwait, if it happened, and that nothing would ensue beyond a verbal reprimand or disapproval.

stay, unless you have an extremely convincing reason. It is polite to stay and share a meal with the host family.

As we were visiting with our hosts over a cup of sweet tea, the conversation veered toward war and its consequences.

"I am praying to Allah that Saddam will be toppled by the Americans," said Saman's mother. "Allah willing."

"Yeah, Auntie, then we can all celebrate and have a party," Sallam responded. (We usually called her Auntie or Saman's mother according to custom. It is considered impolite to address an older woman by her first name.)

"I don't know. This whole thing looks like a scam to me," said Saman in a pessimistic tone. "I'm not so sure they will really try to remove Saddam."

We three friends hung out under the light of lanterns and played charades. The visit turned into a sleepover as both Sallam and I spent the night. The next morning, after having breakfast, we parted. I had to go visit my brother Omid's family and check on his wife. She lived by herself these days. My brother, like many Iraqi men, had been drafted into the service. He was stationed on the border of Kuwait.

"I hope you are doing well. I am here to see if you need anything, heavy lifting, any tough work you need to be done," I asked Shna, my sister-in-law, half-jokingly.

"Oh, Ari, you have always been so gracious to me," said Shna. "By the way, the neighbor girl is asking about you." She teased me, a grin on her face. "I am okay so far. My brother was here yesterday and helped with a few things. I just hope Omid comes home quickly, even if he has to desert the army."

"I know. I do not understand why he would even consider serving in this system of government. I hope he will flee before it is too late," I agreed.

I lingered and had lunch with my sister-in-law and her two daughters, Sarah, five, and Rozha, three. The children were delighted to have an uncle with them. They usually hung all over me and requested to be lifted up high and thrown in the air. It was always enjoyable for me to take time to play with the girls.

In the evening, I decided to go visit my older brother and see how conditions were at his house. My elder brother Hemen worked as an auto mechanic in a large garage for one of my mom's relatives. He had been married for ten years at this point and had three children—a daughter and two sons. He came home that evening with an exasperated look on his face.

"I can tell you, business is not the way it used to be," said Hemen. "People are broke, no money to fix cars anymore. We stood around most of the day with not much to do. If things keep going this way, we will not have money to support our kids."

His wife and I could hear that he was frustrated.

"We'll see, Hemen. I have faith that things will change for the better once the Americans beat up on Saddam and make him either relinquish control or kill him and rid us of him forever," I proclaimed.

"I don't know. It is already the 15th. What are they waiting for? Why aren't they striking?" my brother wondered.

"Maybe it is the time difference. America is almost a day behind," I said jokingly.

That night, the sixteenth of January, I stayed at my brother's house. Around four o'clock in the morning of the seventeenth, my brother woke me.

"By Allah, they started it," he said. "Wake up."

"Started what?" I exclaimed as I rubbed my eyes, trying to wake up. "The raids have started?"

"Yes, BBC radio announced it," he said.

I was ecstatic, enthused beyond description. Finally, it was happening.

That morning I took the bus and went to my friend Sallam's house, and as I saw him leaving his home, I ran to him. We hugged and shook hands and shouted.

"This is it! It is the end! Saddam is done. They will smash him!" I said to Sallam.

My love for everything American increased on this day tenfold. I had always admired America and its history, and the freedom that Americans enjoyed fascinated me. I wished that my people had that kind of freedom, individuality, and the ability to express themselves.

Kurdistan, and specifically my city, has never experienced air raids. We would hear on the radio that Baghdad and the southern parts of Iraq witnessed massive amounts of coalition air strikes, but not a single jet fighter came toward our region. Strikes continued for the next month, the Iraqis were suffering huge losses.

Around February 24, my brother Omid suddenly showed up.

"Your brother is back, go see him," said my neighbor. "He is shook up a bit, but he is fine."

I did not hesitate to take the first public transportation to Sarchnar, a suburb of Slemani, where my brother and his family lived. My brother Omid and I hugged and kissed on the cheek for a long time. I had not seen him for over six months. Now, as we sat down, he started telling me about the battlefront.

"Oh, brother, those American airplanes were just harvesting everything in front of them," he marveled. "Our radar could do nothing to detect them. Anti-aircraft couldn't do much. There were just too many of them." He made an effort to describe the scene. "The highway that leads out of Kuwait toward Basra was littered with burned-up cars, trucks, tanks, dead soldiers…everything, just a big graveyard." He spoke in a fast pace. "It took me two days to get back here. I ran and jogged for ten miles until I finally caught a ride back to the town of Emarra. From there, I caught a ride to Baghdad, and from there back here."

We were aware that the ground assault had begun on February 22. News stations reported massive Iraqi losses and damaged infrastructure. The coalition fighter jets, smart bombs, and satellite-guided missiles hit almost every bridge and strategic location. The rockets were directed to where they wreaked havoc against Saddam's army. Ironically, the Americans, somehow, spared Saddam's Republican Guard, Iraq's elite fighting force.

It was clear that the regime had already lost the war. On February 15, before the beginning of the ground assault, George H. W. Bush made a compelling declaration, *"There is another way for the blood-shed to stop, and that is for the Iraqi military and the Iraqi people to take matters into their own hands and force Saddam Hussein, the dictator, to step aside and then comply with the UN resolutions and rejoin the family of peace-loving nations."*[5]

This announcement now resonated in the ears of the retreating and humiliated Iraqi soldiers attempting to escape the inferno of the American firepower. A young Shiia Iraqi officer took matters into his own hands after his retreating tank reached the city of Basra. The officer eyed a large portrait of Saddam in the city center, turned his tank around, aimed at the portrait, and fired a series of shells, smashing it to pieces. Thus, *the popular uprising* began from the south, largely led by Shiia, who had had enough after suffering from Saddam's brutality against them for the past twenty years.

---

[5]   February 15, 1991

The Popular Uprising

March 8, 1991, was a gloomy day. Rays of the sun hid behind a thick layer of clouds. The skies of Slemani city and the mountains seemed to be lifeless, deprived of energy, as if they begged for a glimpse of the spring sun. The inhabitants had no idea that the city of Raniyah, 150 miles north of Slemani, had become the gateway for the Kurdish uprising. Just two days ago, hundreds of scraggly Peshmarga fighters descended from the surrounding mountains into the center of Raniyah city. They faced minimal to almost no resistance from government troops. The uprising spread like wildfire in dry brush. Most residents of our neighborhood expected Slemani to be next and shootings to occur near us.

We were not disappointed. At around 10:00 a.m., distant gunshots could be heard. I was with Sallam, near his house, which was closer to the foot of Mount Goyzha. This mountain, located in the northeastern part of the city, is visible from anywhere in town. As we heard the gunshots, we saw a few men, holding on to their headscarves, run toward Goyzha.

"I wonder where they are running to," I said.

"Or running from," Sallam remarked.

As I lifted my gaze and looked upon the mountain, there, in the distance, tiny figures moved. They descended toward town. I concentrated my gaze a bit harder, and to my bewilderment, they were men coming down the slope of the mountain.

"Oh my lord, look Sallam! It is the Peshmarga,[6] and they are coming to Slemani," I shouted.

We jumped up and down, shouting, "*Bizhy* Peshmarga! (Long live the Peshmarga.)"

Curious, neighbors stuck their heads out of their homes and stared at us.

My friend and I had just witnessed a historic event that might never be repeated again: the Peshmarga descending on the city of Slemani. Soon, they would liberate her from the control of Saddam's regime and all his symbols of authoritarianism, racism, and control of our nation. An exhilarating feeling of joy, pride, and justice overwhelmed me.

How lucky were we to see this! Thousands of men, women, and children died for the sake of a moment such as this, yet they never had a chance to witness it. We were euphoric about the spectacle until a minivan interrupted our elation. The minivan drove through the neighborhoods broadcasting, "*Attention, my noble Kurdish brothers and sisters. Our gallant and champion Peshmarga forces are going to sweep from the city any traces of the Baathists and Saddam's mercenaries. We strongly recommend that you not carry any weapons! Stay home and secure your doors. Let our fighting forces eradicate every bit of the Saddamists and the Baathists who oppressed us for decades.*"

"Awesome! That means you are stuck with me here in our house," Sallam shouted.

His mom came out and invited me to stay. "I think it is too dangerous to go back to Sarchnar," she said. "Just stay here with Sallam and wait until things clear up."

Echoes of explosions and gunfire filled the quietness for the rest of that day. The massacre of Saddam's agents continued until late and on throughout the night. The next morning, although reverberations of gunfire could be heard, it was sporadic.

By noon, the minivan drove through the neighborhood again, this time announcing exceedingly good news.

---

6   *Peshmarga* is a Kurdish word for "In front of death, or before death," a metaphor for bravery and valor.

"To the citizens of our beloved city of Slemani, we announce to you the very sweet news of victory. The heroic Peshmarga forces destroyed all traces of the Baathist regime in our town. The Mukhabart building has been taken over. All Iraqi informants and Baathists were killed. Every military camp around our city has been liberated. Celebrate the victory!"

The minivan continued its drive to the next quarter of town. Almost everyone was outside, greeting each other, shaking hands, and chanting Kurdish mottoes. Sallam and I sensed the seismic event we had just witnessed and felt lucky to be there, to be spectators of this experience firsthand. Finally, and for the first time, Kurdistan was free of any trace of any kind of central government. I, personally, had much larger expectations and dreams about this *rappareen*.[7]

Figure 1. Kurdish Peshmarga taking over
Saddam's weaponry after the uprising

My mind played all kinds of scenarios about the future of my people, including a homeland we could officially call Kurdistan, to have our own brand of government, universities that studied in the

---

[7]   Uprising

31

Kurdish language, and services provided by Kurds for Kurds. What would it be like to have our own official language, our own style of democracy, freedom of speech, and that of thought?

One of the healthiest developments coming out of this uprising and over the course of the next few weeks was the emergence of free speech and the materialization of more than eleven political parties, ranging from the far left Workers' Party of Kurdistan to the far right The Islamic Assembly.

The bulk of the fighting force during the uprising belonged to the Patriotic Union of Kurdistan (PUK), led by Jalal Talabani,[8] joined by forces from the Democratic Party of Kurdistan (KDP) under the direction of Massoud Barzani. Now president of the Iraqi Kurdistan Regional Government, Massoud Barzani is the son of the historic Kurdish leader Mustafa Barzani (1903–1979). The elder Barzani had been one of the leaders of the first true Kurdish independent country, the Republic of Mahabat, in 1946. He proclaimed independence from Iran under the leadership of Qazzi Muhammad, but that experiment lasted less than forty-six days. The regime of Tehran crushed the republic, captured, and executed many of its leaders. However, Mustafa Barzani was one of the few who were able to escape and take refuge in Russia. He stayed in Russia for more than a decade, not being able to return until after 1958. In the early 1960s, Mustafa Barzani led an insurrection against Baghdad's regime, demanding self-governing authority for Kurds within a united Iraq. It was not until 1970, when the Baathists took control of Iraq, that an accord was signed with Barzani to grant autonomy to the region of Kurdistan. However, the real purpose of that deal was nothing more than Baghdad trying to buy more time and deceive the Kurds. Iraq's Baathist authorities never truly intended to grant Kurds any kind of rights.

The treacherous Accord of Algeria between the Shah of Iran and Saddam Hussein signed and sealed the fate of the Kurds in 1975. That year, 1975, Iraqi TVs displayed thousands of Kurdish Peshmarga laying down arms and surrendering to the Iraqi authorities. I remem-

---

[8]   Current president of Iraq as of the writing of this book in 2012.

ber my mom weeping at that scene. I never thoroughly understood why she was so sad, why she cried every time they displayed those images. Not until I was somewhat older did I understand why she was unhappy at the future of our nation. My older brother had lost his life in the fighting. She was grieving that the blood of my brother had been spilled for nothing, for the sacrifice of thousands of young men sold out for a piece of land and half a river. She was sad that Barzani gave up easily, got on a plane, and flew to the USA, instead of staying and fighting.

This currant *rappareen* gave us hope of reestablishing a formidable force and a tangible government. We, as a nation, felt confident this time. After all, the most powerful nation on earth, the United States of America, had our back, or so we thought. G. H. W. Bush had called us to take the matter into our own hands. We were just responding to his call. Finally, there was a US president who was backing the Kurds, who was not going to deceive us. After all, he said it publicly. The love and respect my people displayed for G. H. W. Bush was indescribable. Pictures of Bush were displayed in almost every marketplace. People pronounced his name as if he were a hero. Some people named him Hajji Bush out of admiration for him. His popularity among the public made any Kurdish leader jealous. Banners reading "We love Bush the Senior" were displayed and posted everywhere. Other signs read, "Long lives the USA. Long live George Bush," and "Long live Kurdistan."

From March 8 until the end of that month, my city lived a dream. People smiled and sang patriotic songs. Books and biographies of legends of the Peshmarga were displayed and sold on street corners. Poets penned lyrics about freedom.

"Do I want bread or freedom?" one of them said.

"I will take freedom any day. I don't desire the bread that comes from Saddam, and I would rather die free than serve under Saddam's authority again," another posted placard quoted.

It was exhilarating to see posters go up, demanding the right for women, equality, justice, freedom of speech, and democracy. I felt like I was living in a fairy tale.

"We will make Kurdistan into a mini Europe, mini USA," I said as I shared my thoughts with Sallam.

"I love this, positively love it. I cannot believe we are free. I can scoff at Saddam and the Baathist regime in the town square without being arrested," said Sallam.

As a nation and as individuals, we had never experienced this before. I had read about it happening elsewhere—the American Revolution, human rights, freedom of speech, etc. However, I never thought I would live to see it happen to us. I did not have faith in utopias, but this changed my mind. It could actually become a reality. During the reign of Saddam, criticism, a slip of the tongue, even a joke could end a person's life. It would have caused arrests and disappearances. Entire families ended up in dark dungeons, tortured, raped, and killed just because of a remark or a joke. To experience such a drastic change was ecstatic, unreal, and dreamlike.

Nonetheless, by March 25, there were whispers about a come-back, a resurrection of Saddam's army. Some claimed that they had met with people who fled Baghdad, Karbala, and Najaf. The word had it that the Iraqi army was alive and well. The Republican Guard had taken back control of Basra, Karbala, and Najaf. The Shiia-dominated cities of the south were no longer in the hands of Shiia rebels. Saddam's troops had taken control of them, and now they were heading toward Kurdistan. Saddam was more threatening than ever before. Most of us, including myself, took it as propaganda of a dying regime, a scare tactic to intimidate us, to rob us of our new-found freedom.

There is no way Saddam can come back to Kurdistan, I thought. *He has no formidable army to fight for him. He has no clout. The Americans will not let him come back. Bush is on our side.*

So did most Kurds believed.

However, these rumors never stopped. On the contrary, they increased. By March 30, a Kurdish radio broadcast spread the word of a regime comeback. They described the brutality of the admin-istration's revenge, the indiscriminate retaliation of the Republican army, killing thousands of men, women, and children. Whether one participated in the uprising or did not, they were considered guilty.

That evening I hurried to Sallam's house to see what he had heard.

"I get the same stuff. If this is true, I don't know what our future will be like," he said grimly.

"I can't believe this! Where are the Americans?" I exclaimed.

"We need to think of an exit strategy. What are you going to do? Can you find a ride or a way to escape town in case they come back?" he asked.

"I have no idea." I answered. Like most, I had no car, nor did I know how to drive. "Wait, my older brother has a semitruck that all of us could fit in. I should go pay him a visit and see what he has in mind."

After a short exchange of thoughts with my friend, I decided to head to my brother's family who lived in the Sugar project houses located on the south side of the city.

My brother Hemen wasn't home when I arrived, but my sister-in-law told me about their plan of exit. "We will furnish the back of the semi, load everyone in, and drive to the border. Your brother wants to go to the Penjwen exit point," she explained.

"Well, that is reassuring. Just please don't leave me behind, okay?" I pleaded.

"No, I don't see your brother leaving without taking everyone," she assured me.

Penjwen, a border village with Iran, east of Slemani, is a small village. Nevertheless, it has always been an active arena for smugglers and merchants to buy and sell goods from Iran. Smuggled goods from Iran made good profit when sold in Iraq. War and hostility between the two countries played into the hands of smugglers, who took advantage of the lack of official border monitoring during the 1980s.

I had rented a room from a family of a widowed mother of three in the Zargata area. Zargata was in fact near the main highway that led to Penjwen, even more reassuring because my brother did not have to go out of the way to pick me up.

Later on, I wrote in diaries recalling these last days.

March 31, 1991

The reality of an imminent attack is becoming more and more tangible. For the first time, I saw people walking toward the east. Men and women carried their children on their backs.

Some hauled large sacks full of necessities thrown over their shoulders. Wearing frightened expressions, they walked aimlessly.

I never dared to ask them questions, never wanted to stop them and look for answers. I still wished to live the remnant of my dream of an independent homeland. However, there was no denying it any longer—the dream was over.

Today, a man shouted in the middle of the central marketplace, the bazaar in Slemani, *"The Iraqis are coming!"* Paul Revere like.

Joy and jubilation rapidly turned into sadness and panic. Everyone is on his or her own now. The Peshmarga forces that victoriously walked in and liberated the town are now retreating before the Iraqi counterattack. They abandoned their posts and recoiled back from where they came in a chaotic and directionless retreat.

April 1, 1991

Today is a cloudy day. I heard thunder, but I cannot see lightning. The sun, peering from behind the clouds, climbed halfway into the sky. The day is halfway through, and it has not rained yet. Spring flowers are everywhere, thirsting for rain. Red tulips and the white petals of nerges cover the meadows. The fields and the mountains take cover behind a green blanket of wild grass.

Not today, the sky has not bestowed its rain to quench the thirst of the meadows. I was sitting in my room, reading, when suddenly my thoughts drifted to the sound of the thunder. I listened carefully. It did not seem normal. The echo did not sound natural. I decided to go outside and look at the sky. I waited a few seconds, and boom, another echo rumbled. Yet I never saw lightning. That is when I realized this was no thunder, but Iraqi artillery bombing the villages and towns on their way to my city.

I recall the scene of people fleeing. Many were on foot. Cars and trucks began to crowd the highway.

I sought out the son of my landlady.

"What has happened, Shoorsh? How far is the Republican Guard?" I asked him.

"By Allah, I don't know, but we are thinking about leaving tonight. My mom was going to talk to you about that," he responded.

I went to talk to his mother about their plan of escape. She told me they were heading to the village of Chwarta, northeast of the city. She was originally from Chwarta and had a few relatives who still lived there.

"I wanted to let you know that we will lock the outside door. I can leave a copy of the key with you, if you're planning to stay longer," she informed me.

"Oh no, my brother is going to pick me up tonight," I replied. "He has a large semi, and there is enough room for all of our family members. I will be fine. Don't worry. I will lock the door behind me."

I had no doubt in my mind that my brother was coming to pick me up that night. The night of April 1 was dark and bleaker than normal. The resonance of the bombing grew louder and closer. With every minute that passed, I fretted a bit more. My brother had not shown up yet. Almost all my neighbors had evacuated their homes and fled toward the border. The neighborhood looked and felt like a ghost town.

If he does not come to pick me up, I do not know what I will do, I thought. I had never been to the border area. Sallam was not available. He was fleeing along with his brothers and his mother. Every now and then I would go outside, looking to see if I recognized my brother's semi coming up the road.

"Greetings, young man," a woman directed her words to me as she stood behind me.

The darkness of the night prevented me from seeing her clearly.

"Hello, what are you doing here?" I asked her. "The city is almost empty."

"Can you please come help us? We have a heavy load to throw in the back of our truck. My husband can't carry it by himself," she asked with a pleading look.

"Certainly, where is it?" I asked.

"We live behind your house. Come, just follow me. It will be brief, I promise," she claimed.

I followed her to her house. The back of their red pickup truck was full of bags and luggage. Her husband attempted to lift a large sack onto the back of his truck. Apparently, he did not have the strength to do it alone.

"Thank you for coming to our aid. Allah protect and keep you safe," said the man.

I helped him lay his load on the back of his truck.

"Thank you very much," he repeated. "If you have no one to give you a lift, come with us. You have to compete with my children, luggage, and sacks in the back of the truck, but it is better than walking. I will gladly take you with us," the man offered with earnestness.

I looked at the back of his red pickup truck. Two little girls, a boy, a few baggage and sacks occupied most of the space.

"That's very kind of you. May you be well with your family. I have a brother who is coming to pick me up. He has a semi," I proudly replied.

"All right then. I won't worry about you. Allah is with you, brother," said the man.

Ten minutes or so went by until I was done helping this kind neighbor. I quickly ran back to the front of the empty house, waiting for my brother to arrive. The landlady and her children had already left a few hours before. Now I was all alone in a dark, lifeless house.

It's dark outside. I should go back in and stay here tonight. I am sure my brother will not leave without me. I will wait in the house, I supposed.

Echoes and sounds of explosions quieted down that night, and as I waited for my brother, sleep overtook me. I had a dream. In my dream, I was climbing a tall steel tower. I made it to the top, but suddenly an airplane flew by. Her whirlwind caused me to fall off, and in my dismay, I awoke.

It was 6:00 a.m. The sun broke the scattered clouds and shone its energy over the fence of the house. Still no sign of a truck coming along, no sign of my brother. I washed my face, changed my clothes, and filled a duffel bag with some extra clothes, a blanket, and all the money I had stashed. I had one thousand Iraqi dinars. Money I had inherited from my parents who had died a few years earlier.

"I cannot wait any longer," I told myself.

I decided to take flight and avoid the risk of being captured by an invading Iraqi Republican Guard. A Sunni himself, Saddam appointed mostly Sunni men to lead his armies. They were the most notorious department of the military and the most brutal in dealing with the population against the Shiia and the Kurds in particular.

The Mass Exodus

After locking the front gate, I turned around and strode toward the main highway. A sense of urgency pushed me. Goyzha Highway was also known as the 60 Meter for its two lanes and sixty-meter-wide pavement encircling Slemani like a ring. Built by the Baath regime in an effort to control the inhabitants in case of military emergency, Goyzha Highway stretched below a mountain by the same name.

It would take the military merely minutes to besiege a city of 750,000 with the aid of a highway such as this. It proved its worthiness during the 1980s when Saddam's troops enforced several curfews on Slemani. None could leave their homes for up to twenty-four hours while Arab soldiers swept houses and dwellings of average folk, looking for what they called *Mukhrbeen*.[9]

"Reach Mount Goyzha as quickly as possible," I prompted myself.

The three-thousand-foot tall mountain provided protection from troops and infantry, but exposed anyone who climbed her to air attack. Her height and the rocky nature of her ravines and crevasses would prevent tanks from entering. My chief fear was not the tanks themselves but their powerful guns, for they could pull over by the

---

[9]   The Anarchists: a name Saddam and the regime in Baghdad called the Peshmarga.

40

edge of the mountain and shoot any climbers. Infantry did not worry me. I had dodged their bullets before.[10] Starting out at a brisk pace from the room I rented, I estimated that it would take me an hour or two to arrive at the foot of the mountain. Meanwhile, the intensity of the bombing increased. The roads and highways that had been clogged with dated Russian and Polish automobiles now seemed to be wide open. An occasional car or truck whizzed by.

"No car would risk stopping for me," I murmured to myself regretfully. *I am too young to die!* These thoughts, and more, ran through my mind as the failure of our experiment as a *to-be-born* nation sank in. An experiment doomed to fail without the support of the superpowers of the globe. It never had a real chance to succeed.

The Kurdish people never had a chance to show the world that we could make it on our own and that we are a civilized people who believe in human rights and equality. The thought of decades of oppression and suffering saddened and angered me.

The betrayal by my older brother enraged me.

"How could he pass me like that?" I angrily asked myself as I gnashed my teeth.

A few cars and trucks zipped by. Suddenly, a car engine roared and slowed down. An old Polish-made minivan loaded with women pulled over. It completely stopped a stone's throw away without shutting down the engine. The driver, the only man in the minivan, kept waving his hand, encouraging me to step in the van. I ran and opened the door.

"*Salaam Alykoom* (Peace be upon you)," I said.

"And to you as well," replied the driver loudly above the noise of the engine. "I can't take you too far. As you see, my van is too full but I can drop you off farther away from town so you don't have to walk all that distance."

"Thank you so much for stopping," I shouted. "Actually, I would not mind if you drop me off by the slope of Goyzha as I am going to take that route."

---

[10]　That story will be told in a second book supplemental to this one.

"Well, it is a brilliant idea," responded the driver. "Just be careful of land mines. That place is full of them."

"Oh, marvelous. I never thought of that," I said under my breath. *What choice do I have now? My brother betrayed me, and this man cannot take me very far. I would rather be walking my way to safety than be captured by Saddam's soldiers.*

The ride to the foothills of Goyzha was slow and exceptionally quiet. The women, somber and sad looking, bobbled their heads as the old *Polony*, as we called it, slowly drove away. Most of the women were older, perhaps in their mid-forties. One of them seemed to be terribly ill. She was younger than the others were, perhaps in her late thirties. Her face was pale, her head covered with a hijab, the Islamic scarf. She leaned on the right shoulder of the woman next to her. Twenty minutes or so into the ride, we arrived at an area that might have been the closest to the start of the climb of the mountain. The driver slowed down as he pulled his minivan toward the gravelly bank of the highway.

"There, go," said the driver as he shifted his minivan's transmission to park. "Be in the safe hands of God."

"Thank you. I shall never forget your kindness. God bless you," I shouted from the backseat. "God be with you all." I directed my words to the rest of the passengers.

"Don't forget your duffel bag," said the old woman. "And I will pray for you, my boy." She continued to provide her shoulder in support of the ill one.

I nodded my head as a thank you gesture and smiled at her. The minivan shifted to drive and continued on its route as I ran to the other side of the highway. The mountain looked steep in areas but climbable. A large crowd had already made it halfway up the slope. It seemed that I was the last to arrive. From a distance, the congregation of escapees resembled ants climbing a hill.

The 60 Meter had carved a small section out of the edge of Mount Goyzha. Between the steepest slope and the highway there lay a fifteen-degree climb that stretched for at least half a mile.

Around 8:30 a.m., the sun disappeared behind a veil of clouds and the air grew breezier. I began to think of food and realized I had not packed anywhere near enough of it.

Echoes of explosions grew ever clearer. Adrenaline kept me from slowing down even as I desperately panted for some air. The gravelly slopes did not weaken my strides as I ignored the feeling of hunger or fear of whatever lay ahead.

At around nine o'clock, I reached a small shack, about one quarter of the way up the mountain. The abandoned shack did not seem at all amenable. Empty, with nothing to offer but its four standing walls, it appeared to be a ranger station now abandoned. I stepped inside.

Shortly, a man and two girls entered. They leaned against the walls and collapsed on the floor. In his mid-sixties, the man looked like the father of the girls. One of the girls appeared to be in her twenties, the other much younger, preteen perhaps.

"Ah," the man sighed as he slowly pressed his back against the wall.

"Greetings," I said, still gasping for air.

"Welcome," the man answered as if he owned the shack. He set a discolored-looking cloth on the floor and proceeded to unwrap it.

"Here," he said as he handed me a hardboiled egg, already peeled.

"Oh no. Thank you," I timidly said in disbelief. "You need those for yourselves."

"That's all right," he answered. "We boiled about thirty of them. I figured it would be a long journey deep into the mountains. It might be a few days until help arrives. I hope you brought a blanket. You'll need something warm to wear. By nightfall the temperature drops drastically."

"Yes," I responded with a hesitant voice, "I did. I have a blanket, and my clothes are warm." I touched my sweater as a sign of assurance.

He handed me the egg and a piece of homebaked bread. I slipped the peeled egg into the heart of the flatbread and folded the ends to make it resemble a sandwich. My bite was as large as a hungry wolf's. I devoured my meal in a few minutes.

"I'll stay warm," I said, more to convince myself than the old man. "My clothes and blanket shall keep me safe from the elements." I knew, however, that my shoes were not adequate for mountain climbing. As I stared down at them, the man said, "These are my daughters."

"God keep them," I gave him the usual response.

"I have four daughters," he went on. "Two of them went back to the house. They went to fetch more blankets. We live at the foot of the mountain. I wonder what is taking them so long. We began our climb this morning around 6:00 a.m., but as we approached this little shack, I realized we didn't bring enough blankets."

The flapping of a helicopter's main rotor interrupted his words. I rushed outside to check out the noise. A blackish helicopter slowly flew against the gray sky of Slemani. Like a hawk looking for prey, the helicopter floated carefully toward the far side of town.

Rooom. It fired a barrage of small rockets. What did it target? I could not tell from where I was standing. Shortly after, a flash of explosion scorched the area where the rocket had fallen. A thunderous boom followed. The pilot instantly made a 180-degree turn and fled westward.

"Looks like an RPG!" shouted the man. "Perhaps a few pockets of resistance continue fighting." He narrowed his eyes and shielded them with his palm in an attempt to gaze at the sight.

"Peshmarga are bunkered in the city center," I responded. "I hope they will get out in time."

"Oh my god," said the little girl, her mouth quivering. "They are going to kill us all!" Tears began streaming down her cheeks as she shifted her gaze westward. "Oh no! Are those tanks?" She pointed her index finger toward the gleaming objects.

I followed her finger toward the west. Below us, yellow-and-brown-hued objects advanced. Tanks and armored vehicles sprang out of the westward bend of the highway. They progressed slowly yet steadily.

Shouts and screams arose from the climbing women and children behind me. Terrified by the scene, they panicked. Some ran, climbing haphazardly over the rocky and green slopes of Goyzha as quickly as their weary legs could take them. Thick clouds stood still over our heads, stretching as far as the eye could see, preparing to dump large amounts of rainwater over the land. At once, I noted two figures laboriously climbing the gray slopes. They carried a load over their shoulders.

"Are those your daughters?" I asked the man, who stood to my right.

"Oh, Allah!" he called out in distress. "Yes, that is them!" He broke away and hurried down the harsh slopes in an effort to reach the girls.

"They are never going to make it up here in time," said the older girl as she wept. "I see the tanks. They are here!"

"Father!" cried out the younger girl. "Do not go down, please!"

Without hesitation, I began to descend the rocky slopes of Goyzha, now and then jumping like a gazelle in the meadows.

"Go back!" I yelled at the man as I passed by him like wind through grass. "I will help them."

The girls struggled under the weight of the blankets. A good two hundred yards separated me from them yet.

"Your blankets," I said with a raspy voice as I panted for air. "Let me carry them. Run now. Flee! They are close!" I urgently encouraged the girls to keep climbing.

"I can't," one of them said. "I am so scared I have diarrhea." She wept and took a seat on the pebbly slopes. "Please don't leave me here."

A moral dilemma faced me. The man and his two daughters needed the blankets, but these two girls needed help climbing. I attempted to carry the one girl on my back simultaneously with the blankets, but the size and the weight of the task was too great for even my broad shoulders. I directed my eyes toward the west as the enemy troops drew ever nearer. Less than a mile separated us from them.

"Please," I begged the girl. "Hurry, you must stand up and continue. If they catch you, God knows what they will do to you." I tried to push her to continue.

The second daughter picked herself up. She crawled at first, then stood and continued upward. The angle of the incline was not terribly steep, perhaps fifteen degrees. Nevertheless, fear paralyzed the girl, struck her with feelings of sickness. A heavy burden and a vicious enemy on your heels would have frozen anyone.

She collapsed and lay down in the dirt. I had a difficult decision to make. I either lug her on my back and forget about the blankets or haul the blankets and hope she will follow me.

"I am sorry," I regretfully said to the girl. "But lingering here is not a brilliant idea. The Iraqi soldiers will shoot us for sport." I threw the blankets over my shoulders and took off, running uphill. My heart sped and fluttered. My mind raced with thoughts of guilt and shame. What was I doing? Meanwhile, I expected a bullet to pierce my back at any second. A bundle of blankets over my shoulder created an unusually large target for gunners and snipers to lick their lips at.

The man and the other two daughters waited at higher ground. They wept and stared at me as I ran crazily away from the girls I had left behind. The older one pointed at them. She blurted out a few words, the distance made it impossible to hear her. Exhausted and out of breath, I wavered and paused. I looked back. To my dismay, the girls lingered still and enemy troops approached steadily. Now only a few hundred yards of stony ground kept the girls from the hands of wicked men. The yellowish-green steel-plated vehicles of the Iraqis were unmistakable now. Their large coaxial guns protruded like chimneys filled with black smoke. A sudden warm gust of air overwhelmed the atmosphere, as if someone had switched on a hot-air engine. A few steps separated me from the waiting man and the two daughters. He moved down from where he stood.

"Come," he said, "give me those damn blankets."

I threw the blankets on the ground near his feet. Mouth wide open, my heart fluttering like a live fish on a riverbank, I bent over, placed my arms on my knees, and gasped for air. Meanwhile, the enemy attained more ground.

Suddenly, they halted their advance. An unknown man had shot a bullet against one of the giant iron horses and brought it to a temporary halt. Guns drawn, Iraqi soldiers jumped out of the iron trap and scattered over the ramps and sidewalks in precaution.

"Now!" I shouted at the man. I turned around and resumed running. However, this time, I faced the troops and my back was to Goyzha.

"What are you doing?" the man cried out. "You are crazy!"

The girl who was feeling sick kept on coming uphill. She took two steps up, then stood still, wavered side to side, and continued to walk like a drunkard time and again.

While the delayed Iraqi troops searched for the perpetrator who had shot at them, I reached the girls.

"Come!" I called out. "Hop on my back!"

Feeble and frightened, the ill girl jumped on my back without saying a word. She was tall but thin, and her long wavy hair covered her face while her long legs dangled beside my thighs. Her sister kept pace, but I struggled with the uneven slope. This time I faced the right direction.

The fleeing crowds climbed higher as enemy troops drew nearer. Moments crawled by like hours. My muscles screamed from underneath me, my lungs were aching for some air, and my tongue was parched for a drop of water. I continued my march until we reached the girls' father.

"I would never have blamed you," he said as he walked a few steps down to receive us. "You could have left and gone off on your way to safety."

"Thank you," the sisters said in unison. "We shall never forget this."

"I shall wait here," said the man. "The two girls need a breather. You go, keep climbing."

The man urged me to continue marching to higher ground lest I fall to enemy fire or hands.

"You are young," he said. "If they arrest you they might execute you. I am old and have no fear of dying. Now that you saved my girls I would rather die with them by my side."

On the Wings of the Clouds

T he weather grew colder, and the clouds sank lower. The atmosphere turned oppressive. I lifted the heavy duffel bag, swung it over my shoulder, and gave the man and his four daughters my back. I set out toward a thin trail, barely visible in the distance.

I never caught any of their names, I thought. It bothered me slightly, but urgency pressed me onward. I wanted to get out of there before troops began crawling up the mountain.

The trail ended. The mountain grew suddenly steep. It looked like a monster in an old story, both forbidding and challenging.

I craned my head back to determine the distance to the top and saw that a multitude of people had already reached the summit. As I took another step, my foot betrayed me. I began to slip and fall but regained my footing. I sprang forward like an animal before the hunter, never daring to look behind me. I told myself that if I could not see the enemy, perhaps they could not see me.

Shrubs grew alongside the slopes, and a large boulder loomed ahead. I began to notice droplets on my cheeks as the rain began slowly to fall. Pebbles acted as marbles beneath my feet, causing me to slip and fall. I was forced to scuttle on my hands and feet like a crab.

Suddenly, a voice blared from a loudspeaker somewhere below.

"Brothers and sisters," announced an Iraqi officer in Arabic. "I ask you to come forth and surrender to us. You and your families shall be safe, for His Excellency Saddam Hussein, Allah preserve him, has issued an amnesty to all."

I turned slowly and carefully toward the announcement, taking care not to lose my footing. To my horror, a long trail of mechanized enemy troops occupied the pavement of the highway like a giant centipede. A row of saffron-yellow-and-brown-colored armored tanks now faced us. A man in uniform stood over the turret of a large T54 tank with a loudspeaker in his hands. I was struck by the scene, an image of Saddam's devilry as he scorned the resources of this vast and beautiful country in a mad desire for weapons to fight unjustified and aggressive wars against his people and his neighbors. The sweet scent of the rain fumed and filled the air. The irony of the officer's public announcement and the view of hundreds of machine guns mounted on steel vehicles rattled me enough that it slipped my mind to enjoy the scent.

"Who in their right mind would surrender to these butchers," I asked myself incredulously.

"We have given you a chance," repeated the officer. "Submit and spare your lives and the lives of your family members. I carry orders to shoot on my discretion. Come now, and get down off that mountain."

At the end of his announcement, he turned the tank's main gun so that it faced us. The glass from the optical periscope gleamed against the gray sky.

Boom! A rocket scudded over the space between the tank and the foot of the mountain. A massive explosion followed. It shook the stones and rocks about me. That was our warning.

The air grew heavier, as if someone had thrown a thick blanket over the fading daylight. The smell of gunpowder hung heavily in the damp air. I breathed with difficulty, as if a heavyset man sat on my chest, and saliva slowly poured down choking my throat. My heart quickened, and fear overtook me. A thousand and one thoughts ran through my mind.

I don't want to die! I am too young to die! My mind repeated over and over. Like an imprisoned animal, I glanced around anxiously, searching for a way out. My only hope was the boulder that I had spied earlier. It sat proudly on the tilting ground, as it had for perhaps the last few thousand years. Would it shelter me from bullets? I peeked toward the pyramid-shaped mountain peak. It seemed a long way off. Would I have enough time to make it up there? I could not tell. Moments passed by with excruciating slowness, each one an eternity. Then it hit me—*eternity.*

Where do I go if I die here? I thought. *Will I dissolve into dust and sand? What comes after life? Is there existence beyond?* Questions about heaven, hell, and God roiled in my frightened mind like boiling water bubbles in a cooking pan.

I had lost my faith in gods, heavens, and hell some time before, when I was in high school. There I had built a friendship with a newly transferred student who introduced me to the work of Charles Darwin. I read Darwin's *Theory of Evolution* with fascination, determined to find out what lay behind this theory.

In the same month, my mother suffered a massive heart attack, which required her to stay at the hospital for over a week. I had already lost my father, and I begged Allah to save her life, for she was the only one left who was close to me. Another friend, a Muslim scholar, urged me to pray a specific prayer invoking the healing powers of Allah, who I believed was omnipotent.

In spite of my earnest prayers to Allah, my mother died a week later. The loss of my beautiful and loving mother was devastating to me and destroyed my faith in Allah. I embraced the theory of Darwin's book that eliminated the need for a creator and drifted away from religion. Secretly, I left Islam and became an atheist.

As I crouched on the slopes of mount Goyzha facing imminent death, I was not so sure about atheism. Perhaps this was a good time to change my mind.

Out of nowhere, another memory came to me. I flashed back to the time when I was only five years old. Spring had come. The nerges bloomed wildly, birds sang, and the sun shone longer every day. Longer daylight hours translated into one thing in a little boy's world—longer hours to play.

Margret, my little Christian[11] neighbor, had come to our doorstep with two of her Christian friends. She carried a basket stuffed with colored eggs in dazzling shades of yellow, red, blue, and green. I stared at them in wonder. I had never tasted colored eggs and couldn't wait to find out the flavor of each different color.

As I quickly peeled an egg, the children spoke in Assyrian,[12] a language I barely knew. They mentioned the name Jesus, the word *Mashicha* and *God*. "Jesus is God the Messiah."

As the words flooded my memory there on the slopes of Goyzha, I bowed my head so low it almost touched my feet. Sincerely and wholeheartedly, as I had never prayed before in my life, I said, "God, whoever and wherever you are, the real and true God, please help me. Save me from this danger, or if you don't want to save me now, then take me to wherever you are. Thank you."

Because of my anxious heart, I hadn't noticed that it was raining steadily now. I slowly, cautiously, raised my head as if watching a horror film but did not want to see the next clip. Unexpectedly and gradually, mist began to steam out of the earth, swirling around us as the rain fell from above us. It formed a cloud, swathing the area where my fellow Kurds and I were wedged in.

I could hardly believe it. *Now is my chance!* I thought. *The mist shall cover me.* Swiftly, I lifted the duffel bag, turned my back on the troops, sprang out of my crouching position, and took off, climbing as fast as my anxious legs could carry me. My back to the troops, I climbed like a mountain goat on my four limbs. Arms and legs raced to gain every inch as quickly as possible. The freshly dampened ground afforded more traction. It made the upward strides more effective and quickened my pace. Under cover of the cloud, I reached the peak.

I heaved a sigh of relief. Joy overtook me as if I had drunk a cold cup of water on a hot summer day. I stood on that elevation and

---

[11] About 1 percent of Iraq's population is Christian.
[12] An ancient language similar to Aramaic

looked down at the hovering mist, or cloud, or whatever it was—it could not be explained!

Fretting men, women, and children continued to emerge out of the fog below me and climb upward. One woman, whose swarthy complexion reflected her southern Kurdish ancestry, struggled to carry her baby on her way up. She stretched out her arm, and I grabbed it and gave her a tug. The baby broke into a loud cry as the droplets of rain struck her face, and the mother shivered and shook her unyielding body. She wept along with her child. They had no belongings, nothing to shield them from the weather. I reached into my duffel bag and took out my blanket.

"Here, cover your baby with it," I wearily spoke.

"Thank you," she said with gratitude in her face. She quickly wrapped her baby.

Soon, more brazen Kurds heaved over the grounds of the peak, fleeing from the advancing enemy troops. They murmured and muttered words of indignation. One man raised his lips to the sky as if he spoke to God directly. He shook his head as he walked away from the peak. Suddenly, the sound of a hail of bullets filled the air. A Kurd carrying an AK-47 had shot it toward the cloud-saturated sky in a mad attempt to down the helicopter that flew in the distance.

"What the hell are you doing?" I angrily screamed. "You're only going to attract its attention to us."

With an uninviting look on his face, he silently walked away. The crowd continued to move past me, and I thought of the man I had met with the four daughters. I wondered if they were among the group. Had they managed to escape beneath the cover of the cloud?

I marveled at the materialization of this cloud that had appeared to shelter us all. The event had a profound effect on me. Had it been an element of nature, or a miracle, as it had seemed?

There was not much time to ponder from where I stood that day on the peak of the mountain. I was relieved that the ghastly Iraqi menace was not an immediate threat to us, although a helicopter still lingered in the distance.

A flood of refugees emerged from the western part of the mountain. Like branches of rivers, every one joined the march.

"These people walk as if they know where they are going." Not knowing where to go next, I asked a short, stout man, "So where is everyone heading?"

"Iran," he answered hurriedly. "You see those peaks?" He pointed to the east.

I looked, not much to see but an eerie view of black dark peaks crowned by gray clouds.

"Follow the crowd," said the stout man. "If you are quick enough, you might get there in two days."

Figure 2. Clouds covered the mountain as I prayed to God

The peak of Goyzha consisted of a grassy plot, narrow and flat. It stretched its arm and bent toward the north to form a second peak. In between lay a large chasm filled with broken stones and large boulders. I joined thousands of refugees, turning from the city of my birth and marching into the unknown. I felt like a stranger in my own backyard. The throng walked wearily, lashed by rain. I buttoned my sweater, gathered the ends of my jacket around me, and followed them away from the edge of the summit. The farther I walked, the quieter it grew, as if no enemy troops lurked below. The somber and quiet faces of strangers exhibited fear and frustration. Only the sound of crying babies broke the creepy hush that hung in the wet atmosphere.

"Enemy troops surrounded the person who surrendered," said a man talking to another.

"No violence?" asked the second man.

"Obviously a trick," responded the first. "They will get him afterward."

Apparently, someone had surrendered to the enemy, crumbling under the pressure of the moment. In that instant, anger, fear, and uncertainty raged through me. Why would God allow such things to happen? What had we ever done to deserve this kind of punishment? Why me? I had nothing but the clothes on my back and a bundle of cash that I had stowed in my duffel bag. The cash is not going to buy me much in these mountains. In fact, it was a source of worry rather than security. If anyone found out I carried that kind of cash, who knew what would happen?

My nearly-empty leather duffel became heavier with each step I took. I decided that it was an annoyance and in a swift decision emptied it of its contents, shoving the cash into my side pocket. I flung the duffel bag down the descending slopes of the mountain, clapping my hands like a child. *Good riddance*, I thought.

Feeling lighter, I continued to walk with the others. In time, we reached the descending end of Goyzha. It was not as accommodating as I had hoped. The back of the mountain, although not as steep, was quite rocky. At the end of the slope, we encountered an ancient paved highway. Brittle tar and large potholes testified to years of neglect. Perhaps no one, or no vehicle, had utilized it in years. It was much smaller and narrower than the 60 Meter. A large division of the mob followed the highway heading toward the east. Another division went straight on, totally avoiding the highway. I was at a crossroad at this point, one of many to come in my life. I had to make a choice: go to the right and follow the highway or go straight and continue deep into the valleys and mountains. I decided that the risk of being overtaken was greater on the highway, however unlikely that it would be used in that condition. Therefore, I chose to stroll straight on deep into the mountains and the valleys. The hidden sun stood almost at noon. No one expected lunch service, and in fact, I was not even hungry. Adrenaline had kicked in, and the instinct for fight or flight overcame any other bodily need at this point. The rain was pouring down now, and we were soaked to the skin. Pools of water accumulated near the side of the unshaped road. The soil, saturated with rainwater, slowly began to turn to mud. People walked single file in long lines. The crowd separated, with the younger, stronger ones considerably ahead while the weak, women with children, and the elderly fell behind.

Just two miles into the valley, a group of women gathered around a large boulder, tending to the needs of another woman. Three men waited anxiously a few feet away. Later, I learned that the woman was in labor, and others huddled around her to help her deliver. One of the men was her husband.

What a tragedy.

This event punctuated for me the determination of my people so victimized by Saddam's treachery.

Noiseless and resolute, the crowd strode on alongside a rivulet. No one spoke much. There was not much to say.

Five long, drawn-out miles were behind me, and the yellow sun was still absent, but I guessed that she was westward by now. The rain did not seem to give way with the setting rays of the sun. With no food in my stomach to give me energy and heat, it felt much colder than normal.

Many continued to walk on through the night. Others decided to delay. Somehow, these desperate refugees collected twigs and wood and lit fires. They flickered bravely here and there against the dark, wet background of the valley. I jostled my way until I was able to get closer to one of the fires. My cold, hungry body much needed the heat. Reduced to survival mode, I pondered how crucial it was that something as simple as a fire could mean the difference between life and death. I marveled at the ingenuity of my people.

As if in answer to this thought, a man standing near the fire broke into spontaneous conversation.

"My truck broke down on the highway," he said. "Therefore, I took a gallon of hydraulic oil and carried it along with me. My wife and three kids are with me. I knew I'd need to be able to start a fire to warm them, especially at night."

A pack of refugees formed a circle around the fire. Most stretched out the palms of their hands and held them over the flames appreciatively. A white light illuminated the place for a brief period. The clouds now were charged with lightning and thunder. To my left a child lay still, sleeping on the wet ground. I wondered to myself who the baby's parents were. A dark-haired woman approximately in her late twenties picked up the baby and then called out plaintively, "Khalil, Khalil?"

"What? Here I am," answered a man with a stringy mustache, appearing out of the darkness. He wore a yellow jacket and black pants, thoroughly drenched. His thin hair was plastered to his face.

"Come," said the woman in a disgruntled tone, "take the child."

Khalil gently took the baby, who, despite the rain, slept deeply. He quickly walked back near the fire. Someone else had taken his coveted spot, and Khalil ended up standing next to me. Cradling the baby in one arm, he held his free hand over the fire.

"By Allah,[13] this is not a condition to live in," he said. "I owned an auto mechanic shop back home and made a decent living. Now I am struggling to find a place near a fire just to keep warm. God knows what those soldiers will do to my house and equipment."

"How old is the baby?" I asked, ignoring his comments.

"She is eighteen months old," he replied.

"Is she going to be okay? She is thoroughly wet," I asked out of concern.

"Yeah, well, what are we going to do?" said Khalil in a disconcerted tone. "She is no worse off than the rest of us. We are all in the same boat. I wonder what time it is."

I had no idea what time it was. Time and schedules did not seem to matter. I was glad to survive my first night in the wild. Khalil and I struck up some more conversation and got to know each other. An ever-flowing stream of refugees passed by us as we conversed by the fire.

---

[13]   In the Islamic culture, the name of Allah is used excessively.

When the flames died down, the crowd dispersed, and everyone resumed the march. Khalil, who was now my walking friend, urged his wife to pick up her duffel bag and start moving.

"Come, let's go!" Khalil shouted at his wife. "We have a long way ahead of us. Join us." He invited me. "Come and walk with us. Do not go alone."

Tarried by the fire, we had not walked away from danger yet. On the other side of Goyzha, Iraqi troops lay ready to pounce. I kept hearing sporadic echoes of explosions, as sound waves traveled easier through the quiet, dark, and rainy night. We began walking again through the dimness. It might have been close to 2:00 or 3:00 a.m. Except for the babies, no one else got any sleep.

The mud and rain made it difficult to lie down or even sit anywhere. Deep into the valley, we encountered a patch that the rainfall had softened and mud gurgled under our striding feet. A few had brought along kerosene lanterns or handheld torches. Red light flickered from these lanterns as we strode on together in the early morning darkness.

Figure 3. I marveled at the materialization of this cloud

Under the Roofless Abode

Dawn was about to break. However, the rain did not show any sign of slowing down or stopping. Khalil and his wife soon demonstrated that they did not have the best communication skills. They argued with one another for a long time. His wife blamed him for shunning her extended family; he blamed her brother for permanently borrowing his car.

The invisible sun climbed her way behind the gray ceiling. During a temporary break in the rain, I took shelter under a tree that looked up to a large mountain with a snow-covered peak. Tired and hungry, I did not take time to admire the breathtaking scene; instead, I loathed the circumstances. Clouds began to spread over the horizon once more. Just like that, the rain came down. My clothes had nearly dried out, but this bout of rain dampened them again. I stood under the tree and watched the rainfall while groups of refugees passed me eastward. I wept at the scene. Khalil and his wife joined me under the tree. He did not seem to be interested in the reason for my tears.

"I heard there is a village behind that hill," said Khalil as he pointed toward a looming knob. "Maybe we can find some help or something to eat."

"What is it called?" I asked.

"*Gorgayer!*" shouted an old man as he walked by. "I hope the wolves stay away from us."

"*The Place of the Wolves.* I never knew wolves lived in Kurdistan," I exclaimed.

"Even bears made dwellings in the mountains," said the old man with a prideful tone. "That bastard...He killed all of them off with Xardal[14] gas." The old man was referring to chemical weapons produced by Saddam's technical staff

Clouds increased in density as we headed toward what we hoped to be an inhabited village. As soon as I reached the prominence of the hill, the view of the small valley became clearer. To the dismay of all the refugees, the village was nothing but ruins. Mud homes with no roofs, half-broken walls, and lumber dangling where once had been ceilings. It was disappointing, to say the least, but a reminder of why we fled.

The Anfal military operation in 1988, led by Saddam's cousin Ali Chemical, razed five thousand Kurdish villages to the ground. One hundred eighty-three thousand captured villagers were led out of their homes and hamlets and buried alive in mass graves. Iraq's western desert became a graveyard for living beings.

In spite of the sight of such desolation, one thought consumed my mind—rest. I had not slept a single moment since leaving my rented room. An opportunity to relax a bit by the ruins attracted me. A group of men and children stood around a fire.

"Greetings," I said to them all.

One of them invited me to share lunch with them.

"What are you having?" I asked.

"Roasted onions!" shouted a man. "With kebab." He gently laughed.

"Oh, well then I would like two shish kebabs, a plate of tomatoes, and roasted onions, please," I responded with a teasing grin.

"Oh, brother," said a second man, "you will only get roasted onions. I found this sack of onions by that creek. Looks like someone

---

14   Mustard gas

left them there, so we decided to eat them. Of course, roasting them in the fire makes them more flavorful."

I tried a roasted onion. "Hmm, not bad actually."

I turned in circles and looked for Khalil and his family, but I could not find him. Apparently, he had continued his walk without me. *Oh well, I will catch up to him.*

Right behind me lay the ruins of an entire village that had once bustled with life with humans and cattle. The adobe behind me had a missing roof. The eastern wall was still intact though, and two supporting pillars faced the west. The idea of resting against the wall lured me. I ate half of the roasted onion but could not finish the other half. All I wanted was to rest by that wall. Perhaps I could catch a quick nap.

I left the men roasting more onions and headed toward the lone wall. Slowly, I leaned my back against it and gradually lowered my hips as my weary legs bent down. Just moments later, the sky's doors opened up like a floodgate and the rain came pouring down. This time lightning seared the cloudy sky, followed by the thudding of thunder. The rain came down in buckets such as I had never seen before.

The roofless house did not afford much shelter. I pulled my knees up to my chest and rounded up in a ball to reduce my size and exposure to rain. Others seeking cover soon joined me. The fact that this had once been a house gave the wrong sense of security to all. Soon there were five of us huddled against the walls.

Figure 3. A typical Kurdish village before
Saddam razed them to the ground.

A single woman emerged out of the soggy atmosphere a few strides away. She held a black umbrella over her head.

"Ugh," she muttered, "this umbrella is a cheaply made piece of garbage." She threw it on the ground.

The umbrella flipped upside down from the impact with the inside facing up. Within a few seconds, the cavity of the umbrella was filled with water. Unexpectedly and out of nowhere, a burro stood up next to the umbrella and turned around so her rear end was just above it. She simultaneously urinated and defecated in the middle of that umbrella. Every one broke into laughter.

"Now I *really* cannot use it anymore," the woman commented ruefully as she joined us.

Hours went by until it was fully dark. The silvery moon hid her light behind the rainy clouds. Some of the men felt we should get moving and not waste time. Despite the heavy rain, the group stood up and moved up the sopping hill again.

"Does anyone know the direction?" asked the woman. "Which way we should be heading?"

"Yes," a fellow announced. "Follow me. I know it's pitch-black out there but stay close to each other." He was a sturdy-looking man, dressed in dark-gray traditional garments, baggy pants, and a vest. "Please understand that I am only trying to help. I am a former Peshmarga, so I know these lands like the back of my hand."

That moonless night was extremely dark. I could not see my own feet. In circumstances like that, it is difficult to walk at a fast pace. We all crept along incredibly slowly to prevent a slip or to fall off a cliff. Anything was possible.

It had been two nights now since I last had a few hours of sleep; and other than a half-roasted onion, nothing else had passed into my stomach, or out of it. My body had gone into shutdown mode. The body is smart. When food is scarce, thinking it is facing famine, metabolism slows and normal functions stop. I had had no need to use nature in almost three days now.

Picking one's way in pitch darkness soaked in rainwater is extremely slow and frustrating. I was never so happy to see the light of dawn as I was the next morning. It was now my third day in the wild as a refugee in my own home country. The light of dawn and decreasing rain gave us a chance to increase the speed of our walk. I welcomed the movement. I was still utterly soaked and feeling very cold. Sitting down or resting would have intensified the feeling.

Around midmorning of the third day, the clouds dissipated and the sun finally raised her warm head to greet us with a cloudless morning. Seeing the golden light of the sun and allowing its rays to touch my face and my wet clothes was a sensational feeling that I had taken for granted all my life up to this point.

Soon we reached the valley of Barzinja. A creek flowed through it with fast-moving water. I thought about taking my shoes off and rinsing my feet since my shoes were filled with mud and my socks were soaked.

I approached the creek. There I saw two girls sitting on the bank. I recognized the girls. They were the ones I had met by the shack on the slope of Goyzha with the affable older man who gave me boiled eggs.

"Greetings," I said. "How are you holding up? Do you remember me?"

"Oh yes!" shouted the older one with a surprised look on her face. "I do remember you. My dad was very thankful that you risked your life to save my sisters."

An attractive girl with large dark eyes and a wide smile, she might have been in her early twenties. She wore a long brownish wool coat that made her seem even smaller than her tiny size.

"Not exactly," I said sheepishly. "I never did risk my life. Actually, I am ashamed that I didn't stick around."

"Hey, you didn't have to," she proclaimed. "You did not have to go back at all. You tried to rescue my sisters and the blankets."

"Well, it doesn't matter now," I said. "We are all alive. Where is the rest of your family?"

"I don't know," she said and suddenly broke into tears. "My dad and other two sisters got separated from us."

"Oh no! What happened?" I asked.

"Iraqis began shooting," she explained. "My dad insisted that my little sister and I continue climbing while he awaited my other sisters who were struggling to cope. She and I kept on going. Then fog emerged unexpectedly, and we were cut off from them. We didn't want to risk waiting for too long. I trusted my dad would find us somehow."

"He will be able to find us later," the younger girl said trustingly.

"But it has been three days without a sign of them," said the older sister as she wiped tears from her cheeks.

"Oh, I am so sorry," I said. "I hope they are all right and somewhere behind us."

"I don't know," whimpered the older girl. "I think they took a different course. They carried a heavy load of blankets, duffel bags, and all the food. My little sister here is extremely tired, and the bottoms of her feet are entirely scoured from walking."

The little one had removed the small sturdy boots she was wearing. I examined her feet. They were in bad shape. The skin looked swollen and puffy with pebble cuts scattered on her pale skin. "Maybe if she soaked her feet," I suggested. "The creek's cold water might help reduce the swelling."

The little girl wordlessly set her boots aside and plunged her feet in the stony creek. "Ah, that feels wonderful!" the little girl exclaimed. She gave a sigh of relief as she closed her eyes.

Soon I followed her example and soaked my own weary and aching feet. Finally, her older sister followed suit.

"This was a brilliant idea! It feels so good," she said with enjoyment as she gazed at the mountain to her right.

"I know," I said to both girls. "But I am afraid that I have to move on real soon. I heard that the border is not that far."

"Can I ask you a favor?" said the older girl. "You seem to be a pleasant man."

"Possibly," I responded hesitantly. "In these circumstances, I'm not sure how I could be of help, but go ahead and ask."

"Could you please walk with us?" she timidly asked. "I don't want people to think that my sister and I are alone. At least with you beside us, no one would think of taking advantage of us."

I thought about how these two might slow me down. After a moment of consideration, I decided this was a chance to help someone in need. Besides, after Khalil left me, I had not relished being alone myself.

"Yeah, sure," I answered. "Of course, you two can join me."

We gathered our half-dried footwear, put it back on, and continued the walk.

The sporadic trail of people continued on, mostly in groups of twos and threes. I soon noted that the pace at which we traveled was unmistakably slower. The little girl seemed to walk somewhat faster than her older sister did. She still did not say much.

"I am sorry," I cleared my throat. "I didn't catch any of your names back by the hut."

"I'm Nasreen," the older sister said. "And my sister is Noreen."

"Nice names," I said. "They even rhyme."

"My mom," she said as she rolled her eyes. "She was into rhyming names. She wanted all of us to have the same ending letters. What about you? What's your name?"

"Ari," I politely responded.

"Ari?" she repeated. "Interesting name."

"Yeah, interesting indeed," I replied.

I wondered what the names of the other sisters were, but I restrained myself from asking, and she did not volunteer them.

We walked on that way for a few hours, none of us thinking of much to say. Clouds began to gather once more. "Not again!" I exclaimed in frustration as the rain began again.

Soon we were once more enveloped in a torrential rain. There was nowhere to run for cover atop the grassy hill. Open fields stretched for some distance with only a few trees directly ahead. In the far distance, a mountain lay in wait with a path leading up toward it.

About fifty feet to my left, a petite girl sat on a stone, her head in her arms. Soon, she laid her head on her thighs and curled up like a ball. She rocked back and forth. I wearily approached her, and as I came closer, I heard her gently weeping.

Right across the trail, a few people congregated about a fire, stretching their arms over the comforting heat of the burnt logs. A man kept stoking the fire so that it kept burning in spite of the rain.

I asked the crying girl what was wrong. She said she was so cold that she could not move. I asked her if she knew any of those who huddled by the newly ignited fire. She said one of them was her mom, her sister, her aunt. Her aunt's spouse were among them as well. I was surprised that someone left this child alone.

All those relatives and none of them cared to take this girl's hand and bring her near to the fire? I wondered.

"Come," I cried. "Let me carry you closer to the fire."

She slowly stood up but quickly sat down again. "I can't," she whined.

I grabbed her arm and tried to give her a lift. She barely stood up. I put my arms around her shoulders and walked her toward the fire.

"Kahzhaw?" one woman shouted. "Where were you?" The woman appeared to be in her mid-to-late forties and had the appearance of a wealthy person. Traces of makeup stained her face.

"She was sitting back there,"—I pointed to the site—"on a rock under the tree. She was shaking from cold. "

"Oh, my girl, I am sorry! I didn't mean to leave you on your own," said the wealthy woman.

I assumed from her response that she was this girl's mother. The group of five people also included another couple, a second daughter, and another man, who was a bit older, perhaps in his mid-to-late fifties. I thought he was the girl's father, but it turned out from my conversations with the group that he was just a close friend of the family. The husband was left behind in Slemani because he was much older and ill. A journey like this would have proved to be fatal.

"Our Volkswagen broke down right on the 60 Meter highway," the wealthy woman explained. "We left it behind and began climbing Goyzha from the west side."

"A Volkswagen?" I exclaimed. "How did you all fit in a small car like that?"

"The two girls sat in the trunk," answered one of the men.

"Poor girls, they were remarkably calm," said the second woman.

While we were in the middle of the conversation, Nasreen and Noreen arrived. They also wanted to benefit from the warmth of the fire.

"I'm sorry. I didn't forget you," I explained. "I was just trying to help this girl to the fire."

"That's all right. Actually, we'd walked ahead but when I noticed you were held back here, we decided to come back and warm up a bit."

"Welcome! Come and stand by the fire," said the second woman.

"Thank you," I responded. "We have been without fire of our own the last three days. Others have allowed us to stand by theirs."

"You two are a cute couple!" said the older wealthy woman to Nasreen and me. Before I had a chance to explain, she grabbed my arm and held it. "Walk with me, please? I hope you don't mind that

I grabbed your husband's arm!" She turned to Nasreen. "I would appreciate his help in climbing."

Obviously, she assumed Nasreen and I were married. We couldn't blame her. Anyone would have thought as much, since in Islamic culture, a man and a woman may not walk together unless they're married.

"Go ahead," Nasreen answered with a sassy grin at me. "I don't mind."

Nasreen and I were now in an awkward predicament. Out of concern for her well-being and reputation, I hesitated to try to clarify the situation. Both of us would have been regarded very negatively. Muslim culture does not look favorably on any female who has an unmarried companion, and there are no exceptions. She would be called profane names. She would lose her reputation and might even be a victim of an honor killing.

After resting by the fire for a little over half an hour, the man who identified himself as Karim, the friend of the family, urged us to continue our walk.

"This is not a picnic," he complained. "We need to hurry. At this pace it will take us an extra three days to reach the border."

I had learned the names of the others while we conversed. They seemed to be a terrifically upbeat group of people. It would have been fun to hang out with them if it were not for these dismal conditions. Roonak, the wealthy woman, was accompanied by her aunt Sheereen and her husband Hassan. Besides the fellow Karim and the girl Kahzhaw, whom I had helped, there was also the girl's younger sister Azheen. In all, there were now eight of us: five new friends and we three, a fellowship of refugees.

We addressed each other in the formal traditions of our Kurdish culture. Men of similar age address each other as *kaahk*, or big brother. Thus, my new friends became Kaahk Karim and Kaahk Hassan, etc. With much older men, I would have used the prefix *mam* or *khaal*, which means "uncle." Ladies' names include the suffix *khan* after their first names, short for *khanem*, or lady. Older women would have the prefix *poora*, meaning "auntie."

Little did our company know that as we trod the muddy slopes of these remote mountains, our case was gaining the attention and the sympathy of the international communities. The mass exodus of refugees made the worldwide news. Long after it was over, we learned that efforts had been made by countries from around the world to help the Kurdish refugees. Coalition forces and the UNHCR[15] worked in the forefront of that effort.

Coalition leaders also engaged in negotiations with the UN in an effort to establish a no-fly zone, a safe haven that stretched from the northern border of Iraq down to the 36-degree parallel. The purpose: protect the Kurds from any future attacks via chemical or conventional weapons by Baghdad. The world was alarmed by images of cold and hungry Kurds desperately trying to escape Saddam's wrath. Major news agencies, including CNN and BBC, continuously and closely covered the events. Celebrities such as Chris De Burgh and Madonna held concerts to raise funds to help the Kurdish refugees. Supposedly, food, water, and medicine were flown onboard large planes and dropped among us. However, my friends and I never saw a pinch of anything.

---

[15]   United Nations High Commissioner for Refugees

The Shallow Grave

Wet and cold, our fellowship of refugees struggled up the hill. Mud built up deep pockets and potholes thick into the ground. Rain kept falling at a slower rate although lightning scorched the sky above and thunder shook the stones. In one instance, I witnessed lightning hitting a lonely tree on the side of the upcoming hill.

Roonak Khan worried me. She walked uphill slowly and wearily. Then she halted for a minute, pulled a pink umbrella out of her bag, and held it with her right arm. The metal cap atop the umbrella caught my eye, and I worried that she would be struck by lightning. She was two hundred feet ahead of me. I tried to warn her, but my cries were in vain. The barrage of lightning struck sporadically. I thought for sure she would be hit. Yet somehow, she made it to the top without complications. It was a prodigious relief to see her safe and in one piece.

A midsize river flowed north and south, cutting the trail below the ridge. Roonak stood there and stared at the water as it streamed down between the banks. She did not move, as if she were frozen in time or as if she were a victim of a powerful hypnotist.

"What are you waiting for?" I shouted.

"I can't go in," she cried, raising her arms as if in surrender. "That water is too fast! It will sweep me off my feet."

Both of her daughters and Nasreen and Noreen arrived at the same time. All four girls had similar reactions.

"Women," I muttered as I shook my head. I took my shoes off, threw them to the other side of the riverbank, cuffed the legs of my pants, and stepped into the water to test it. I took a few more steps. By the time I reached the middle, the water was waist deep. Large rocks gleamed under the clear water. Moss and algae grew on their surfaces.

"Okay, my back is ready," I declared. "Anyone need a piggyback ride?"

Noreen was first to take advantage of my offer. I was glad she did. She needed it the most. Carefully placing my feet, I avoided the slippery surfaces of the rocks. She had her first piggyback ride across a streaming river on the back of a stranger.

"Who is next?" I asked, slowly wading back through the deep water toward the group.

Only one of Roonak's daughters took advantage of my offer. The rest of the women, hesitant to ride on the back of a stranger, waded into the river themselves and made it to the other side. Because my clothes were already wet from constant rain, I climbed out of the river only a little wetter than I had been when I walked into it.

The trail bent toward the left and headed into a rocky canyon. Rain and flooding water from the river conspired to create a large puddle of mud just around the bend in the trail. With no room to maneuver around it, I walked straight into it. Just as I took my next step, the mud gurgled and my right foot came out bare. I realized that I had just lost my shoe. Panic set in. A frantic search of the muddy water resulted in nothing. Now I had only one shoe on and only God knew how much longer I would need to walk. This episode made me terribly frustrated. I lost it.

"Why are you doing this to me?" I screamed at the top of my lungs to the Almighty, who continued to allow this misery to take place. Finally, I looked around, searching for something to cover my foot. Pieces of ripped bags and plastic floated around the muddy terrain. I used them to construct a makeshift shoe. The rain continued to pour down, as it had for nearly all of the past three days. Would it never stop?

A wide open field nestled between two musty green hills that loomed beyond the ridge. In the field, I noticed a three-foot-deep hole had been dug, which I realized was a grave. Soon we came to learn that an old man had died and some of his family members had dug the shallow grave to bury him. Passing by the freshly dug grave reminded me of my dad's funeral, a gloomy time in my life.

I remembered his untimely illness and subsequent death. It was years ago in December. I had barely approached the age of puberty at the time. Only three days before, he had awakened abruptly and shouted my name.

"Ari, Ari!"

"Yes, Reb Emma." I used to call him that nickname, meaning "the leader of one hundred men." Reb Emma reminded him of his glory days when he was a leader of a team of one hundred men in the British army.

"Get me a cup of water," he asked, as if I were one of his soldiers.

"Yes, sir." I went and filled a glass cup with water and walked back to his room. "Here, I'm sorry it isn't cold. I got it from the tap." He loved icy cold water.

"That is unacceptable." He gazed at his cup as if he were inspecting it. Then abruptly, he said in a low voice, "They will all come."

"Who will come?" I asked.

"My relatives—my dad, my brothers, my sisters," he added, nodding his head.

"But your parents are dead. Your sisters and brothers are too. How can they come?" I asked him with a tone of surprise.

"In my dreams. I dreamt of my mom last night and I know my dad and my siblings will come to visit me in my dreams," he explained. "A sign. It is a sign."

Confused, I asked, "A sign...a sign of what?"

"I am going to die," he ominously declared. "My days are numbered." His chilling assertion made the hair on the back of my neck rise.

"Nah, it's just a dream, nothing more." I jokingly tried to dismiss him.

"It is not...just a dream. I know this," he stated with a bit of annoyance in his voice.

I slowly walked away, thinking about what my dad had just said.

He had recently retired from his work. I knew this was not easy for him. Saddam's regime had robbed him of his severance. They had cut short his military record by ten years and accused him of being a British agent. This affected the amount he could collect from his retirement pay. The monthly paycheck he received as a retiree reckoned him much less than what he deserved. Nevertheless, we could not do much about it. We were Kurds and did not know people in the high areas of government.

Three days after he recalled his dream to me, his health declined and his mobility lessened. One early December morning, clamoring noises awoke me. I sprang out of my bed and went to my dad's room to see him. He lay on his left side and faced the wall. He made unintelligible noises, sounds that sent a chill to my heart; and at that moment, I had a sense of discomfort, as if his dream was coming true. That morning he passed away.

These memories seemed as bleak as the circumstances I was experiencing as I recalled them here in the rainy open field. I shook myself to try to come back to reality.

Suddenly, two men nearby flew at each other. One of them was extremely aggressive. He hurled profanities at the other man like there was no tomorrow. Swear words and threats poured down like the rain falling around us. One of them ran toward a tractor parked nearby. He pulled out an AK-47. He ran toward the other man and pointed the gun at him as if he was about to shoot him. There was a scuffle. Somehow, a few decent men hurried over and broke it up.

"Thank God, he didn't shoot," I said to Kaahk Karim.

What had triggered the fight? That answer we never knew. I had a hunch that, somehow, it was related to the dead man and the fresh grave to my right. Here, I had beheld both childbirth and death all on the same journey.

The day wound down, the sun sliding westward behind the clouds.

"It will be dark soon," said Karim with a concerned look on his face. "And it will grow much colder."

Kaahk Karim assumed the role of the pack leader, and he scoured the area looking for a place to settle for the night. Closer to a group of hills to my right, a shepherd was leading his sheep back to wherever he came from. Karim spoke to him. I did not hear what they exchanged. However, he came back with a small sack in his hand.

"The shepherd gave me this sack of cracked wheat (bulgur)," said Karim.

"Thank God," said the teenage girl. "I haven't eaten anything in two days."

"How are we going to cook this?" Roonak wondered.

Karim found an abandoned tank dugout that looked like a small room with no roof. He thought that would be a decent place to stay for the night. All eight of us searched the land and looked for something to fix the bulgur in. Eventually, Hassan found a rusty metal canister that must have been a bullet container. One of the girls cleaned and removed the accumulated mud out of it.

"Here," she said. "It's clean now."

Now we needed wood to start a fire.

The Stealthy Assassins

Across the dugout, a few birch trees stood motionless. Karim commanded Hassan and I to go get some wood with him.

"By the way," he warned us. "Be careful where you tread. This side of the hill is laid with land mines. The shepherd warned me about them."

The thought of stepping on a land mine was horrific. There was little hope if, God forbid, something of that sort would have happened to any of us. Karim tugged and pulled with difficulty on a couple of wet branches, trying to snap them. Hassan and I collected some twigs. Then we went to help Karim. I was fixated on one branch that I tried to sever. Finally, after wrestling with it, I was able to snap it off the tree. I turned around, but to my surprise, Karim and Hassan had left me all alone. They were already off by the dugout.

All of sudden, fear overcame me. My thoughts froze me in place, my eyes searching the ground for any signs of a mine. I began to walk with slow cautious steps back toward the dugout. I kicked the ground in front of me with the hope that I could expose any buried landmine before I stepped on it. Then I placed my foot softly, as though somehow that would eliminate my weight on the pressure point. The tremendous stress affected my thinking, but it gave me a sense of safety at that moment. Ten slow and agonizing minutes later, I found myself near the dugout with no recollection of how I got there.

While we were busy collecting twigs and branches, the girls had collected some rainwater to cook the bulgur. Dusk had just fallen as the fire began to blaze. We boiled the water and then dumped the bag of cracked wheat into the rusty old can. A few minutes later, the boiling water softened the wheat and it was ready to eat. We each had one scoop of cooked wheat. Without silverware, we ate with our fingers. The scoop of cracked wheat was dirty and filled with small pebbles and perhaps many other things since we could not quite see what we ate. Although the amount was small, it did me extremely well. In the last four days, I had eaten nothing but the broiled onion. I had gotten no sleep, nor used the restroom in all that time.

Tonight I might be able to catch a quick nap, I thought.

We tried to bed down for the night. The dampened ground, the falling raindrops, and the girls' occasional complaint that crawling things touched them kept me awake. Once again, I could not get a moment of sleep. Surprisingly, it still did not affect my cognitive thinking, at least, not yet.

After a couple of hours, Karim roused us. He thought that the border was not far away now. There was no way of telling what the hour was, and I did not care. The idea of spending more time in these mountains had long ago lost its appeal. Earlier, I had accepted the challenge, hoping to see how long I could last. Now weary and hungry, I was ready to go home. I wanted nothing more than to take a hot shower; eat a home-cooked meal; sleep in a soft, warm bed; and, above all, stay dry. I had not been thoroughly dry at any given moment in the last days. The weak light of the sun hid behind the clouds as dawn approached once more. It was the fourth day of my refugee life. How many more days were ahead? I had no way to know.

The mountaintop ahead gleamed under the light of the gloomy dawn. A broad ridge looked down on a vast valley. The trail led us to the left, down the hilltop. A spectacular and a massive valley separated us from another series of mountains. Far down the valley, by the foot of the other mountain range, I saw a row of lustrous objects.

"What do you think those are?" I asked Hassan. I squinted and examined the scene further. They looked like car windshields.

"I think that is the border crossing of Penjwen," he said.

"Yes, it is Penjwen," a passerby confirmed. "There is a dirt road that leads into Iran. That's where most cars await permission to enter."

The Iranians were exceedingly careful to regulate those entering their country. The UNHCR was setting up refugee camps inside Iranian cities and towns in preparation for the arrival of hundreds of thousands of refugees. In the meantime, they had set up makeshift camps on the border to distribute food and medicine. The scene below gave us hope.

"Perhaps by the end of this day we could find ourselves in a refugee camp," I said to Hassan.

We headed down the slope along the side the mountain that we had just climbed. To my left, a tall wall of rocks was hewn out of the mountain. It went straight up and was so awe-inspiring that despite all my misery and anger I had to stop and stare at the scene. In the center of the mountain wall, a cavern was hewn and a thin flow of fresh water fell down directly to the grounds below. It was a waterfall, the like of which I had never seen. Years later, a visit to Yosemite National Park in California would remind me of the scene. The waterfall was breathtaking, and I admired its natural beauty.

Moments later, my reverie was interrupted by a small voice calling, "Khalil, Khalil!" I turned around, and to my surprise, it was my old walking friend Khalil with his wife and little girl. The child had called his name. I was dazed to learn that the little girl spoke. She looked too small.

"Hey, brother Khalil!' I greeted him. "It's great to see you again."

"Oh, you are still alive," he jokingly responded.

We shook hands, and he put his left hand on my arm as a sign of respect and alliance.

"So where did you guys end up?" I asked.

Khalil explained that on the day we were separated he and his wife had been fighting continuously and that he was embarrassed to expose me to their problems.

"There is nothing to be embarrassed about," I assured him. "In times like these it is understandable. We need to support each other and stick together."

This fellowship of mine had grown larger as the days rolled by. Now I had several companions. One was misconstrued as my wife.

The trek down to the valley was not strenuous. A downhill stride gave relief from climbing in the past four days. Noreen, however, looked extremely exhausted. She wobbled sideways like a drunkard. At one point, she gave up walking altogether. She sat down on the ground and began to cry. I walked up to her and asked if she was all right.

"My feet hurt so dreadfully," she whimpered.

"Come," I said, "climb up on my back, and let me carry you."

"No," she wearily responded. "I am not going to burden you." She lowered her head and quailed on the stony ground. Although only twelve years of age, she had shown a great deal of stamina and pride and I was determined to help her. She had not complained in the past four days. The situation was finally taking a toll on her.

"I am so terribly hungry," she went on.

I scanned the crowd for someone who might conceivably have food of any kind. Half a mile below, a woman made her way down the rocky slopes. She hauled a large sack on her back. I figured she must be local to the area, perhaps a farmer or a shepherd. Quickly, I sprang up and strode my way downhill toward her. In desperate tones, I pleaded, "Peace be upon you. Might you have a piece of bread that you can spare? It's for my little sister up there." I pointed to the spot where Noreen sat curled up on the ground.

The woman set down her sack. She reached inside for a loaf of bread and tore off a piece. "Here," she said. "I am sorry, but it's all I can spare. Too many of you ask for food."

I thanked her much and quickly returned to Noreen. She took the bread and ate it ravenously. Then she silently climbed on my back. This made me supremely happy. I was touched to know that she now trusted me. I felt a connection with this little girl. Although I was too young to be her father figure, a big brother would do. I wanted to take care of her. With her on my back, I sprang to my feet and set forth strolling down the slope of the mountain. From that day on, Noreen and I developed a silent understanding between us.

To my right, vast flats lay quietly, unaware of the stream of thousands of refugees treading across their soil. To my left, the tall wall of broken rocks stood proudly facing eastward. Paradoxically, the pastoral scenery bore a sinister image. Below and to my left, hundreds of landmines stuck their ugly heads out of the soil. These stealthy, nonhuman assassins threatened havoc even in the absence of their master.

I looked away to avoid further thoughts of a detonating landmine[16] and what it could do to the flesh of its poor victim. Rushing winds swirling in from the valley ran through Noreen's hair.

Hours later, the sound of streaming water was audible. Perhaps a creek ran among the trees down below. We came into the lush area of trees and discovered that a small creek indeed flowed through them. Here and there, folks pitched tents and some spread their rugs over the sward. The deeper we travelled into the trees, the more people stationed and pitched tents. One could have mistaken it for a picnic area. Busy men and women among the tents gave the place a vibration of energy.

I put my load down on the musty, rain-saturated ground. Noreen hopped gingerly on one foot and then the other, as if she did not want her boots to be muddied. She and I strolled around, gawking at the hustling families as they struggled to prepare for their day. Some cleaned the grounds around their tent. Some threw rugs down to furnish and warm up the cold grassy floor of the tree-filled area.

Figure 4 Cluster Landmine

---

[16] From 1979 to 1988, Saddam's regime had buried thirty million land mines across the borders of Kurdistan with Iran and Turkey.

A woman who wore traditional clothes was cooking something in a large pot on a campfire. It smelled like rice pilaf. Mesmerized and yet famished, Noreen and I greedily inhaled the fragrance of the freshly cooked pilaf, while daydreaming of consuming a plate full.

The rest of the group arrived minutes later. Roonak walked up to the woman, and they hugged and kissed each other's cheeks. Soon Roonak waved her hand to us, signaling everyone to come and join them. I was too hungry to show interest in anything but eating, and the woman's name escaped me. I was tremendously grateful when she politely invited all of us to eat from her freshly cooked pot of rice. In a normal situation, a Kurd would resist and there would be insistent and repeated invitation from the host, only to be politely declined by the guest. However, in this case, we were so ravenous that traditions were dispensed.

As we ate our fill of rice, we learned that this generous and amiable woman and Roonak were related. She and her family had arrived at this spot a few days before. They drove their own truck. That explained why they had been able to bring so many necessities, such as cooking pans, pots, a kerosene heater, lanterns, a tent, blankets, rugs, and an AK 47. These people had traveled on the gravelly highway that continued northerly toward the border of Iran.

Those who were blessed with cars or trucks did not suffer the impact of the exodus as much as those who walked. This noble family made this ordeal feel more like a picnic or a camping trip. More than half a dozen other families pitched tents similarly nearby, living out of vehicles loaded with equipment in this valley near the creek.

Suddenly, gunshots were heard. I sprang up off the ground and found my way to Noreen.

"Come," I called out to her. "Hurry! Hop on my back." I was certain that enemy troops were nearby, firing shots at refugees.

Our hostess gestured at me. "Relax," she said. "It's only my husband hunting."

Her husband had shot a rabbit running through the woods. From a distance, he came striding toward us, carrying his prey on his shoulder.

Nearly an hour and a half later, we were told that more food was ready. As I ate an additional plate of red rice seasoned with onion and tomatoes, I savored every bite. It was the first real meal I had eaten in five days. The husband of the cook struck up a conversation.

"We camped here because water is readily available," he explained.

They also came from my city, Slemani.

"I did not desire to move my family across the border," he continued. "I don't have much faith in the Iranians. They would treat us as badly, if not worse, than the Iraqis." He paused for a short time. "Here, we're only half an hour away from the border. I have the option of staying right where we are or crossing into Iran if things escalate." He recommended that we all stay there overnight and reconsider crossing the border. "Don't walk all the way to the border yet, I have heard rumors that they (meaning Coalition forces) are negotiating with Saddam. There might be an accord to help us go back to town without threats of arrests or executions by the Iraqi army."

"Another amnesty? No, thanks. I don't need one."

I was determined to leave life in Iraq behind me, this time for good. I would register myself in a refugee camp in the hopes of being interviewed by a European country, perhaps obtaining political asylum. Any of the countries of the EU, Australia, or the USA would be superior to my prospects in Iraq. Many Kurds had earlier fled Iraq back in the 70s and 80s and obtained asylum in Europe or Australia. In fact, there are more than two million Kurds scattered around EU countries today.

As I pondered whether to cross the border, dusk arrived swiftly. The large mountains to the west shielded the light of the sun, causing nightfall to arrive prematurely. Nasreen and Noreen kept close to me as the sun slipped away westward. Khalil, his wife, and child strolled aimlessly about like lost souls.

Bone-Chilling Night

Campfires went up as the temperature dropped. It seemed much colder here than it had been up in the mountains. Whether it was because we were in lowlands and near a stream of water or because we had stopped moving, I could not tell.

Someone had thrown a large rug on the grass beneath the trees. I snuck in and lay on the rug. A frigid breeze blew in from the area of the creek. It made me shudder. I folded half of the rug to cover over myself while I lay on the other half, hoping this would keep me warm. I closed my eyes and drifted off to sleep.

I have no idea how long I slept before I was awakened by the sound of an explosion. The campfire was about ten feet away, its red light flickered dimly. Yet I was so cold and stiff that I could not move my arms or my legs. For a moment I wondered if I had become paralyzed. I struggled in an effort to give myself a boost out of the folded rug but to no avail. My attempt failed to move even a single finger on my hands. My body and mind drifted off to sleep again. The last thing I recalled was the flying cinders from the fire pit. My sleep was fitful.

Soon I was awakened again by my body's sense of urgency to move. This time I strove to call for aid, but my tongue felt frozen also. For a brief second I believed that I was passing into the land of the dead, imagining that this was how death creeps upon the living. The basin felt like a deep freezer, motionless and cold. Other than glimmers of lanterns and torches, nothing else moved. Eventually, I gathered all my might and gave it a last push and my left shoulder moved ahead. Then my right leg budged under me. Finally, I was able to crouch on all fours, still trapped under the rug. The weight of the rug felt as if an incubus lay on my back. Turtle-like, I stuck my head out of the rug only to be struck by a gust of frozen wind that came from the creek. My whole body shook and shuddered. I was unable to move away from the accursed rug. I had never experienced anything like this before, being so cold that I literally could not move.

Once more and with a Herculean effort, I began crawling my way out of the folded rug. I made my way desperately towards the fire, moving with great effort. No one seemed to pay attention to me heaving and pulling my way painfully across the ground. None viewed my struggle with the elements of the Kurdish valley. How long this went on? I have no idea. However, it felt like an eternity.

At last, I made it. The warmth from the burning twigs and logs enveloped me like a thick, smooth blanket drawn over my body. The fire loosened me up. As though I were a great hibernating animal that had just awakened from its slumber, I sprang up to stand on my feet, checking to make sure that I was not paralyzed. The invigorating scent of burnt wood gave me a sense of life once more.

From that moment on, I sat next to that fire pit and never stepped away from it. I was determined not to fall asleep for fear of going through the same experience again. I watched the night slip away, and the grey dawn creep up on the camp. Life began extremely early in this unofficial campsite. Folks awoke before sunrise. The sounds of labor could be heard in all corners. Some fetched water from the creek; some performed ablution (ritual washing) in anticipation of Islamic morning prayer. Others were busy loading and unloading items into and from their vehicles. One man tried to tune in his radio so he could receive BBC or Voice of America in Arabic. News updates played a prominent part in people's decisions about what to do next. The old man did not seem to be terribly successful. Perhaps we were too far in the mountains to be able to pick up decent reception. Rumors and hearsay had been our only source of news for the past five days. Dawn arrived quickly. Soon everyone was awake. The sun dispelled the grey mist that had risen from the creek, and for the first time in five days, we witnessed a sunny dawn. It gave a sense of security and optimism to the group.

Nasreen and Noreen exchanged morning greetings with a few other women. Hassan, Karim, and Khalil relayed the news they'd heard from another man, that the border was merely three-hour's walk away. We decided that the four of us men should go and check out the situation. That morning we walked to the border and left the women behind in the dell.

The gravely trail twisted sharply in some areas and undulated like a roller coaster in others. As we walked along, we chatted about various topics. Four hours later, we arrived to the border near the passage point. To our surprise, enterprising merchants had turned the area into a market place. They sold everything one needed to survive in the outdoors. Tarps, blankets, fire starters, canned food, fresh fruits—all were displayed before us.

"Wow," gasped Hassan, "this reminds me of *Ber Darky Sara*."[17]

"Kurds!" said Khalil as he shook his head in amazement. "They always find a way to make money, even in these types of situations."

"Actually, this is not a bad idea," I commented, then paused. "I sure wish I'd had them a few days ago!"

"Hey," said Karim as he gently tapped me on my shoulder, "now you can look for a pair of shoes." He laughed softly.

"I know," I said. "I was just thinking of that!"

It did not take long to find a pair of cheaply made plastic shoes. I paid for them and quickly snatched them from the merchant. The flip-flop I had borrowed from Roonak had held its own quite well over the past several days. However, it was a few sizes too small. It was luxurious to have a real pair of shoes again.

We began to ask people questions about the situation. We soon learned that about two miles away, there was a crossing point, a UNHCR reception site, and a mobile hospital. The Iranians controlled the situation, and they only let in forty thousand refugees

---

[17]   Slemani's largest open bazaar

a day. Later, I learned that, based on UN numbers, there were 2.5 million refugees scattered across the mountains of bordering Iran and Turkey. The influx of refugees overwhelmed the Turkish and Iranian governments. The UN pressured both administrations to absorb the impact more quickly, but Iranian authorities did not respond to the pressure at first, which contributed to worsening of conditions. US Chinook helicopters dropped tons of protein bars, water, and medicine over the exiting refugees. We did not see these relief efforts in our area, but rumor had it that they rescued many at the Turkish border.

The situation on the border of Turkey was most dire. The Turkish government dealt with the refugees harsher than the Iranians, refusing to allow any to enter their country. Pushed away by the Turks, thousands of refugees became stranded in the snowy peaks of the Amedi and Zakho mountains and suffered greatly.

Turkish officials excused their behavior, citing their prominent problems dealing with their own Kurdish population and the PKK. The PKK, short for Party Krekarany Kurdistan or Labor Party of Kurdistan, is a secular, communism-advocating, and anti-Turkish government militant movement whose goal is to liberate Kurdistan from Turkey and establish an independent nation of Kurdistan in the southeast. Founded in 1978, the PKK did not begin its armed struggle against Turkey until 1984, under the command Abdullah Ocallan. Since then, thousands of Kurds and Turks have been killed in skirmishes, guerilla fights, and ambushes over and in between the mountains of Turkish Kurdistan. These issues caused the Turks to be extremely cautious in dealing with the mass exodus of Iraqi Kurds on their doorstep.

Our reconnaissance trip to the border was a success. We purchased fruit and other supplies to distribute among the people in the makeshift camp in the dell. As I bought a couple of pounds of fresh oranges and waited for the others to make their choices, I thought about the land around me, once dwelt by hardy men and women with short rugged bodies and deep brown eyes. They grew rich vineyards, and crops were garnered abundantly. Now they lived an uncertain existence, constantly threatened by the red hand of Saddam spreading poison and death indiscriminately. The living and the dead endured under his brutality. My chain of thoughts was interrupted by Hassan and Karim. They were determined to return and stay in the glade near their relatives and friends. I, myself, missed Noreen. She had become like a little sister to me.

We set out again. As we walked, my mind drifted away from conversation with the others as new plans and ploys germinated in my thoughts. Iraq and all of its wealth did not appeal to me anymore. I desired a new life, a new beginning in another country far away.

The light of the day grew dimmer, and three and a half hours later, the valley loomed from the distance.

Noreen smiled broadly as she saw me approaching. "How was it?" she asked with an excitedly giggly voice, taking my hand.

I told her an abridged tale of my account at the border and the bazaar. "See!" I pointed down at my shoes. "Look, I bought new shoes."

"By Allah! That's great! Now you can carry me better!" she cried.

I handed her an orange to eat. Swiftly, she took it and stuck it in her coat pocket, chattering about her day. Her sister Nasreen soon joined us but was much more reserved in showing emotions. I was in shambles trying to figure her out. The two girls spoke about their uneventful day, expressing relief that they had been able to rest.

The bleak shadow of the mountain grew larger as the sun made its way westward. To my dismay, another night impended ahead.

"Well, we should collect some wood for a fire before night falls," I said to the girls.

Noreen came along with me to collect twigs and fallen branches far from the shallow creek. Most of those were dried out, unlike the ones we had struggled with on the rainy mountainside. With relative ease, I kindled a large fire to keep us warm while our companions went on attending to their own business.

Roonak and her group had met relatives and set up camp at some distance. Khalil and his wife had done the same. That night, as the girls and I sat at our fire away from the others, I discussed Karim and Hassan's choices.

"They want to stay here," I whispered. "But, honestly, I am not thrilled about that option. I've decided I am going into Iran, and beyond." I explained to them that it was my intention to leave the country and that this was my opportunity to seek asylum elsewhere, possibly even in Europe.

Upon hearing this, Noreen released a little squeal.

"Oh! I would love to live in Europe!" she cried.

Nasreen, however, had an ill view of my plans.

"I am only telling you this because I want you to make a decision of your own," I whispered to the two sisters. "I am leaving whenever the opportunity arises."

The two girls continued to whisper among themselves. However, I overheard Noreen excitedly telling her sister how delightful it would be to live in Europe.

We dozed near the fire for a few hours. Sometime around midnight, I was awakened when a pickup truck pulled over by the campsite. The driver announced that he was heading to the border.

"Anyone needs a cheap ride?" he shouted.

The revving of his engine disturbed the somber air of the night, and I sprang to my feet, as alert as a sentinel. I saw him and his truck as an opportunity for a ride to the border, but the two sisters lying on a rug nearby made me think twice. The truck rested there while its engine ran idle. The smell of diesel filled the atmosphere. The driver was not in haste, which gave me a few moments to think. I reconsidered briefly, but the lore of my age did not aid me in making a decision, for I was young. In the end, I followed my haughty heart and decided to leave.

"I have to go," I whispered softly, lowering my head to crouch next to little Noreen near the fire pit. "You two are in safe hands here."

Her lips trembled, and she began to weep without a sound. Nasreen slept undisturbed.

"Say good-bye to your sister."

The child nodded her head in agreement. Without hesitation, I sprinted to the back of the pickup truck and jumped in. A few people had climbed in ahead of me. Some stood still while others sat with knees drawn to their chests. The driver made a final call, and then he hopped into his seat, revving the engine a few times.

Suddenly, Khalil and his family jumped in, followed by Nasreen and Noreen.

"Hey," I called out with a smile on my face, "you guys are coming?"

"Yes," Nasreen answered hesitantly.

Her younger sister clambered over to me. "You just can't go alone," little Noreen said. "And you can't get rid of us that easily!" She smiled broadly, her large brown eyes emitting excitement.

The truck rolled out gradually. Its headlights pierced the thick darkness of the night, illuminating what was ahead. I swiftly stood up so my head was above the edge of the truck bed and waved good-bye to the folks who had hosted us the preceding night and day.

"Allah goes with you!" I shouted as others joined in the farewell.

We heard a few faint replies as the truck left the glade. Then we fell silent, each lost in our own thoughts. The trip was quite uncomfortable. We bumped along the rough roads, but it was still better than walking the same distance on foot. It was a moonless night on the plains of Kahni Sur, and little was visible other than the dark mass of the mountain behind us. The hours, or perhaps the minutes, rolled by heavy and slow. I lost track of time. This was my fifth night without adequate sleep. Heads nodded as the wobbling truck bed rocked some to sleep.

After a while, I stood up once more to try to determine where we were. In the distance, multiple campfires flickered and twinkled. We were close to the border.

Suddenly, the truck slowed down, and the driver pulled over. Off his truck he came and announced that he was going in a different direction. He was not taking us all the way to the border after all.

Voices rose in complaint.

"We are paying you for this!" one male voice cried out.

"Get of my truck!" shouted the driver angrily. "And I don't need you to pay me!"

Reluctantly, we stepped down off his truck.

"How far is the border from here?" I asked.

"Not too far. Two kilometers, perhaps less!" he answered. "I would stay on the border if I were you. The Iranians won't let you cross over anyway." The driver hopped back in his vehicle and drove off.

Some of us stood there for a few moments while others wandered away immediately and began walking toward the flickering lights.

"Well, I guess we have to get going again," I said.

The girls, Khalil, and his wife and child followed.

Figure 5. Some families cooked food
while camped in the dell.

The Unwilling Witness

Onward we went, a company of six strangers now bonded via fateful events. I noticed Nasreen limping, but I didn't think much of it at first.

Perhaps she is tired, I thought.

However, no more than twenty strides later, she halted, stretched her arm, and sat on the cold hardy ground. She began to weep, swinging her head back and forth, as children do when reading the Koran in Islamic Madrasa.

"Are you all right?" I asked with concern.

"My hip hurts," she answered faintly. "I had hip surgery as a child. Now the pain is back. Walking the past few days has taken a toll on me."

Khalil and his wife kept on, slowly strolling away from us, heading in the direction of the looming campfires. After some consideration, I decided I had no choice but throw Nasreen on my back and carry her.

I had never suspected she had any issues regarding her legs, but now I realized why she fell behind her little sister constantly. We headed toward the first visible campfire. Although cloudy, the night was not as cold as the last, but it was certainly moonless. We stayed in one line and walked cautiously. On a hillside, a family of three—an older man, his wife, and their son—were gathered around a lovely blue fire. I took Noreen by the hand while Nasreen remained on my back and headed toward them. The older man stood erect and straight. His lean body gleamed in the light of the fire, and his face was rugged and hardy. He welcomed us, along with Khalil and his family.

Heads hanging low, we sat down near the bright fire.

"It's oak," said the old man. "Only oak wood gives off such bright blue light."

None of us had any clue as to what time it was. The night was folding away its dark layers, yet no sleep came to me. The shadows gradually gave way to the pale light of the rising sun in the east. Suddenly, the peaks and the edges of the surrounding mountains reared their heads. A shaft of golden yellow light shone on the opposite side of the dale as the sun rose behind the border mountains of the once-embattled ravines and dales. Blue smoke levitated from multiple campfires, and it shimmered in the sunlight as it rose in the ether. The yellow disk of the sun felt much closer to earth today, closer than usual. The morning dawned with new promise. I sprang up on my feet.

"Based on our last visit here, we should be just minutes away from the border," I said to Khalil.

We thanked our hosts, and our company got up and began walking once more toward the border, leaving dejected faces behind us.

A neatly flattened trail stretched beyond the upcoming hilltop. It looked as if someone had made sure the roads were capable of carrying armored tanks and the individuals that drove them. As we walked, I could vaguely overhear Khalil and his wife mumbling antagonistic words to each other. Their bickering accelerated. Finally, Khalil called out to me.

"Kaahk Ari! I want you to be the witness. Right here and right now, I am divorcing this woman," he said, waving his arms in frustration.

"What?" I responded with disgust. "Please, Khalil, this is downright childish! We're in the middle of nowhere, for god's sake. You two need to support each other, not separate from each other. This is shameful! I am certainly not going to be your witness or give my approval for any such thing. Don't be ridiculous."

"Brother," his wife cut in, "let him! I am sick of it too. If he wants to divorce me, let him." She paused briefly. "Just wait until we get back home. Then you can answer to my brothers, you half a man!" She scowled at him in disgust.

I was floored. "Seriously, you two, let it go. This is not the time and place for a divorce. Think about your child. What are you going to do with her? Besides, the Iranians will not let you stay together, if you are divorced. You know how they are. It is an Islamic republic, might I remind you. This is no time for foolishness."

Nasreen stepped in and ushered Khalil's wife and daughter away from him. I had no idea what had brought them to this point, but it was no laughing matter. Wasn't it enough that we were fleeing with a brutal enemy on our tail? To top it off, we were facing entry into an Islamic republic that was not exactly welcoming.

I couldn't believe that Khalil was serious. For one thing, according to Islamic law, no witness is needed for a divorce. I wondered whether Khalil had called upon me in the hope that I would mediate and prevent him from following through.

Islamic Sharia law declares that a man has a right to divorce his wife for any reason, whatsoever, at any time. All that is necessary for divorce is that the husband pronounces the words "I divorce you." It can be spoken or written once, twice, or thrice.

If the words are uttered once, or even twice, reconciliation is still possible. However, the marriage is ended permanently if the words are proclaimed three times. In the event that the woman marries another and the second husband dies or divorces her, the first husband may remarry her.

As I pondered our companions' disturbing behavior, we approached a grassy knoll. Iranian sentinels watched over a barbed wire gateway. Droves of refugees were entering Iran ushered by the UNHCR.

To the right of the gate was parked a white ambulance with the UNHCR logo on its sides. The wheels disappeared halfway into the tall growth of lank grass that had sprouted in the abundant rain.

Next to the ambulance stood a large sand-colored tent with a canopy in front of it. Medical personnel commuted in and out of the tent. A line of bedraggled refugees in tattered clothing waited to be seen by doctors and nurses.

"So this is it," I said to Khalil. "Are you guys coming across?"

"Of course," he quickly responded. "To hell with Iraq and Kurdistan. I am leaving, even if Gholala doesn't come along. I will just take my daughter Ashti and leave."

I believe this was the first time I heard Khalil speak his wife's name. A lovely name meaning "tulips." I had known him and his wife for five days and not once had he called her by name, nor had she introduced herself to me. Although it was our culture, I had never gotten used to the treatment of women in Islam. In a society built on Islamic traditions, women enjoy little status. To me, it had always appeared that women were feared by men, who concealed and controlled them under the excuse of "protecting" them.

"Come, my friend," I gently said to Khalil. "You are not going to leave them here. They need you, and you need each other."

He didn't respond.

By then, the women had caught up with us and passed us. Khalil surveyed them slowly hiking their way, reeling under the grab of earth's gravity. Then, like coordinated dancers, they propped up on the grassy knoll.

Khalil had asked me earlier about Nasreen. He was glad to know that one of them was my wife and the other was my sister-in-law. "At least you two seem to have a better marriage than mine," he murmured ironically.

The women paused briefly before we crossed over to the Iranian side.

An Iranian female guard came up to us, and she distributed Islamic scarves to each of the women, including the twelve-year-old Noreen.

"*Zanan bayad serytoon be posheed* (Women must cover their heads)!" she shouted in Farsi.

"*Ary mefahim, xaily memonoon* (All right, we understand. Thank you)," I responded.

Gholala, Khalil's wife, was the most disgruntled. "Ugh," she muttered, "I hate head scarves, and my dad never forced us to wear one. He was a nonpracticing Muslim, and he always told us, 'What counts is what is in the heart, not all the rituals that people do to please Allah. He shouldn't need our rituals.' So we never truly practiced much at home."

Noreen and Nasreen gently placed the headscarves over their hair.

"I don't really know how to put this on either. We never wore one except at prayer time during Ramadan," Nasreen commented.

By now it was almost noon. The sun had climbed its way into the middle of the bright blue sky. Now we consented to enter the territory of Iran as refugees. One by one, we were searched at the barbed-wire-topped wooden gate of the border. Iranian sentinels wrote down our names and ages and gave us each a paper slip with a number. One of them kept repeating, "*Baray Urdugay Abbasabbad* (this is for Camp Abbasabbad)." Then a sergeant commanded us to walk over to the Iranian area and wait for *miniboos*, a minibus, that would take us to the camp.

In the meantime, a beige Toyota pickup truck approached. It drove its way through the carefully carved hill. The Toyota pulled over, and a man in civilian clothes jumped out. With both hands, he lifted up a load of freshly baked Iranian bread. "Biscuits, wafers, and bread!" he shouted. He claimed he was from a nearby village and that this was a donation from the dwellers of the tiny hamlet. An Iranian Kurd, the man's accent was a bit strange to us. However, we understood him clearly. The particular part of Iran in which we found ourselves is called *Austan Eh Kurdistan*, meaning "Region of Kurdistan."

Originally, Kurdistan was one piece of land and the Kurds lived in harmony and peace with their Persian, Arab, and Turkish neighbors. At the end of WW1, the victorious British troops marched into Iraq, then known as the Ottoman Empire. Later, the Brits controlled the population by appointing a local king, King Faisal, to rule over Iraq. This was intended to make British influence less apparent and less odious to the people.

Faisal was an Arab and a Sunni Muslim. Sir Percy Cox, British colonial administrator of Middle Eastern affairs, reported to London that it was in Britain's best interest to have an Arab king rather than a Kurd. According to Cox, the Kurds were more headstrong and harder to control. At his suggestion, Britain mandated the division of the area, drawing borders that separate modern-day Iraq, Iran, Turkey, and Syria, and tearing Kurdish entity apart in the process. The Kurds woke up to this bitter reality and found themselves scattered among four countries. They took up arms and battled for their existence against the far superior British forces and the central governments of Baghdad, Tehran, Ankara, and Damascus. Nowhere was the so-called Kurdish Problem more visible than in Iraq, where Saddam's regime had aggressively sought to wipe out the Kurdish people with chemical weapons early in 1988. These lands lay desolate even today, toxic and barren where once villages and farms thrived. We Kurds had no homeland to call our own.

Our little company lay in wait on the sward, hoping that soon the *miniboos* would come. Exhausted, drowsy, and full, I fell asleep. The grassy knoll cushioned my back, and the rocks served as a pillow for my head. Several times, I awakened but the bus had not yet come.

Hours passed, and when I opened my eyes again, dusk had fallen. The evening light shimmered in the west, and blue shadows hung over the twilight. The nearby hills seemed larger than they had been earlier. The sun had set, yet still no sign of a bus at all. At last, the Iranian sergeant made an announcement. He explained that there had been some logistical issues with their transportation system.

"The bus is not coming. You all have to walk to the village of Hangazhal," he shouted.

The waiting crowd did not respond well to this announcement.

"We have been walking for days. Now you ask us to walk farther yet?" cried out a middle-aged man dressed in traditional Kurdish clothing and carrying a little girl in his arms.

No answer seemed to come out of the Iranian tent. With no other option at hand, we all got up and strode wearily toward the dusty road that descended downhill. It overlooked a remote village. The lighted lanterns placed in the windowsills of the mud homes in the distance encouraged us. Despite the unpleasant circumstances, the view of the quiet hamlet of Hangazhal nestled among tall, dark mountains was soothing.

Camp Abbasabbad

After trekking in the dark for over an hour, roars of car engines were heard. Bright headlights shed their beams over the dirt track, illuminating it like daylight.

Suddenly, three pickup trucks appeared. Dust particles rose in a haze around us. A soldier jumped out and waved to everyone to get in the back of one of the trucks. There was a stampede as people scrambled to grab a spot in one of the pickups. My primary concern was the two girls. I lifted Noreen into the back of a pickup first and then her sister. Nasreen had a harder time climbing in. I searched for Khalil and his family, but it was too dark to see where they had gone. Finally, I jumped in and the three trucks drove off in one line to an unknown destination. Rain began falling again, and the night grew bleaker.

A little over an hour later, we pulled up in front of a gated garrison. A passenger sprang out of his seat and spoke to the guards. A few minutes later, the guard raised the gate and let us in.

The site looked like a military camp. A few concrete buildings were vaguely discernable against the dark mass of the mountain behind the camp. The trucks maneuvered along the road. Freshly wet by rain, potholes filled with newly formed pools of stagnant water.

We dismounted the trailer before a doorless room utterly packed full of bodies seeking refuge from the weather. Hundreds of others aimlessly walked about outdoors in the rain like zombies. The three of us stood by the outside wall of the doorless room, hoping that its narrow concrete canopy would fend off the rain. Irritatingly, the rain fell toward us at an angle. There was to be no relief from its pelting tonight.

Upon inquiring, I learned that we had indeed arrived at Camp Abbasabbad. It was a makeshift camp used for gathering statistics and for the redistribution of refugees to more permanent camps.

I could see the frustration on the girls' faces. My heart went out to them. As the night grew deeper, the temperatures dropped. Chilly winds swirled through the air and twisted the direction of the falling rain. Leaning against the concrete wall, we stood outside of the room, damp and cold. Finally, some women managed to squeeze Nasreen and Noreen into the already crowded room. I remained outside. Legs drawn to my chest, my body shuddered as I leaned against the wet wall.

I lost track of time and drifted once more into unconsciousness, only to be awakened by sirens going off. It was time for the military company to go into morning preparation. They were in the process of a flag-raising ceremony.

Mist and clouds hung over the north, and it crowned the distant mountain chain, when I just remembered the two girls. I panicked, thinking that I had lost them. I sprang up out of my position. My legs tingled since I had sat in the same position for too long.

"Nasreen, Nasreen," I shouted.

No response came. I repeated the call once more, and then a muted response came from the end of large truck covered with a waxy tarp.

"Yes, we are here," Noreen's voice replied. A moment later, she stuck her head out from underneath the tarp. "We are here, do not worry."

"How did you guys get back there?" I asked.

Nasreen flung her right leg over the tailgate of the trailer, then her left, and awkwardly jumped down onto the ground. She adjusted her coat and pulled it down to cover herself.

"Those women were so wicked," she whispered. "They pushed us out of the room last night. We had nowhere to go but climb into the back of this truck. The tarp kept us warm but, more importantly, dry."

I was relieved knowing that they were both okay. I would not have forgiven myself had something happened to them while I dozed off. They had entrusted themselves to my care, and in my care they stood. After the soldiers had finished their flag ceremonies, an announcement was broadcasted over the loud speakers.

"*Thabt namha bezodi aghaz shudeh* (registrations shall begin soon)," said the voice.

Soon, queues of men and women were formed.

"Females nine years and older must cover their hair," the orders came in.

Names, age, and number of family members were asked for by Iranian registrars. Rumors quickly spread that families and singles would be sent to separate camps. We were told that families had priority. They were given better care and food, or so we believed. In order for the two girls to have any chance to stay with me, I had to register Nasreen as my wife and Noreen as my sister-in-law.

The men stood in an extremely long line, but the women's was much shorter.

"Why don't we both stand in line?" I suggested to Nasreen. "You stand in the women's column, and I'll stand in the men's and whoever gets there faster will have us registered."

She graciously agreed to do so. Exhaustion, malnutrition, and lack of sleep took a toll on my body so much that at one point, while standing in line, I fell asleep. My knees gave in, and I fell straight down. But just before I hit the floor, I was awakened. Two hours went by. The rain came and went. At times, it lashed, and sometimes, only droplets fell. At one point, Nasreen came striding toward me with a furious look.

"What's wrong?" I inquired.

"Filthy soldiers," she fumed. "They groped me and every other woman that waited in line." Then she burst into tears.

"I am so sorry." I placed my hand on her shoulder as I tried to comfort her.

"The bastards claim to be Muslims and look how they treat people. We knocked on their doors and sought help, and they take advantage." She wiped her tears. "But I did get us registered," she said. "They gave me a note for three people as one family. We have to wait for another bus to pick us up and take us to a permanent camp." I left the line to accompany her back to her sister, who was alone and anxious and needed to know what came of things. By midday, the whole *urdugga* (military camp) had turned into a puddle of mud as hundreds of soldier and thousands of refugees trampled on and kneaded the muddy landscape.

Three Iranian-assembled, midsize buses arrived. They came to deliver refugees to distant camps. Older versions of Toyota Coasters, these buses housed twenty-one seats besides the driver. Soon, a guard, the driver, and twenty of us were loaded onto one of the minibuses, and off it went. None of us had any idea how long the trip would take. However, we heard the name *Urdugay Saqqez* mentioned a few times. The driver and guard spoke Farsi. I understood some of the language, but not enough to comprehend complex conversation. Today was day seven of my journey out of Iraq. Perhaps it was not the end yet. A great deal of time had passed when the driver pulled into a roadside tea shop that neighbored a restaurant.

"Break time!" he shouted.

No one responded, for sleep had crept up on most of the passengers. The tiny roadside place emanated a welcoming vibe. The owner gave away food and drinks for free to all of us. Noreen jumped out of the bus and walked up to the tea shop's display stand, a truly humble one.

I went over to her. "If you want anything, feel free to get it. I will take care of it, okay?" I said.

"I know you would, but thank you. I don't want anything," she assured me.

Nasreen soon joined us. "Hey, look," she said, "dried figs! You love those, Noreen."

I picked up a small plastic bag of figs. "How much?" I asked the shop tender.

"Twenty toman," he replied. "But it's free for the little girl."

Iranian currency is known as *rial*, but is more commonly called *toman*. A group of ten rial equal one toman. Ironically, despite the eight-year war and the Gulf War, the Iraqi dinar still was worth more than the toman. The exchange rate at that time was twenty toman to a dinar. The one thousand dinars in my pocket would have lasted me at least four to six months. I took out a five-dinar bill to pay for the dried figs, but the shopkeeper would not take it because he knew we were refugees.

"No, please keep it. You are our brothers and sisters," the shopkeeper said politely and generously.

"May you be prosperous and safe. Thank you very much," I responded.

Our rather formal remarks were customary in such an exchange of speech. Courtesy and friendliness are highly valued as virtues in that culture. The guard came out of the restaurant, signaling to us with his hands to get back into the minibus.

"*Bya, bya bereveem,*" he repeated.

"Come on, let's go."

Slowly, unhurriedly, passengers began to board.

"We are near Baneh," the driver told us. He had just learned that an avalanche of snow had blocked one of the passages to Saqqez. Because of it, he was forced to divert to an alternate road.

I took in the scenery around us as we jostled our way back into the bus. It was breathtaking. A large tree-filled valley sat softly between two towering mountains with glistening white snow covering their peaks. The whiteness of the snow contrasted sharply with the rich green hue of the trees and the velvety dark-brown earth that surrounded them.

"No, it's all right," remarked Noreen as we squeezed our way back to our seats. "You sit next to my sister." She gave me a pert little smirk.

"You little devil!" I mussed the veil up on her head.

The passengers fell asleep during the second leg of the trip, but I was not one of them. Various thoughts and emotions sprinted through my mind, keeping me awake. Now that we were essentially out of danger, I had no inclination as for what to expect. These two girls were complete strangers just five days ago, but now one of them is publicly known as my wife. *How am I going to handle this? What are the expectations?* I wondered. Fears and worries stormed through my mind. I closed my eyes to relax a bit. Then I heard a voice telling me, "I will take care of you." Did my own mind make up this voice? Was it actually the voice of God? I could not tell.

Four and half hours later, the minibus arrived at the town of Saqqez. Dusky evening veiled the narrow streets of this small town, and folks closed up their businesses and began to head home. Scores of people walked up to the bus and conveyed words of affirmation and encouragement to us. The largely Kurdish population displayed compassion and overwhelming emotion for our plight. The minibus pulled into the backyard of a school building. A tall wall surrounded the school from three sides and painted murals of the Ayatollah garnished the walls, bellow them quotes from Khomeini covered the interior walls of the school. Columns of refugees stood before the main entrance. Two additional sentinels joined in the head count.

"*Dwestw beest* (two hundred and twenty)," one of them announced.

After the head count had been completed, we were taken into an indoor basketball court. We were not the first to arrive, and it was going to be difficult to find a place to rest. The rubbery[18] floor heaved with people. Bodies of weary refugees occupied almost every inch of space.

"Looks like we're spending the night here," I said to Nasreen.

As I stepped onto the rubbery floor, a hand touched my shoulder. I turned around, and my good friend Kamaran stood before me. He had been my classmate in high school for two semesters of my sophomore year. We hugged and kissed each other on the cheeks. He explained that they had arrived around noon that day with his entire family, all of whom had managed to flee Iraq together.

"Come." He tugged my arm. "Let me introduce you."

His dad, mom, three sisters, three brothers, and two of his sisters-in-law were there. His dad and I exchanged friendly banter. He

---

[18]   A green rubbery substance that resembled an Astroturf

was quite a jokester. I went along with him and kept pace with his jokes while his children and his wife thought he was trying too hard to be funny and attempted to ignore him.

A moment of silence hung in the air. I looked to my right, and then to my left, and there was my own *family*.

"Kamaran, I must introduce you to my wife," I said rather sheepishly. "This is Nasreen and my little sister-in-law Noreen." I felt like everyone knew I was telling a lie and that we were not actually married.

"You got married?" said Kamaran with an exaggerated look of surprise on his face. "When?"

"Yes, I did, just this March," I responded softly.

"Oh my god, so you are newlywed!" his dad shouted out in his booming voice, and then he broke into laughter. "Ha-ha, so this is your honeymoon? Oh, my boy, you could have done better. You should have taken her to Switzerland or Paris."

His sense of humor made the situation much easier to bear. I did not experience as much trouble thereafter, and we all began to get acquainted. The girls all seemed to be taken with each other from the start, which I was glad to see. I knew they needed female companionship. Iranian guards hauled in large cans of feta cheese and bread and served it for supper. Kamaran's brother eagerly ate his feta sandwich.

"Mmm," he murmured as he smacked his lips. "My body needs fat from the cheese." He commented on the sandwich the entire time he ate it.

It was uplifting to see my friend and his family and to know that no matter what we would remain together at the same camp. This calmed my fears a bit. I did not feel so alone and knew I had someone to rely on in the event of an emergency.

Around 8:00 p.m. another batch of supplies arrived. This time, each person received two blankets. Some blankets were tattered and emitted a stench, one similar to hospital wards. Later, I learned that the US alone had donated $600 million in relief, yet not all donations made it to their intended targets and not all were of the best quality. Perhaps someone replaced new items with old ones or perhaps some of the donors simply gave old items. Yet we did not complain and bicker about the quality of supplies. At this point, any kind of assistance was appreciated. Half an hour later, lights were turned off. Candlelight illuminated parts of the basketball court, and voices spoke faintly in the background as the road-weary refugees went to sleep one by one.

I spread a blanket on the rubber floor and lay on it, grateful for the chance to stretch out at full length for the first time in six nights. Nasreen and Noreen joined their blankets and lay with their backs touching each other. It was wonderful to be able to sleep while protected from rain, rocks, dirt, and the cold air.

Wakeup call came at around 6:00 a.m., as shouting soldiers kicked the doors open. Breakfast was leftover feta cheese from the night before. We ate very quickly, for another group of refugees was on its way to the same building.

"We, as the Islamic Republic," shouted an officer, "apologize about the quality of service. Our government has been overwhelmed with the sudden influx of refugees, and it is not only you people but Afghani refugees as well."

The sound of hurried labor was heard as everyone began to gather their belongings and prepare for the next trip. Kamaran's family requested from the officer that we travel with them on the same bus. His dad was especially adamant. The officer granted the request, and I expressed my gratitude to Kamaran's father. Interestingly, and despite the fact that I knew his first name was Usman, I never actually called him by name. However familiar they may be, it is considered extremely rude for a younger person to call an older man by his first name. The proper title would be uncle, or "the father of so-and-so."

With engines running, a handful of minibuses were parked out in front of the school. A line was quickly formed as we waited to board. A quick head count began, and then we were hauled into the vehicles. Nasreen and Noreen went in first, then Kamaran's mother and sisters, followed by us men. Together, we occupied almost half of the twenty-one available seats in the bus.

About ten miles or so outside of town, we arrived at a large fenced area with buildings of various sizes. Once more, Iranian soldiers guarded the gate. A tightly fenced area of about one square mile stood beyond the metal entrance, guarded by two sentinels. More of them occupied the small watchtower room to the right of the gate.

The Cozy Cot

As the minibuses parked closer to the gate, large rectangular buildings came into view. The metal roofs gleamed as in the light of the eastern sun. I counted six of them while the driver awaited permission to enter. Then orders came allowing us to enter the camp.

"All stand up here," called out the captain of the guards. "Welcome to Urdugay Saqqez. We apologize for the uncharacteristic format of this camp. I invite you to feel free to occupy any building of your choice."

A dirt road went down toward the other end of the camp, and it forked in the middle like a wishbone. Each road led to three massive rectangular buildings. A foot race began as each sought to find the perfect spot, with both men and women running as fast as they could.

Quickly, Kamaran and I sprinted to the first building that looked solid from the outside. This one was near the westerly fence of the complex. Kamaran was the first inside. I followed him, almost slamming into his back as he suddenly came to a halt.

"Sons of dogs," he shouted. "This is an oversized barn!"

The large floor was divided into long lanes. An area of concrete formed the entrance, perhaps ten feet deep. Then two troughs ran the length of the building, separated by a walkway about six feet wide, all coated with concrete. The doorway was hewn sloppily, and the hinges seemed to be loose. Multiple small windows were open, high up near the ceiling. Kamaran and I realized that there was no point in checking out any of the other buildings, for they were all designed in the same manner. Dismayed and desperate, we chose the spot closer to the door for better ventilation. The rest of our folks arrived, looking grim and unable to conceal their disappointment. By now the sun had climbed to the middle of the sky, and we were weary and hungry. Kamaran, his brothers, and I hauled in half a dozen metal sheets that we found lying at the eastern end of the fenced camp. We used them to make an enclave, a private room for both of our families. It was a delightful feeling to know that now we had little homes constructed out of metal sheets and some blankets. Soon others followed our example, and a frenzy of metal-sheet hauling began. A haze hung over the afternoon sky, and empty stomachs ached for food. At last a Toyota pickup, painted in Iranian army colors, pulled over by our gate. It carried bread, cheese, and boiled potatoes.

An officer walked in and asked if one of us would volunteer to act as a liaison between them and the refugees. Hamid, Kamaran's elder brother, agreed to do so to his father's dismay. Usman was concerned that Hamid would become the object of complaint and dissatisfaction among the refugees. However, Hamid assured Usman that it would be fine. After all, he (Hamid) was the general manager of the electrical department for the city of Slemani and knew how to handle people.

By dusk our barn housed at least twenty families Hamid counted eighty-six souls in total. Relief items came in later that night. These included blankets (two per person), a kerosene heater per family, one liter of kerosene, matches, and few cooking utensils, as well as an empty plastic container.

Kerosene heaters are versatile. They could be used for heating and/ or cooking. Kamaran's mother was glad to have one. She promised to cook a meal for us as soon as we acquired what she needed.

Figure 6. Kerosene heater

In the next few days, water tanks were installed in between the barns. Now people could fill up their plastic container for cooking and cleaning tasks. Public restrooms made out of metal sheets and lumber helped clean up the camp from human refuse.

Six feet of concrete floor between the inner wall and the trough was barely enough to accommodate three people, let alone to lie in. Between the two families, we occupied about thirty feet of length and, of course, only six of width.

Sleeping was particularly awkward when Nasreen and I, with Noreen between us, tried to make it look as if we were married. The whole time I would be consumed with concerns about her reputation and the importance of it in Islamic society. Had the Iranians found out about us, they would have stoned us to death. All it would have taken was for a rumor to circulate. Therefore, I impressed upon both Nasreen and Noreen the importance of keeping their mouths shut. Nasreen and I even pretended to disagree on things from time to time in order to give the impression of being married.

Women who lose face and standing suffer tremendously in that society, physically as well as socially. It is extremely rare for a woman with a bad reputation to marry or remarry. Unwed mothers are in danger of *honor killing* by parents or brothers, or sometimes even a zealous cousin, in the name of reclaiming the lost honor of the family. Adulterers are stoned to death in remote villages and isolated communities. Loss of virginity prior to marriage, or even falling in love with a non-Muslim could bring the wrath of punishment upon the offender.

With this in mind, I grew intensely weary of acting the part day after day. Surprisingly, it did not seem to bother the two sisters. One day I confronted Nasreen as we filled our water jug at the tank some distance from the others.

"So what is it with you?" I asked Nasreen quietly.

"What do you mean?" she wondered.

"Why is it that none of this bothers you?" I whispered.

She understood. Looking up into my face, she brought her lips closer and closer to mine until she was so close I could feel her breath.

"Because I trust you," she whispered.

That only complicated life in the refugee camp. Mr. Usman didn't make things easy either. He kept joking about my good looks and the girls flirting with me by the water tank. I made sure Nasreen knew that he was joking. In spite of her repeated assurances that it did not bother her, she acted like a jealous wife. Her facial expressions and body language exuded jealousy.

The water tanker came in once a day. It distributed water to the tanks installed in the floor of the camp. Girls were the primary collectors of water. They stood in wait by the tanks and then pushed and shoved their way to the forefront, which rendered men like me helpless.

Both of our families made up our own schedules for responsibilities such as gathering water, taking out trash, cooking, and sweeping the front of our housing area.

Only a week into the inauguration of this camp, it was quite full of householders. Every barn was jam-packed with refugees. I dare not number the total population of Urdugay Saqqez, but I could estimate it to be in the thousands.

Local merchants expanded their business into the camp. Numerous booths and awnings went up. The merchants sold anything from necessities to accessories. Items such as shampoo, cleaning supplies, meat, eggs, oil, fruits, and vegetables were a lovely break from the potato-and-cheese diet the authorities fed us. I allocated Noreen a daily allowance of twenty toman. Most of the time, she spent it on dried figs. Now and then, she would have leftover change from the day before, so she would not take her twenty toman. Nasreen expressed her gratitude for the generosity I showed to her little sister and always reminded me that she will pay me back once she went home or we had made it into Europe.

"I never think of giving Noreen a daily allowance as a burden or a favor," I told Nasreen. "On the contrary, she is more like a little sister to me than a charity project or a chivalrous thing I should brag about so please relax."

By the end of the next week, Hamid was ready to quit his volunteer role as a liaison. Sentinels would dump food and relief items on the front entrance, and it was Hamid's job to distribute them. It was the same in each of the other five barns, as well. Each building had a representative they called *masseoul*,[19] who distributed food and supplies to the householders. In Hamid's case, some accused him of hiding the best and most desirable items for himself and his family. Hamid had enough of that and quit his position. Another man took over the position of masseoul.

Little by little, the sleeping area looked more like a tiny home. I bought a rug to throw under the blanket. It insulated us from the cold concrete floor. We had accumulated a small silverware contingency, a knife, and a small radio.

The first day of May brought in a surprise. Snow covered hills and the surrounding mountains like white dust. Cold winds rushed through Saqqez valley, but luckily, the snow melted by noon.

News spread about delegates from European countries visiting refugee camps in early May. We learned they had been sent to make reports on the conditions of the camp. Conditions were deteriorat-

---

[19]   Liaison

ing. As the population of the camp swelled, so did problems with its restrooms and drainage system. The one square mile fenced camp felt more like a prison.

There was little to occupy my time. Reading was a welcome diversion, but books were few. I spent many long hours walking and chatting with others. One May day, I strolled up to the front entrance to gawk at the cars driving by. I noticed that a tall blonde man had entered the camp along with a veiled woman with European features. The tall blonde man had a camera with large lenses attached to it. Slowly, I approached them as they spoke to an Iranian officer through an interpreter. Minutes later, two other Europeans joined the conversations. I snuck behind the man.

"Hi, where are you from? Germany?" I whispered.

"No, I am from Sweden," he responded.

"Can I show you something?" I asked.

He looked to his left, then to his right, as if trying to excuse himself; but as he realized no one heeded him, he promptly agreed to come with me.

I thought this was my opportunity to tell him about the deteriorating conditions of this camp. The first place I took him was the restrooms.

"Do you see how bad it is? There is no running water, and they have not cleaned it, ever," I spoke to him in weak English.

He quickly began taking pictures with his large black camera. After he had snapped few, I grabbed his arm and asked him to come further. Next, I took him to our housing area. As I brought him into the barn, a few onlookers gathered around us, clamoring with questions. The Swedish man had no time for questions. He asked me to tell them that he would try to produce a report about the bad conditions of this camp.

Moments later, we were joined by Iranian soldiers and a plain-clothed man. They had noticed the reporter's absence, and they tracked him down. An Iranian official politely asked the Swedish reporter to leave the barn. Nonetheless, the reporter took several more pictures. I hoped and prayed that this episode was not going to get me in trouble with the authorities.

At one point, the men of our barn decided that it was time we took matters into our own hands and dug a hole to use as a restroom. I borrowed a shovel from the front watchtower. Three men and I began digging a large hole near the eastern fence. Not long after the digging began, five Iranian soldiers surrounded us and arrested all four of us. They accompanied us back to the front office near the front gate to be questioned by an officer.

"Did you know you were performing an illegal act?" asked the short, chubby-faced officer.

"*Agha,*" I answered. "No. We only tried to dig a hole so it could serve as a restroom."

He let us go this time, but he also made it clear that we must inform them in all circumstances.

An Offer I Had to Refuse

The next week, a strange man came to visit our barn. *Aghay* Nizzami was his name. He was Iranian, lean and taller than average with fairer skin. He had an air of authority about him. He was accompanied by a photographer and another man robed in black-and-green Shiia-Islamic garments and wearing a turban.

I had taken on teaching myself Farsi in the past few days, with the assistance of the soldiers. I taught myself ten words a day. As I caught snatches of conversation, I would write down the words that I did not comprehend and then ask one of the guards what they meant and how to pronounce them. The Farsi radio was a tremendous help too. This was a hobby for me, and it gave me something to do.

Nizzami asked if someone spoke Farsi. I volunteered immediately. It felt fantastic to know that I had learned enough Farsi by now that I could interpret. I was virtually the only interpreter available.

Aghay Nizzami informed us that each family would be photographed by his photographer. Each family had to line up and a photograph of them was taken.

Later, Nizzami showed me an article that he had hand written. The article read, "*Last night, Jalal Talabani (leader of the PUK) and Saddam Hussein met in person. They kissed one another on the cheek.*"

"What do you think of this?" Nizzami asked me.

I wasn't shocked by the account. Kurdish dignitaries and leaders went to Baghdad often, attempt to reconcile or negotiate a deal with Saddam Hussein, only to be disappointed and double-crossed by Saddam later.

"I hope he (Jalal Talabani) has done so to help his people," I remarked.

"Perhaps it's a political maneuver," Nizzami commented. "You know, Talabani has the nickname of The Fox."

The conversation then diverted to me. Nizzami expressed frank admiration for my mastery of the Farsi language. "Truly impressive," he said, shaking his head. "You learned this much in such a short time. You must be adept at languages." Nizzami encouraged me to return to visit and talk with him. "Tomorrow afternoon!" he called out as he walked away. "Come up to my office. I have something I need to discuss with you."

For the rest of that entire day, I thought about my upcoming meeting with Mr. Nizzami. I speculated about his intentions. The man seemed to be of stature and influence within the authorities, yet he sought to chat with me? It was mystifying. I couldn't understand why he seemed to want to befriend me. Not knowing what to make of it, I kept my thoughts to myself and told no one about my meeting with him.

The next afternoon was warmer than usual. A haze of dust particles filled the air near the main gate. By four o'clock I stood in front of Nizzami's office, nervous and leery. The complex was constructed in a straightforward style. A large open space was surrounded by a nine-foot fence with a single gate serving as the entrance. Two small buildings stood flanking the gate, one on either side of it. One served as an office; the other, as a watchtower. The larger of the two was occupied by Mr. Nizzami and his company. I informed the front guard of my arrival and gave him my name. The guard walked inside, and just a few moments later, Nizzami himself stepped out. He walked up to me with a smile and shook my hand warmly. He came across as a supremely humble man. In spite of his seniority over me, he came out, shook my hand, and welcomed me in. Typically, in Islamic cultures, the young walks up to the old; but in this case, it was a demonstration of humility and respect.

"Sweet tea?" he asked as I sat down inside his office.

"Sure, that would be fine," I politely responded.

Within seconds, a traditional cup of tea was set before me, along with a beaker of diced sugar. Iranians love to drink pure tea while serving cubes of sugar on the side. A cube of sugar is placed in the mouth, and the tea is drunk over it. They say one uses less sugar this way.

Nizzami was curious about my living conditions. He asked questions about the accommodations and whether I liked them or not.

I tried to be polite. "Honestly," I responded carefully, "it's a refugee camp. There are plenty of deficiencies, but it's better than being tortured by Saddam."

"Exactly," he replied. "I agree with you."

Then there was a moment of silence between us.

"Which is why I want to offer you an opportunity," he continued. "Perhaps it will change your life. I want you to give it some thought before you respond."

Excitement and doubt simultaneously rushed through my mind as I attempted to guess what he would say next. "All right," I said hesitantly, clearing my throat. "Could you elaborate, please?"

"You are obviously a bright man," said Nizzami. "Someone who learns Farsi as well as you did in a matter of weeks must be a smart man."

"Thank you," I unassumingly responded. "It's kind of you to pay me such nice compliment."

"No," he said, waving his arm. "I am not saying this to be courteous. We need people like you to help us." The expression on his face changed from soft to stern.

"Help you?" I exclaimed. "What kind of help, may I ask?"

"Help us to weaken Saddam's leadership and defeat the American-Israeli agenda in the Persian Gulf. Saddam is an American agent. He works for them," Nizzami stated.

"How do you want me to help? What is it that I can do?" I asked curiously.

"Join the *Etellat*," said Nizzami. "We will teach you, develop you into a superb agent. You are young. You are smart and nice looking. You will make a great addition to our staff. You will even have a chance to apply for Iranian citizenship," he said as he gently pumped his fist.

I had heard of the term *Etellat* before, and I knew it was the Iranian version of the CIA, basically a spy agency.

"You mean the *SAVAK*?" I exclaimed.

"No, the *SAVAK* belonged to the old regime," he explained. "The Islamic Republic has *VEVAK*. *VEVAK* stands for *Vezarte Etellat Ve Amnyate Keshvar*."[20]

A spy...for a foreign country? My thoughts drifted to images from James Bond movies: beautiful women, nice cars, travel around the world, money, and adventures. Then, in a matter of seconds, I was back on earth. *This is the Islamic Republic of Iran,* I thought. *There are no fast cars, and cars are locally made and assembled. Women's beauty is concealed. It's against the law for women to walk in public without proper hijab (covering). Their money is not even worth the paper it's printed on.* I shuddered as my thoughts jerked me back to reality. "What do you want me to do, *Aghay* Nizzami?" I said aloud.

"Simple," he said as he adjusted the collar of his shirt. "We want you to draw maps, take pictures, and write reports. One more thing, we shall provide you with counterfeit money, denominations of the Iraqi dinar. We want you to distribute them in Iraq."

"Oh," I adjusted my voice. "You want me to go back to Iraq?"

"Yes. Trust me, it's safe now," he claimed. "They have established a no-fly zone. Iraq's army cannot attack the Kurds."

A moment of silence fell upon our meeting room, and the air grew thicker. My mind was reeling. I had imagined so many other plans in that busy head of mine, so many ways to go, yet becoming a spy had never been one of them.

"Can I think about this," I politely asked, "and let you know later?"

"Albateh," said Nizzami. "Yes. But don't make it too much later."

There was a threatening note in his voice. I knew this was not going to be easy. I excused myself and left his office and made my way

---

[20] The Ministry of Intelligence and National Security

to my living quarters. Night had drawn its curtain over the earth, but stars shimmered in the pitch darkness. Apprehension filled my mind as I labored through the possibilities and the consequences of this situation. My thoughts churned in every direction. I even blamed myself for picking up the language so quickly. Was my affinity for languages a blessing or a curse? I had heard plenty of frightening things about the Iranian Etellat. Their interrogation tactics rivaled those of Saddam's *Mukhabart*.[21] Torture and forced confessions were routinely practiced. Some of their torture methods made water-boarding look like horseplay among friends. Human rights were completely disregarded.

Lanterns flickered like fireflies from afar as refugees prepared for the night. I walked along, wondering whether anyone else shared in my plight. Had the Etellat asked any other man, young or old, to assist them?

Mr. Usman observed my heavy steps and grim face, but he greeted me with a generous welcome. "So what were you doing?" he joked. "Meeting up with pretty girls in secret?" He laughed softly.

"Oh, Uncle Usman," I said wearily, "you are always in a good mood. I wish I could be like you."

The others soon noticed that I was not in the best of spirits.

"What happened?" Hamid inquired. "Did Nizzami tell you something?"

"How did you know that I talked to him?" I asked.

"I saw you walk into his office," said Hamid. "I tell you, man, this guy is in the Etellat. Stay away from him. They are notorious people."

Kamaran's mother had prepared a heartwarming dinner, a casserole of potatoes and rice. The fragrance made my mouth water and momentarily distracted me from my predicament. We all sat together in the small restrictive space we shared. After giving thanks, we broke bread together and enjoyed a home-cooked meal.

---

[21]   Iraqi intelligence agency during the Saddam era

I took Kamaran, his father, and his brother into my confidence and told them about my encounter with Nizzami and his proposal. I confessed my fear and hesitation.

Hamid's wisdom was evident as he counseled me.

"Listen," he said. "Do you think this is a job? This is not a job. If you work for these people, they will own you forever. You cannot just walk away or quit. They will not allow that. What will happen if the Iraqis seize you? Have you thought of that? You will be put to death. It might give the impression of a glorious job, but you are too young to understand the complexities. Don't forget your family, and soon you might have a child, or two. Where are you going to live? Here in Iran or Kurdistan? I care about you, Ari. That's why I say do not do it."

"He's right," Mr. Usman commented. "And another thing, you have no way of knowing who else is in this camp. There might be Iraqi agents or spies who are watching things. The way Nizzami took you to his office and talked to you was careless. It shows that he is not an expert spy."

"I don't know about you," said Kamaran. "You have always been…different and rebellious. I don't doubt that you could do the job but at what price? Besides, you dreamed of going to Europe or America. This kind of work would kill all your chances."

"Thank you," I said. "You have displayed genuine concern and friendship. You're right. This is not what I want to do with my life." I had made my decision. All that was left was to face Aghay Nizzami and tell him that I could not accept his offer.

As I had feared, Nizzami didn't take my answer in a sportsman like fashion. Instead, he threatened that if I didn't cooperate, he could recommend that I be put under surveillance. "You have no idea what prisons are like in Iran," he said with ominous coolness. "Once you're in, it's almost impossible to get out." His threats frightened and disturbed me greatly. My heart was filled with anxiety.

Suddenly, my humdrum life in the refugee camp had turned into an unexpected drama. A game of cat-and-mouse began. I avoided Nizzami and his office, taking care to hide whenever he was about. Nizzami continued to page me over the loudspeaker. I did not always respond, and when I did, the visits were stiff and short. Thankfully, however, he never mentioned his offer again; and eventually, my situation began to change.

Trip to Saqqez

The Allied Forces had established the no-fly zone for several weeks now, and their fighter jets patrolled Iraq's air space constantly. People began to leave the refugee camps in Iran and trickle back into the villages and the towns of Iraqi Kurdistan. Urdugay Saqqez was no exception, although, at first, only a few families left the camp to go back to their homes. Iranian authorities, alongside UNHCR staff, supervised and provided resources to enable people to return home. Although going back was voluntary, the UNHCR encouraged people to return, dropping them off at the nearest border to make their way back into Iraq. The atmosphere in Urdugay Saqqez lightened up. Competition for food and water lessened. Guards loosened up security measures, and word went around that for a small bribe the front gate sentinels would let people go out into town.

Nasreen, Noreen, and the women in Kamaran's family desired to go into town, as did I. All of us had our reasons. Mine included the fact that I desperately longed to take a shower since I had not had one in over a month. Nevertheless, more importantly, I wanted to inquire about smugglers. I wanted to find someone who would help us get out of Iran and into Turkey, then, hopefully, to Europe.

Early one morning, around four o'clock, we got ready and made our way to the front gate. It was chilly, and the scent of spring filled the air. I volunteered to do the bribing since I spoke Farsi. After a brief conversation with the guard and two hundred Toman later (ten Iraqi dinars, about two dollars at the time), he let us leave the compound.

"Go to the other side of the highway," he whispered. "Minibuses will pick you up."

An orange minibus approached from the distance. The driver pulled over for us. He was talkative and engaging and very helpful. He volunteered information about where to find local bathhouses, a decent restaurant, and other things of interest. He let us off in downtown Saqqez. I, the only male, along with five females, walked in the narrow streets of Saqqez in search for a bathhouse.

Bathhouses existed prior to the Islamic period in the Iranian culture. However, their number seems to have been limited due to the Zoroastrian religion's reverence for the holy element of water. Nevertheless, after the invasion of Islamic armies of the Sassanid Empire and with the conversion of the population of Iran to Islam, ritual purity (*tahārat*) through washing one's body (*ḡosl* and *wożū*') became a requirement of religious life. Subsequently bathing became an integral part of life. Besides, baths were frequented not only for purity and hygienic reasons but for health reasons as well.

We had strolled along for several blocks when I noticed a boy who seemed to be following us. He would stop as we did. Then he would continue to follow as soon as we resumed walking. I asked the group if anyone else had noticed him. Noreen noted that the boy had also drawn her attention. Eventually, the boy gathered up his courage and approached us.

"Forgive me," he said. "My mother asked me to scour the town and look for refugees. She wanted to share the *Eid* with someone."

"Oh wow," said Noreen as she placed her hand on her forehead. "It's *Eid!* I completely forgot, and I am supposed to be good with dates."

We had all, in fact, missed the date. It was the first day of *Eid El Ftr,* an Islamic celebration at the end of the month of Ramadan. In this month, Muslims fast from dawn till dusk for thirty days. Fasting in Islam mandates that the individual must abstain from eating, drinking, and having intimate relations with a spouse during the hours of fasting. Once the fast is broken, which is around dusk and after the prayer of Maghreb (sunset) have been called for, they are free to eat and drink until the next morning just before dawn. This feat is repeated the next day until the thirty days are completed. Enthused, everyone readily agreed, and we eagerly followed the boy to his house. After walking through several narrow winding streets, we arrived at a well-built home with high exterior walls that looked like ramparts and a small metal front gate. The boy stretched his hand through the metal bars and opened the gate from inside. A brown wooden door separated the inside of the house from the narrow cemented front yard. The boy rapped on the door with its metal knocker. A pleasant-looking woman, wearing a loosely laid covering over her dark hair, opened the door.

Immediately, she welcomed us with kind words of courtesy and hospitality. She hugged the women but, of course, did not touch me or even shake hands. Her husband soon approached. He was tall and slim with short hair and slight mustache. He shook my hand and welcomed us in the same gracious way, as had his wife.

The man introduced himself as *Aghay* Akbar. His wife's name was Zereen. They had a young daughter whom they said was nine years old. She sat watching Iranian dubbed cartoons as we entered the room. Zereen explained that she was a stay-at-home mom who took care of their daughter and the teenage boy. The boy was not her son but her younger brother who lived with them. He called her mom because he had no one else to take care of him. Our hosts were exceptionally courteous, welcoming, and friendly.

Zereen informed us that she had heated up the bath for us to bathe. In that society, most homes do not have private baths. Instead, people bathe at public bathhouses. Those fortunate enough to have a private bath must heat them with gasoline or kerosene burners. The burner is lit and then placed into a small opening in the exterior wall of the bathroom. Inside, a water tank is built directly over this opening; thus, fire warms up the water stored in the tank. It is an effective but risky way to heat up water. Every year, many are victimized by fire.

We soon learned that Akbar was the sole breadwinner of the household. He worked for the government, as do the vast majority of Iranians. Islam teaches a socialist approach to the economy rather than capitalist. Therefore, private enterprises are limited in Iran. We talked for many hours. Our hosts were very interested in hearing about our ordeal. Zereen even wept at one point when I told her about our journey and conditions at the refugee camp. She felt terrible that anyone had to endure in such conditions.

Lunch was incredible. Zereen was a fantastic cook. She made *ashbaza, korisht sabzy,* and *khorisht gaimah* (Persian lamb, rice, and stew). *Halva,* a sweet made with sesame *tahini,* and flakey pastry served as a delicious dessert. Then more black tea and cubed sugar. We drank it gratefully, but had we refused, we might have offended our host. Black tea is a cultural staple throughout the Middle East. The Brits brought tea with them when they colonized the area, and ever since, it has been the most popular of beverages.

When the time came, we each took a warm bath one by one. It was luxurious to feel clean for the first time in over a month. Zereen and Akbar insisted on keeping us overnight.

"It would be an insult if you'd leave," said Akbar. "You must stay and be our guests tonight."

"One night away from the camp," said Zereen.

Since Kamran's mother was the oldest person among us, we looked to her to make the decision. We were more than happy when she agreed. When time came to go to bed, Zereen took Nasreen and me aside. She led us to a separate room, where she had laid a cotton mat.

"I want you two to take this bedroom," said Zereen. "You are newlywed, and you need your time together."

Rendered speechless, I had no idea how to behave.

"You don't need to give us a separate room," Nasreen politely objected. "We will sleep where everyone else is."

No argument would have convinced this spunky hostess.

"I insist," she said. "And when I do insist, it must come to pass." She smiled a friendly smile.

Soon Nasreen and I were left alone. We had never been alone during the past weeks while in camp. The tight living space did not allow it. Suddenly I found myself facing a night alone with a woman I had met on a slope of a mountain. In spite of the fact that I knew we had developed a liking for each other, I was determined to keep my boundaries. The full-size pad Zereen had laid on the floor was not large enough for both us, so I decided to sleep on the floor. Embarrassed and shy, both Nasreen and I could have described the situation with one word—*awkward.*

Nasreen seemed less nervous than I was. She had displayed this type of calmness around me before. As my brotherly relationship with her little sister had grown stronger in the course of the past many weeks, Nasreen had been more reserved and harder to read. Sometimes I wondered what her feelings were. At times, I had noticed her efforts at trying to get my attention and her thinly concealed jealousy listening to Mr. Usman's teasing.

"Please understand that I am not blaming this on you," said Nasreen, blushing. "We are victims of circumstance." She paused. "It's not that I don't want to be in the same room with you. I do. I am concerned about the future. You know, we are not married and I do not think you want to get married. You have dreams of your own."

"I do think about marriage, but I have always dreamed of marrying someone that I'd fall in love with. You know, stay up at night at the thought of her, write poems for her, stand under her window and serenade her. The fairy tale romance we read about in books," I timidly replied.

"Of course, I want that too," she responded. "What woman doesn't want a romantic relationship? Nevertheless, I also realize that we live in an oppressive society where women are killed on a daily basis if they lose their virginity. Honestly, cows and goats are valued more than women."

"I totally agree with you," I told her. "Society in general has no mercy on women. It has been this way for over 1,400 years. Both men and women disobey the rules, but the ones who pay the price dearly are women."

We continued to whisper to each other in this vein for some time, before turning out the lights and trying to sleep. The next morning was quite uncomfortable. The rest of the household was already awake as we stepped out of the bedroom, and we were greeted by the cheerful faces of our hosts. Zereen boasted about her superb breakfast and the quality of her homemade yogurt, butter, and fresh bread made from scratch. Indeed, breakfast tasted sensational, something I might never forget in my life.

Nasreen and I were quiet most of the day. As we left the Akbar's home and made our way back to the camp, we spoke no words to each other. Akbar himself drove us back. His Iranian-made car did not seem to have much horsepower. He asked about Japanese made cars and told us he wanted to buy one someday. Iranians suffered from a lack of international goods due to successive embargoes. Imported cars were a luxury that most people could not afford. Common people had little access to foreign made goods. Iran is one of the wealthiest countries in the world in terms of resources. It sits on gargantuan oil reserves and is rich in agriculture, easily able to produce its own food and grains. Yet the average person sees little benefit from the wealth. Except for the Gulf area, this is typical of all the tyrannical Islamic/secular countries in the region.

When we arrived back in camp, folks swarmed us and pelted us with questions about our trip into town. I was preoccupied with thoughts of what would happen if they knew the truth about what had transpired between Nasreen and me.

The next day, after Nasreen and I were alone, she asked me to come out and talk to her. "Please don't tell anyone about last night," she whispered.

"No, I promise," I quickly responded. I extended my pinky to do the *pinky swear*.

Nasreen smiled in relief, and we resolved to leave things as they were.

Soon after, I ran into Kamaran. He stood by me with a grimy face and downcast eyes.

"I am sorry," he said. "My dad has decided to go back. My family and I must return to Kurdistan."

The news of Usman's family returning to Kurdistan was depressing to us. Noreen, Nasreen, and I had developed an emotional attachment to them. We had been virtually like one family throughout this experience.

Usman and Hamid were the two who primarily wanted to go back. Both of them had left good jobs behind, and they could not see how it would improve any of their lives to stay longer in the camp.

"My business and household are back in Iraq," said Usman. "That's where we belong. Now that the no-fly zone has been established, I trust that the world is watching and Saddam won't dare to attack again. Plus, my daughter needs to go back to school. They have extended the school year until the end of June, so I heard."

"I have my managerial job,' Hamid followed up. "The whole city is waiting for the electricity grid to be turned on again. I need to go back and help my town and the people."

Their situation was understandable. They were in an entirely different position than Nasreen, Noreen, and I. We were single. I, personally, did not feel an attachment to that city any more than if I had been a visitor. With the death of my parents and the betrayal of my brothers, I carried so much resentment and anger. I did not want to revisit the pain. Instead, I looked forward to starting a new life in Europe. I hoped that Nasreen and her sister desired the same. Of course, they had their father and sisters to think about.

The Usmans left the camp with the next convoy. Hugs, tears, and words of farewell lingered in our memories long after their bus drove off.

"Come visit us if you are back in town," Mrs. Usman called out from her window as they pulled away.

By the end of that day, the camp felt even emptier than ever. Our site was quiet and forlorn. The six-by-thirty foot space we occupied now seemed lonely without their company. Even the sun emitted low-energy rays from the west.

Meanwhile, Aghay Nizzami reestablished his harassment. He contacted me every day, making small talk, perhaps as a psychological tactic attempting to break me down now that the Usmans had left my side. Nizzami never again came right out and asked me to join him, but he consistently showed himself and made his presence known to me in a way that was very intimidating. Heavy, dreary, and without relief, Nizzami's pressure continued.

Then terrific news came over the loudspeaker. The announcement was made that the remnant of this camp would be moved to a different camp—one with real rooms. The UNHCR had filed a complaint to the Iranian government regarding the poor living conditions at the refugee camp. Forced to provide a more humanitarian alternative, the Iranians decided to move us out of the current camp. I was relieved and hoped that this would rid me off Nizzami.

In a matter of three days, the remnant of camp Urdugay Saqqez was moved to a new location on the south side of Saqqez. An abandoned multistory apartment complex was our new home; however, most of the apartments had no doors or windows. When we inquired of the guards about what had caused the damage, they said that this place had been struck by Iraqi jet fighters during the eight-year war with Iraq. Registered as a family of three, we were given a doorless room with a glassless window, along with another family.

As soon as the guard heard me speak Farsi, he immediately appointed me as masseoul (liaison) between them and the group of five apartments for a total of one hundred people. They would call me once a day and assign me the distribution of that day's ration. The head officer, who was a Turkmen from the region of Azerbaijan, was impressed when he found out that I also spoke Turkmen dialect in addition to Farsi. For that, he gave me a special privileges—extra cans of chicken, extra bread, cheese, eggs. Best of all, he gave me permission slips that allowed me to leave camp whenever I desired. Life was grand, drastically different from the previous situation. Nasreen and Noreen also took leave into town over the course of the next few weeks.

Then one day, I ran into Nizzami while shopping in town. We were attempting to cross a side street when he purposefully cut us off by stopping his car in our path.

"*Salaam* (peace)," said Nizzami, after rolling down his window and sticking his head out. "I hope things are going well for you." Then, just before hitting the accelerator, he snapped, "You know, I could report your woman. Her veil does not match the code." Then he drove away.

His final threatening remark disturbed me and once more proved that we were not yet rid of him or his ilk while we remained in his country. Although he was no longer in our camp, we were reminded that the long-term threats of staying in Iran remained.

Back at camp,[22] Nasreen and I had a lengthy discussion about the pros and cons of escaping from Iran. Should we go back to Iraq? Should we stay in the refugee camp a bit longer, then attempt to escape to Europe? It was impossible to foresee an answer. With Nizzami lurking on street corners, things did not look merry outside the camp. No country had sent delegates to collect asylum requests. We had no way of knowing when, or if, that would happen. Smuggling operations were also a possibility. The preferred route was from Iran into Turkey, but it was very risky and sometimes fatal. Even if we made it to Turkey, that is only the first leg of the journey. From there we would have to find another human trafficker to smuggle us into Greece, then to Western Europe. I did not have enough money to pay off two different sets of smugglers for three people.

Nothing is truly guaranteed when it comes to the business of smuggling. Although hundreds of thousands of Kurds had successfully reached Europe in the past decade, thousands of others had been arrested and deported back to Iraq. It would have also been a difficult trip for us, involving long walks, mountain hikes, and endurance across both borders of Turkey and Greece. At this point, we were left with two options—either we could stay in the refugee camp and wait for delegates of asylum or go back to Kurdistan and hope for the best. We decided to go back to Iraq.

---

[22] Although they were apartments, we still called camp since it was fenced and surrounded by Iranian guards.

The Journey Back to Iraq

We spent the next few days preparing ourselves for the trip back to Kurdistan. Although disappointed that I would not fulfill my goal of escape to Europe or beyond, I considered it temporary. I was determined that one day I would try again. I justified it by telling myself that I was still young and had many years ahead of me.

I officially submitted our names to the camp UNHCR representative for a return trip. He informed me that we should be out of there within several days. Two days later, our names were called. And on a sunny morning, along with eighteen other passengers, we boarded a red minibus and began our journey back to Kurdistan. He drove steadily for the next three hours, stopping only once at a roadside tea shop. The bus arrived at the border about late afternoon.

The sun had already drawn back westward, and the pale evening spooled. This time the border was not black and foreboding but was covered in a carpet of green lush grass. The sounds of hurried labor were dampened by the greenery, and business bustled in the makeshift marketplace. Commerce was booming. Everything from herds of sheep to heavy equipment, such as bulldozers, was being traded. A makeshift garage for buses and trucks was established on the Iraqi side of the border.

"Where can we get a ride back to Slemani?" I asked a man, who busily stuffed his merchandise back into a gray sack. He paused and elongated his neck, looking to the left and to the right.

"Unfortunately, all of the buses have already left the garage," he said.

We began to walk away in disappointment.

"Oh, wait," he shouted. "There is a truck!" He pointed down to a silver truck that had wheels caked in mud.

Left with no options, we decided to take the truck and leave the border behind us. The westward sky turned from pale to deep orange and blue as the sun hid behind the horizon, and we boarded the tall truck. A few others were already waiting in the back. The pungent smell of diesel saturated the air as the driver pressed on the accelerator.

Little Noreen struggled to keep her balance while trying to make her way toward me across the back of the truck. By now, the eastern star flickered above the dark outline of the massive mountains of the east. The passengers were tired. Everyone dozed, and sleep overtook some.

Suddenly, the truck pulled over. We were only halfway through the journey, but our driver claimed it was time for a break. He ushered us off the truck and disappeared.

No sign of a city or a village was in sight, only the black shapes of the hills and the mountains that surrounded us. We spread our few blankets on the thorny ground and waited for the driver to reappear. Weary and apprehensive, we spoke very little.

Finally, the driver returned. When he attempted to start his engine, it stalled. It looked like we were going to spend the night in the open after all. Tension thickened between Nasreen and me as she became more conscious of the perilous path that we were taking. I was unaware of what triggered her change in attitude. Perhaps it was a conversation between the two sisters or the broken-down truck. Questions and uncertainty swirled through my mind like winter snow, cold and relentless. What was next?

We lay on the thorny ground protected only by a blanket, whispering for a long while.

A faint glow had begun in the eastern sky when the driver finally reappeared. He had managed to find a ride into the nearest town. He had brought back tools and a helper to repair his broken truck. After what seemed like an endless amount of work under the hood, the engine finally roared into life once more. The twenty-four passengers, including the three of us, were crammed back into the vehicle again. The sun pressed its way against the blue horizon and slowly brightened the sky with golden rays. However, our stomachs growled with hunger. None of us had eaten dinner the night before, so we hoped the driver would pull over at one of the roadside tea shops. However, he pressed on. Thankfully, only three hours later we approached the edge of Slemani.

During the final leg of our journey, Nasreen and I had not spoken. As we neared our final destinations, the two girls readied themselves to disembark and we made plans to meet again in two days' time.

"We should meet in the main market place," I told Nasreen.

The spot was known to everyone in Slemani, and it would be a good location to meet. We were back on the 60 Meter highway. The familiar slopes of Goyzha appeared, now lush and green. The trees seemed unusually beautiful, covered in blooms. It had been only two months since I had climbed my way out of danger while a white cloud blanketed me and blinded the eyes that attempted to locate me. It was hard to believe. The two girls were dropped off at almost the exact spot where we had once met. Little Noreen wept as she hugged me good-bye, and Nasreen wept as well.

Traffic moved normally over the paved highway. It seemed that many refugees had already come back to town and resumed life as usual. I threw my bedroll on my back and leapt out of the back of the truck. I hailed a minivan and made my way back to Zargata quarters where my rented room was located. I took stock of the amount of money I had spent within the last two months. It came to three hundred Iraqi dinars. A reasonable amount, I told myself. Upon my arrival at the one room apartment, I found that the proprietor had already come back. Their daughter was baking bread in the front yard. The key to my room still rested in the right pocket of my black pants, the same ones I wore the day the enemy attacked. I opened the door and found myself home.

In my room alone, I reflected on the events that, at this point, felt as if they had been nightmares—long dreaded nightmares that had come to an abrupt end.

It is remarkable how much this experience changed me. To flee death for six days and six nights and survive the elements, hunger, thirst, and sleeplessness had made me appreciate being alive. I appreciated small things that I had once taken for granted, like fresh food and the bed I slept in at night. I also had a new understanding of the importance of human solidarity and collaboration. I had experienced the way vulnerability brings groups of humans together and seen how the need to survive melts away differences in age, gender, religious beliefs, and social traditions no matter how deeply rooted and well preserved they may be. I became stronger and wiser than I had been before the exodus. Difficulties build character.

That night, as I lay in my bedroom alone, I wondered what the girls were doing at that moment. I sighed. My eyelids grew heavier and slowly sleep crept up on me, and I drifted into dreamland.

Figure 7. Six days and six nights, my first journey out of Iraq

PART 2

Coming to America

Home Sweet Home

I opened my eyes to the morning light pouring through the window of my bedroom. The sound of tweeting sparrows had awakened me.

Amena Khan, the proprietor, released a loud yawn while she lazily strolled down the hallway outside my room. I had grown accustomed to her loud yawns in the early morning. Moreover, I knew she was coming to talk to me. I was not surprised when she knocked on my door.

"*Kaahk* Ari," she called out.

Although older than I was, she called me *kaahk* as a sign of respect. I promptly put on my pants and opened the door.

"*Salaam*, Amena Khan," I said as I smiled at her.

"*Salaam, Kaahk* Ari," she responded. "I just wanted you to know that I am not charging you rent for the duration of the refugee episode."

"Why, that is extremely thoughtful of you," I said. "Thank you very much! May Allah grant you wealth."

A few moments later, she came back with a bowl of fresh yogurt and a piece of homemade bread.

"Here, take this," she said. "My daughter baked bread yesterday."

I hung around my room for a few hours, cleaning and rearranging the little furniture I possessed. By noon, I decided to head out to the marketplace and check out the extent of destruction the invading army had left behind.

The blitz invasion had left behind unsightly devastation. Homes without walls or roofs, broken doors, and looted stores were the visitors' hallmark. Barricades of sandbags and Iraqi soldiers patrolling the streets of Slemani made me question my decision to leave the refugee camp.

Although the no-fly zone was in effect, Saddam's army still roamed the area and drove in and out of the city at will. However, bribery was rampant among the low-level soldiers and their leaders. The international sanctions had made it extremely difficult to survive on one salary, especially the way Saddam paid his personnel. To survive, Iraqi soldiers established numerous checkpoints and harassed people for any reason in order to extract bribes from them.

While I walked around the *Mizgaouty Gawra* area, an Iraqi private asked for my ID. He began to pester me until I paid him five dinars. Then he let me go. I purchased a few grocery items and went back home.

The next day, I was unable to meet Nasreen at the marketplace in downtown Slemani. The fact of our situation involving her family and fearing social scrutiny briefly sunk in, but the hope of getting together again was real. Meanwhile, in a culture where religious dogmas dominate people's minute living details, reality and hope are separated by a chasm as thick as the size of the Koran and the Hadith. I was ready to accept the fact that I may never see her again.

Dating is a thing of fancy in the vast majority of Islamic societies. The main reason for this is drawn from the religious scriptures. No man may visit a woman unless a *Dhu-Muharam* is present during the visit.

The concept of isolating women from men is associated to the concept of *Namus*, or *Ard*.

A family's name or *Namus*, which means ethics, is directly connected to the way their women behave. The family's reputation, good or bad, depends on their women's chastity and behavior.

In the Islamic society, if your sister, mother, aunt, or a daughter has a bad reputation, then the entire family is looked down upon.

The women will have a hard time finding husbands, and the men have a hard time finding wives.

Namus is so important that women lose their lives over it in a tradition known as honor killing. This is the reason it is strongly recommended that men and women be separated at all times, except when they attend the Hajj.

(Warning: This section is for adults only.)

Typically, when a man and woman are engaged, or even married civilly, they still will not live together until a moving-in date has been set. That is the date when the marriage is consummated.

First-time brides must be celibate, but the same does not apply to the groom. The culture and religion place a heavy emphasis on female virginity. She must be found to be a virgin on her wedding night, or else she will face defamation, instant divorce, and shame to her name and her family's name, and possibly even honor killing. Grooms do not face the same standard. In fact, men will brag about their premarital sexual adventures to their peers and friends.

In addition, since Islam allows polygamy exclusively for men, it is much easier for a man to get away with multiple sexual partners than for a woman. Moreover, since there is no physical method to determine a man's virginity, it is impossible for men to be indicted for premarital sex. Girls, on the other hand, are a different story. Since virginity of a girl is judged by the integrity of her hymen, anything physical that could tear into it puts her in jeopardy, even the simplest thing, such as riding a bike.

"On the wedding night the man must sever the bride's hymen. He shall allow the bride to bleed on a sheet of white fabric, and the next morning he shall confirm (to his family) her chaste honor by displaying the bloody fabric." This was the lesson my grandaunt taught me as she attempted to explain the wedding night to me.

If a girl enters a marriage under the condition of being a virgin, she must be found to be a virgin or she will face calamity. Sometimes the groom decides to keep the secret of his bride and shelters her regardless of what his family and community think.

More problematic is the fact that a husband can accuse his wife of being *nashaz*, an Islamic term that means "in an odd place or out of bounds." A nashaz wife is not entitled to a dowry in the case of divorce. A nashaz wife has no choice but to accept a reduced amount of dowry or nothing at all. The idea of nashaz allocates much power to the man and keeps the woman at bay.

Muslims do not frown upon abortion as strictly as Christians do, simply because, in Islam, it is believed that every dead child will go directly to heaven since they have not committed any sins. The age of accountability in Islam is seven years old. A child is supposed to begin the duty of worshipping Allah and participating in other Islamic rituals, and the age at which sin can be attributed as well. Early human life is not regarded with the same reverence in Islam as it is in Christianity, and abortion is not considered murder.

No matter how dysfunctional and psychotic the culture's social boundaries are, an individual or two, or even thousands, cannot change the reality. When such a society appoints itself as the prosecutor, judge, and jury over individuals' lives, it is almost impossible to change it because the society borrows its power from the religion. Even if such a culture may not follow or practice every religious ideal, it is quick to enforce its cruel and patriarchal rules when it comes to women. It is a way for men to establish their dominance and security and to inflate their shrinking manhood. Women's interests are overruled, and their rights as equal individuals are trampled. In this way, men use religion as their wand to conjure up antifeminine jurisprudence on demand, quoting from the Koran (the holy book of Islam) and Hadith (the written and spoken traditions of Mohammad the prophet of Islam).

The Man Who Knew Everything

On a mild day in September, months after coming home, when the leaves were beginning to change colors, I met my old friend Sallam in the marketplace. We strolled down main street, conversed, and exchanged stories of our exodus ordeals. Briefly, I told him a short version of my dilemma with the two sisters and the consequences that followed. He was amazed and fascinated by my account of events, for his story was not as eventful. Then our conversation veered to the war.

"So what happened?" I asked.

"With what?" replied Sallam with a puzzled face.

"This whole Gulf War and the fall of Saddam," I continued. "I thought the Americans were going to rid us of him."

"I don't know. I guess things are never what they seem," he answered, frustrated.

Then, after a moment of silence, he asked, "Did you hear what George H. W. Bush said?"

"I heard that he called on the people to overthrow Saddam." I paused fleetingly. "And in response to that call, the *Peshmarga* and the people waged the *rappareen*."

"No, I wasn't referring to that. He said something about a New World Order," replied Sallam.

"Sallam, dear friend, may I refresh your memory," I tried to joke. "I was stuck in an abandoned animal barn in Iran for most of the past few months. The news service there wasn't quite up-to-date, so no, I haven't heard anything regarding a so-called New World Order. What about it?"

Sallam suddenly came to a halt, placed the palm of his hand over his forehead, and crunched his face as if trying to recall something.

"He said, 'We have before us an opportunity to forge for ourselves, and for future generations, a New World Order,'" recalled Sallam. "He also said something about a credible United Nations force."

"What is that supposed to mean?" I queried.

"It's beyond me," Sallam said. Then he added suddenly, "I'll tell you what! Let's go see my Uncle Farhang. He has some interesting thoughts about the whole debacle."

"Farhang! Well, sounds like he would be the man to talk to, if he lives up to his name." I chuckled.

The name *Farhang* is uncommon in Kurdistan. It translates literally as *encyclopedia* and reflects the culture's high respect for knowledge and learning.

I shook my head and grinned. "I just hope he knows everything."

A bit defensive, Sallam said, "Believe me, he is a very smart man."

Before long, we had made our way out from the center of the city and into the ancient narrow streets of Slemani. Built by the Babbani Dynasty in 1781, Slemani is the largest among the three major cities of Iraqi Kurdistan, followed by Erbil and Duhok. The name *Slemani*, sometimes spelled *Sulaimani* or *Sulaymaniyah*, means "Solomon's town."

Cloaked women attended to their daily errands while children ran around kicking a soccer ball. Some boys were attempting to fly a kite, which they had constructed rather sloppily using old newspaper. The scent of mud and clay homes mixed with the aroma of cooked pilaf filled the air of the narrow streets of the *Jewlakan* neighborhood, the Jewish quarter.

Not too long ago, many Kurdish Jews lived and worked peacefully in this vicinity. Then, when Israel declared itself an independent state on May 14, 1948, the Arab Muslim countries began a frenzy of removing their Jewish citizenry from their countries and sending them into Israel.

Iraqi and Kurdish Jews were no exception. Baghdad sent off thousands of Jews and dumped them on the newly formed borders of Israel. Then a few months later, the Arab countries of Egypt, Iraq, Syria, and Jordan waged war against Israel. This defied logic, since the same Arabs who claimed to oppose the formation of a Jewish nation had also supplied them with a larger fighting force. By evicting their own Jewish citizens, the Arabs dramatically increased the population of Israel.

Sallam and I soon arrived at a moderately-sized stone home with a white metal gate. Sallam reached in and opened the gate from inside. We crossed a concrete courtyard and reached a brown-varnished wooden door. With his knuckles, Sallam gently knocked on the door. A few moments of silence went by. Then the latch was loosened from inside, and the door opened.

Sallam's uncle Farhang stood before us. He was a striking-looking man with completely white hair, a strong jaw, and a cleft chin. He wore a pair of classy glasses, and his hair was unkempt.

"Oh, my boy Sallam!" he blurted out in a raspy voice. He welcomed us into the house. We removed our shoes on the threshold, as is the custom in all Middle Eastern homes, and stepped inside.

"Come in," he repeated. "May you bring good tidings."

Sallam introduced me to him as we sat down on cotton mats on the floor.

"May you come with good tidings, *Kaahk* Ari," Uncle Farhang greeted me with the traditional Kurdish welcome.

A large bookshelf stood against the eastern wall of the room. A few books lay on the floor, and Mr. Farhang slowly picked them up and put them away. It was evident that he was an avid reader, judging by his extensive book collection.

"So what brings you two here?" he asked as he tapped Sallam's shoulder.

"Well, we were talking about the war," said Sallam as he pointed at me. "We were wondering if you have any explanation of what happened. Specifically, why didn't they kill or get rid of Saddam?"

"Even though Bush called for his removal," added Mr. Farhang.

"Exactly," I pointed out. "Bush gave his tacit blessing by asking the populace and the army to overthrow Saddam."

"Ah," Mr. Farhang sighed as he stood up and walked toward his book collection.

Meanwhile, his wife came in, carrying an aluminum tray with three cups of sweet tea. Conservatively dressed, but without a hijab, she welcomed us in a velvety voice. "Welcome, may you bring good tidings."

"Thank you," Sallam and I replied in unison as she held out her tray of sweet tea to us. We each chose a cup for ourselves, and she placed her husband's cup on the floor near where he sat.

"Thank you, dear," he whispered to her as he stood up to pick out a book from the bookshelf. He walked back to his spot and sat down on the cotton mat.

"You see this book?" he asked as he waved a brown hardcover volume

"This book was written in 1928 by a man named Edward Bernays. It is titled *Propaganda*. In it Bernays says something that you two need to understand," he said as he pointed to both of us.

Sallam and I kept quiet in anticipation of what he was about to tell us.

Farhang opened the book and read in English. He then left the book opened and stared at us from over his glasses as if he was waiting for a reaction from us. After a brief pause, he broke into gentle laughter.

"I know you didn't understand most of it. Let me translate the meaning of this passage for you," said Farhang with a stern look on his face.

"Bernays writes about a conscious and intelligent manipulation of the organized habits and opinions of the masses. He says it is an important element in a democratic society."

He paused to let the statement sink in. Then he asked, "And what kind of system is America based upon?"

"Democracy," Sallam answered promptly. "It is a democratic system."

I thought for a moment. "Wait," I said, "I thought America was a republic."

"Bingo!" shouted Mr. Farhang. "Exactly. It *was* a republic."

"It *was?*" I asked. "Why are you saying it in the past tense?"

"It was changed," he replied. "Slowly and gradually, it was changed to a democracy."

Before I had a chance to ask him a second question, he said, "Let me continue translating. Bernays goes on to explain how the American public is governed, their minds molded, their tastes formed, and that ideas are suggested to the public largely by men they (the public) have never heard of."

I was a bit stunned.

Farhang went on, "Few people understand this fact, but the truth is that Bernays's writing summarizes the American society. You see, the American public is living in an illusion." Mr. Farhang said this statement emphatically.

"Huh?" I questioned his last statement. I was completely taken aback. "How do you know this?"

Farhang looked over at Sallam as if awaiting an answer.

"Sorry, Uncle, I haven't told him yet," Sallam said apologetically.

"I lived in the States," said Mr. Farhang. "From 1975 till 1990, I lived and worked in Chicago, then later in Alexandria, Virginia."

I was amazed to know this about him.

"How did you get there?" I inquired.

"After the failed revolution of Mustafa Barzani in 1974 and as a result of the treacherous treaty of Algiers, the Americans and the shah of Iran relinquished their support for the Kurdish rebels who fought against the Baath Party of Iraq. The Americans granted asylum status for Barzani and his followers, if they chose to move to the States."

"I don't mean to be rude," I questioned him further. "But why did you come back? I think it is insane to leave the USA and settle for Iraqi Kurdistan. America is the land of opportunity! A person can have success and fulfillment over there. Look at us here! Wars, social injustice, religious theocracy, political oppression, unemployment, illiteracy, subjugation of women, and racism are prevalent on this continent. Why would you have chosen to move back here?"

"I can't disagree with anything you listed," replied Mr. Farhang. "In the end, societies are made up of individuals, and change comes from within. I came back after the end of the Iraq-Iran war to make a difference, to help my community move forward."

He paused while his wife invited us to the dining room for lunch. Sallam and I apologized, for we had not meant to linger until lunch. However, no apology sways a Kurd from sharing his meal with a visitor. While we sat at the dinner table, his wife Shaho *Khanem* joined us.

"Thank you so much for lunch, Poora Shaho," Sallam timidly said to his aunt. "May your hands never see the signs of weariness."

I courteously repeated Sallam's words, a traditional phrase of appreciation.

"You are welcome," Shaho Khanemsaid with her velvety voice. "Upon my eyes (another traditional phrase used to show utmost humility), we are at your service."

We enjoyed eating our delicious home-cooked meal and made merry with the host and his wife. After the meal, we men moved back to the living room and sat visiting over another cup of sweet tea.

"I sense that you don't like much about this culture, my boy." Mr. Farhang directed his statement at me.

"Well, there are a few things I am not fond of," I replied, "such as the points I listed earlier."

"Oh, you don't have to be so negative. There are also many good things about our culture." Farhang smiled.

"Like what?" I asked.

"Like you two stopping by unannounced. You could never do that in the Western culture. There is a much closer sense of community here. Children can play outside safely. Neighbors share meals with one another. People are simpler, friendlier." He spoke with passion, as if he was defending his personal honor.

After a few moments of uneasy silence, he continued, "At any rate, let's get back to our subject. Edward Bernays explains many things in his book. He demonstrates how a few powerful men control the perception of the masses."

"You claimed that the American people live in an illusion?" I said with curiosity.

"Yes, most of the time," he replied. "You see, in order for governments to survive and justify their power over the population, they need an enemy. And if they don't have one, they create one."

"Wait, that doesn't make sense. Why would governments create enemies for themselves?" I asked, as his statements began to shock me more and more.

"Well, look at Saddam and America," he answered. "Weren't they friends at one point in time? Donald Rumsfeld shook hands with Saddam back in 1983."

"I didn't know that," said Sallam.

"Me neither," I remarked.

"It's a long story." Mr. Farhang folded the palm of his hand and placed it under his chin like Rodin's *Thinker*. "Have you two heard of the petrodollar?"

"I...no, I haven't," I replied.

Sallam shook his head. "I have not either."

"In the early 1970s, Nixon took the dollar off the gold standard," Mr. Farhang went on to explain. "Prior to that, the value of the dollar was backed by gold and silver. It changed after Nixon's executive order. Henry Kissinger visited the Arab countries of the Gulf. He offered them riches in exchange for buying US Treasury notes and backing the dollar. The Arabs gladly accepted."

"How is that connected to the Gulf War?" Sallam curiously asked.

"Well, the Baath Party took over Iraq in 1968, and then in 1973, Saddam and his cousin Ahmad Hassan Al-Baker nationalized Iraq's oil resources. That meant the government of Iraq kept all the profit from oil. Saddam and his cousin were reluctant about engaging in the petrodollar scheme. In return, the Americans, with the cooperation of the shah of Iran, instigated a war between the Kurds, led by Mustafa Barzani, and the central government of Iraq. The Kurds were used to pressure Saddam.

"Ironically, just as the Kurds gained the upper hand and almost achieved victory over the central government, the rug was pulled out from under their feet. The shah and Saddam famously shook hands in Algiers and signed a mutual agreement. Saddam gave up half of the Shat-Al Arab River and a few acres of land to Iran, and in return, the shah forced Barzani to lay down his weapons and send the Peshmarga home in what was famously known as the *Ashbattal* (a Kurdish term meaning "the mill is empty and sold out, so everyone go home").

"Saddam agreed to get in on the petrodollar scheme until the shah was removed by Ayatollah Khomeini in 1979. As soon as the Islamic Republic of Iran was established, Saddam backed away from his Algiers accord, citing it had been done with a different government. Then he demanded that the new regime give back Shat Al-Arab and the territories lost to the shah due to the accord. Khomeini, a Shiia scholar, refused to yield to Saddam, a secular Sunni. Thus Saddam waged the eight-year war against Iran."

Mr. Farhang[23] paused as he twirled his teaspoon in his cup of tea. His wife entered carrying a plate of *koolicha*, a stuffed dessert very similar to cannoli.

"Does this mean the Kurds were used by the shah and the Americans?" I asked, helping myself to the koolicha.

"Yes, absolutely," Mr. Farhang replied without hesitation.

"But, if that's the case, then why did you participate in the revolution knowing it was a setup?" Sallam asked.

"I was young, naïve, and patriotic, and I didn't have this insider information at the time. Once again, we veered away from our main subject. Now let me explain something to you. The US and Saddam's government are very similar in the way they operate."

This statement made me regret even coming and listening to this man, for it went against everything I held desirable and lovable about America.

"Excuse me,"—I pursed my lips—"but I find what you just said to be outrageous. How could you compare Saddam's bloody regime to the freedom-loving US government? America is the land of the free and the home of the brave. Everyone wants to go there, to live

---

23   The author does not necessarily agree or disagree with the introduced analysis. Please do your own research.

and work in the USA. I would love to have an opportunity to live in the States."

"Yes, yes," he swiftly replied. "I know it is a great place. However, I never mentioned anything negative about the land or the people, but only the government. The US government victimizes."

Irritated by now, I argued and said, "That's hard to believe, the American people are free thinkers. They are tough to tame or control, especially for politicians. After all, Americans changed the history of humanity with their revolution and the Declaration of Independence."

"You seem to know much about the history of America," Mr. Farhang said to me.

"Yes," I declared, my chest puffing with pride. "I read about everything. I love learning."

"Okay," he said as he adjusted his glasses, "you are right. All of that is true. You must also understand that things have changed. America is not the same now as it was originally. It is controlled by bankers who control the career politicians, who care for nothing but their own interests. They lie to their people. They deceive them into going to war." He paused, sighed deeply. "Listen, I must repeat, in order to establish full control, governments need enemies that they can blame for destabilizing the country. Hitler did it, so did Saddam, so does the American government.

"When Saddam's Baath Party took over Iraq in 1968, they executed hundreds of innocent men, citing they were an imminent danger to the newly crowned revolution. Then in the early seventies, the regime invented a fictional character they called *Abu Taber*, the ax man. This alleged ax man used to break into people's homes and kill entire families for no reason. At least that is what the regime propagated through their radio and TV stations. The people gave away their weapons and relied on the regime to protect them from this ax man.

"Then in the late seventies, terroristic acts were blamed on the Islamic *Dawa Party*, and then the war against Iran, which lasted eight years. Finally, the invasion of Kuwait came upon us. Throughout all of this, the regime always blamed outside forces for meddling in

Iraq's internal affairs and the poor government had no choice but to oppress its own people in order to eradicate the exterior threats.

"Similar policies were implemented in America. It was the savage Indians, the South against the North. Then it was the gangsters like Al Capone and Dillinger, who were labeled public enemies. The Great Depression, World War II, followed by the Cold War, Korean War, and Vietnam War.

"Often, the government lies to its own people. For example, the Gulf of Tonkin incident, which led to the invasion of Vietnam in which fifty thousand Americans died and over a million Vietnamese perished. It was all a lie.

"Saddam oppressed his people publicly, but in America, they do it covertly with lies, rules, codes, and regulations. Today, the 'Land of the Free' is the most regulated country in the world. Almost everything needs permission or a license regulated by the government. Now that the Soviets are gone, who knows what enemy is going to threaten the American way of life. Perhaps the Muslim extremists or domestic terrorists will become the next American *ax man*. I don't know, but time will tell."

"But true believers of Islam, not the nominal ones, hate America, don't they? They blame America for helping and supporting Israel," Sallam said.

"That is true," I added. "Orthodox Muslims do blame America for helping Israel. Islamic groups could inflict damage against America. I mean, they defeated the most powerful force on earth in the Soviet Union and the Red Army."

"That is a valid point," Mr. Farhang interrupted me. "Let me ask you this. Do you think a few scraggly, untrained, mostly illiterate Afghan fighters, although brave, could defeat the Soviet empire by themselves? The Mujahedeen were fully supported and aided by the CIA and the US government. That is why they won the war. I realize that Islamic teachings encourage jihad against enemies of Islam. Israel and America are considered enemies of Islam since both belong to the house of war. All of that is true, but those who dwell in the remote caves of Afghanistan do not have the training, the planning, or the technology to wage attacks against America. They can only be used as a tool to further oppress the American public."

The allegations that this man made that day left me questioning why I ever came to listen to him. Sallam and I left his house with more questions than answers. Later, I even scoffed at Sallam and labeled his uncle as either a wacky conspiracy theorist or someone who was angry at America and jealous of its position as the leader of the free world.

"I think your uncle is either a communist or an Islamic hard-liner," I said to Sallam as we made our way back downtown.

"He is neither," Sallam replied in defense of his uncle. "He is just a seeker. He likes to go deep into the core of matters and analyze them."

"Well, I think he is nuts," I commented.

That evening, my third brother, Fareed, came to visit me. It was a pleasant surprise to see him alive and doing well. Feelings of resentment and anger prevented me from asking about or visiting my older brother, who I blamed for my six-day exodus ordeal. Fareed, on the other hand, I did not blame, for he had no part in the promise Hemen had made last April.

Fareed and I had not seen each other in many months. We enjoyed visiting and catching up, as we retold our accounts of events reaching back to January and the coalition strikes. He proudly spoke about his new trucking job. Delivering goods and services between Baghdad and the Kurdistan region made him gloat over the type of money he was about to make. He had rented a small apartment in Baghdad, rooming with a half dozen Egyptian migrant workers.

Since his eight-year war with Iran, Saddam's regime had brought between half to one million Egyptian workers to replace the work-force in Iraq. The Gulf War had cost many Iraqi lives, and more than half of the nation's youth were forced into military draft.

I briefly recounted my own events to my brother and expressed my excitement about the opportunity of traveling with him.

"When are you driving back to Baghdad?" I asked.

"Tomorrow, around midday," he replied as he puffed the smoke from his cigarette.

All my brothers smoked, although I did not indulge. Although it was regarded as cool, I had never been attracted to the habit.

"Be safe," I declared. I gently took the cigarette out of his mouth and extinguished it on the glass plate before him.

Life under Embargo

Months went by, and the Oil for Food program initiated by the UN to help relieve the international embargo imposed on Iraq did not help at all. None of the benefits reached the commoners, only high ranking government officials and insiders benefited from it. The unemployment rates exceeded 60 percent. I was aware that I would have a tough time finding work.

I held a few odd jobs that were only temporary: working in a foosball shop for a few weeks, selling live chickens, and trading non-perishable goods for very little or no profit at all, though I never lost money.

In the months ahead, minor uprisings by the Peshmarga liberated entire cities in Kurdistan. In some cases, Iraqi troops withdrew on their own without putting up a fight. I suspected that this was a ploy. Saddam withdrew from Kurdistan knowing that his replacement would be the inexperienced Peshmarga forces, which had no practical knowledge in running large towns and cities. This also gave him an excuse to cut off supplies.

Saddam gambled that the pressure of managing the affairs of five million Kurds would force the people and the leaders, such as Jalal Talabani and Massoud Barzani, to crawl back to him. He wagered on the fact that without food, electricity, and salaries, the populace would revolt and head back into his lap. To his disappointment, and in spite of worsening conditions, most of the population resisted the temptation at first.

After the troop's withdrawal, the situation worsened. With the cut off in electricity, oil, and salaries of government employees, prices of commodities skyrocketed. The Patriotic Union of Kurdistan, a political party led by Jalal Talabani, and the Democratic Party of Kurdistan, led by Massoud Barzani, vowed to help. However, salaries were distributed every forty-five days or even every other month, and ruinous conditions followed.

The dollar exchanged at a rate of 1:90, which shrank everyone's purchase power. Saddam's move right before winter, the most difficult time of the year, seemed to work. Without a stable income, I suffered from cold and hunger.

Winter was colder than average. Snow fell abundantly. White and pure, it veiled the city and the distant mountains alike. Harsh it was upon those of us who did not have kerosene to burn. The winds blew down from Goyzha, carrying winter chills into the city, freezing the air and water in their path. Icicles, pearly silver, dangled from fireless roofs of houses. Without fire, blankets became the only defense to shield against winter's bitter coldness.

My search for a job grew ever more agonizing. The rise of the dollar caused prices to inflate. Every single commodity rose in value, while the dinar lost chunks of its purchase power due to the double sanctions we endured. The situation was so bad that it resulted in a several diminutive domestic battles among the factions: the Islamic group against the Patriotic Union and the Communist Party against the Democratic Party.

"As if the lack of food and oil is not enough!" shouted an elderly man in the middle of the bazaar. "Now civil war is upon us. By Allah, one day we will wish for Saddam to be back!"

It looked as though Saddam might accomplish his objective. The populace grew angrier as every day went by, and the Kurdish factions had no swift solutions. On the contrary, corruption, money embezzling, and smuggling of goods peaked while Kurdish authorities did little to nothing to stop the onslaught. Men dug phone cables out from the ground, stole the copper, melted it, and smuggled it to

Iran. Electrical wires were brought down, and the aluminum coatings were cut and stolen. Bulldozers, tractors, and Japanese automobiles were smuggled across the border and sold to the highest bidding Iranian merchants.

The days of our lives darkened. Hope dwindled. People looked swarthier by the day as they delayed bathing weeks at a time. Our clothes were tattered. Potatoes once more became our main supply of nutrition. We boiled them, mashed them, fried them, and stewed them.

The food shortage strangled us. In the meantime, the converted garage where I recently moved to save on rent money began to display construction problems. Droplets of water seeped through the living room wall, and with time, a layer of green mold covered it. My attempts to scrape, remove, and repaint the wall resulted in only temporary remedies.

The bathroom teemed with rats. The powerful rodents pushed out through the drain cover and sprang into the bathroom. Even when I placed a sizable rock over the drain cover, the rodents seemingly chewed their way around it. I suspect they were as desperate for food as I was. Malnutrition forced my body into a starvation mode and limited bathroom trips. Then, mice found their way into the interior bedroom, where they nibbled on my toe while I slept at night.

Then, from an unlikely source, help arrived. The withdrawal of the Iraqi army from the area encouraged foreign nongovernmental organizations (NGOs) to enter. Various European, American, and Australian NGOs began arriving in our territories with the intention of rebuilding, rehabilitating, and reconstructing Kurdistan. The British Mine Advisory Group (MAG) came to remove the thirty million mines Saddam's regime planted in the fields and mountains of Kurdistan. OXFAM helped with refugees and human rights issues. ACORN, an Australian NGO, helped with agriculture. UNHCR and Doctors without Borders were among the NGOs, and many more came from Germany, Austria, France, Finland, and Italy.

In addition to bringing much needed services, the NGOs also brought in some greenbacks. However, NGOs did not yield any employment for me other than an on-and-off job as a depot porter for twenty dinars (about $2) a day. My porter job consisted of loading and unloading trucks with bags of fifty to one hundred pounds of wheat and flour. Workers were picked by lottery. Fifty to seventy young men would stand by the fences and gates of ACORN early in the morning, and a staff member would handpick whomever he wanted to come in and work for the day. It was frustrating that I was not picked more often.

The arrival of the NGOs caused a spike in rent. Homeowners, desperate for an income, began charging advance rent, from a year to two years in advance.

NGOs paid in dollars, converted to dinars. A large house that would cost the locals 1,000 dinars a month would cost an NGO merely $50. Overall, the outpouring of nongovernmental organizations into our area only marginally contributed to enhancing the local economy.

Employment

As the popular saying goes, God closes one door, but he opens another. Just as the anxiety of not having a job and the lack of regular employment crept in, my friend Sallam told me of a TV station newly established by the Patriotic Union of Kurdistan. They were hiring for different positions but needed someone for their news department who could read and write Arabic, Farsi, Turkish, and English. I felt confident. After all, I spoke, read and wrote all of the above and understood English enough to make do.

In an interview, the manager of the station explained what his news department needed.

"Not too complicated of a job," assured Mr. Abbas, the manager.

He was a tall man, somewhat heavyset, with dark skin, salt-and-pepper hair, and a mustache that showed signs of aging.

"We need someone who can listen to Arabic and Farsi broadcasts by BBC Radio and VOA (Voice of America), tape record the bulletins, and then inscribe them on paper and submit them to our news editors."

He administered a test to determine my abilities in listening, writing, and translation. I passed with excellence. I was elated. At last I had my first full-time job!

Mr. Abbas gave me a tour of the station. Empty rooms were separated by Styrofoam walls, and scattered furniture lay everywhere. In a corner, a desk a chair and a Sony cassette recorder awaited me.

"Here, this is your office," said Mr. Abbas as his belly shook with laughter.

"A news reporter," I said.

"Excuse me?" wondered Mr. Abbas.

"I am going to call myself a news reporter," I explained. "A glamorized version of my job description."

"Oh, yeah. Ha, ha." He laughed again. "I see what you are saying."

Mr. Abbas excused himself and went back to his office. I sat down at my desk and spread my arms over the entire desktop, as if claiming my property. It was an exhilarating feeling.

"Looks like the newly rented garage brought some good luck," I whispered to myself.

A week later, Sallam was hired for the same position.

The TV station paid me 350 dinars for a starting wage, about $4 a month.

The next six months the station grew horizontally and vertically as they hired more people and opened different departments. Two additional young fellows worked with Sallam and me, and three young women were hired for children's programming.

Two Russian women were also hired. Lydia, the widow of a highly decorated Peshmarga leader during the late seventies, served as an English translator. She had moved to Kurdistan in the sixties after she married a Kurdish man by the name of Aram, who was a leader in the liberation movement of Kurdistan. He was later executed by Saddam's regime. Lydia did not look anything like a native Kurd. She was taller, about five foot eight, and very slender, with pale white skin and light-blue eyes. Even though she had lived among us for twenty-five years, her ability to speak Kurdish was not to be praised.

Valentina was the second Russian woman. We called her Valla for short. She joined us a bit after Lydia. She also had creamy white skin, piercing bright-blue eyes, short brown hair, and a considerably more attractive face. Both women were in their late forties to early fifties.

The management purchased a large satellite dish and opened up a control room with three men who worked around the clock recording programs. During our free time, Sallam and I would stop in the satellite room and watch TV stations from all over the world— Euronews, CNN, BBC English, Discovery Channel, MTV, VH1, and History Channel, just to name a few. After we had been isolated for so many years, it was an incredible experience to be able to view current events outside of Iraq. Every time I saw a city, a street, or a building in Europe or the USA, I told myself, "One day I will walk down those streets and drive down those highways."

The list of employees continued to grow. They hired Smko—a man in his early thirties, clean-shaven, which was uncommon, well-groomed hair, clean shirt, and pants, articulate—and his friend Akko. Although his name rhymed with Smko, Akko was nothing like him. In his late thirties and with unkempt hair, he wore the same clothes days in a row, shaved his beard but kept a rather bushy mustache. He was, however, a benevolent man.

Mr. Nawzad was our branch manager. Shorter than average, middle-aged, and with red hair, he was a former Peshmarga who had been injured in action and released from fighting duties sometime in the 1980s. The PUK transferred him to the radio station while they broadcasted from Mount Handreen near the town of Rawandoz. A mild-mannered and soft-spoken fellow, he came across as sincere. However, he had a hidden side to him. He backstabbed some of us to the general manager, and Lydia was his first victim.

February 26, 1993, the day after my birthday, was a busy day. Terrorists had just attacked the World Trade Center in New York, and the editors needed quick updates. Lydia lagged behind, stuck on some translations. Nawzad, the department manager confronted her. Teary-eyed, Lydia left the building halfway through the day and never came back. Smko and Akko stepped up and covered for her. CNN, BBC, and Euronews continuously broadcasted a series of news stories, and the two men struggled at translating them.

The incident left the duo Akko and Smko to handle translation work full time. Although not impressively adept at translation, Akko did not protest as often as Smko did.

"They should be paying us double salary. We are doing the job of three people," Smko complained. He often vocalized his opinion regarding his job, his ability, and the manner in which the station utilized him.

A couple of weeks later, his friend Akko gave notice, he was moving on to a different line of employment.

"I hope you will like your new job," said Sallam as we scripted the news bulletin.

"Oh, thanks," responded Akko. "I'll be working for an NGO. They pay well—the copious dollar. That is what matters these days. We are paid squat here. Those guys will pay me $100 a month."

One hundred dollars a month was the equivalent of eight thousand dinars a month. How I wished I could find employment with one of these NGOs.

Smko was furious. His friend's decision to leave took him by surprise, which did not sit well with him, and he felt betrayed. Smko's behavior grew increasingly unpleasant, until one night he called in sick, citing fever and a cold. Dr. Shirko, the chief news editor, walked into our room with a frazzled look on his face. He and Nawzad acted panicky, agitated, and concerned. They paced the floor like caged tigers, trying to figure out a way to deal with the evening news.

For the past year, I had worked closely with Smko. This had enabled me to learn a large English vocabulary. On several previous occasions, I had had the urge to volunteer to try my English skills but courage escaped me. I was afraid of making a mistake, but now seemed to be the right time.

"I will do it," I said as I raised my hand and directed my words toward Dr. Shirko.

"Will you?" asked Dr. Shirko with a tremendously relieved look on his face.

"Yes, I will," I responded. "But please understand that this is my first time translating from English."

"That is fine," responded Dr. Shirko.

Nawzad, on the other hand, looked more like a skeptic than a believer. However, since he had no choice, he agreed to cooperate.

I tend to be a bit of a rebel with a few unorthodox methods of my own. Instead of listening then jotting down transcripts in English then translating the transcript, I took a shortcut and directly translated from the mouth of the announcer onto paper. My first bulletin was from CNN. Shirko and Nawzad watched me in amazement as I translated twelve pieces of news.

I could barely contain my excitement. It appeared that my life was headed in the right direction. I had everything I needed.

Unanswered Questions

My new position as an English translator gave me a massive boost in my morale. My life's positive opportunity was self-explanatory at this point. You become what you think about the most.

However, something was still missing, something beyond me, a farfetched reality that I longed for, a reality that seemingly existed only in my fantasy.

The political realities that surrounded my own maturation were causing an increasing separation within me from the ideology in which I had been raised. In spite of having been brought up in the culture and having been quite religious as a teenager, I found myself increasingly a misfit in Islamic society. Social and religious restrictions and unfair judgment of others had always enraged me.

Religious rules and restrictions have had the ultimate influence over people's lives for many centuries. Islam is far more than a religion; it is a complete way of life. For the rules, laws, and regulations of its founder dictate how an individual lives his or her daily life. It dictates everything from the simplest activities such as handwashing and handshakes to more complicated affairs such as running a government, marriage, divorce, inheritance, banking systems, loans, mortgages, buying, selling, profit, and interest rates. One can safely conclude that Islam is not a religion, but more appropriately and fittingly can be identified as a political ideology that includes religion.

Those who are not familiar with Islamic teachings and doctrine or know little about Islam tend to describe it as a religion with two wings— fanatics and moderates. However, those who are thoroughly trained and schooled in the teachings know that that is not the case. There is no such thing as a moderate or fanatical Muslim. Individuals merely present themselves according to the degree of knowledge they have of their religion. The more a person is educated in the teachings of Islamic doctrine and Hadith, the more they tend to veer toward what the West labels as fanatic, jihadist, extremist, fundamentalist, or terrorist.

Most people brought up in Western culture are ignorant about Islam, partly because they tend to be negligent in their attempt to seek answers, to study deeply, or to find sources that will give them the correct answers. The mainstream media in the West are not reliable sources of news, or stewards of conveying the truth either.

Another reason why most Westerners do not understand Islam correctly is through no fault of their own but because of a specific teaching of Islam, an ancient tradition called Tuqyah.[24] Difficult to find and verify, Tuqyah is a teaching that has been passed down from the time of Mohammad.

The *tafseer*, or explanation, of this verse is based on an interpretation by Ibn Kathir.[25]

In another example, al-Bukhari[26] has recorded in *Sahih-Al-Bukhari* and elaborated on how to practice Taquyya.

As an insider, the more I experienced the actual realities, the more disillusioned I became.

I longed to find the answer to my eternal questions: Why am I here? Where is God? My spirit was empty. I sought an answer to the nothingness within.

During those years after the exodus, I often pondered the events of my trip into the mountains. I would recall the prayer that I had

---

[24] Koran 3:28
[25] (1301–1373) a Syrian Islamic scholar, historian, and interpreter of the Koran and Hadith
[26] One of the most reliable Hadith collectors

said in those desperate moments as a hunted animal, and the cloud that had appeared, hiding others and me from our pursuers. I wanted to understand.

One day, I set out alone into another part of the city. I knew where I was going, but I didn't want others to know. I needed to find a Christian church and to ask questions. I arrived at the dingy-looking church and knocked at the door. A short, slightly built door attendant appeared. He asked my business.

"I want to convert to Christianity," I blurted out.

"Really?" the door attendant responded, looking both puzzled and shocked. "I've never heard of that before."

He invited me inside and led me upstairs to an office room. A kind-looking man welcomed me into a chair. He was dressed in the traditional dark robes of an Orthodox priest with a tall distinctive headpiece.

After a few brief introductions, I repeated my desire to become a Christian.

"Why, that's wonderful!" he exclaimed at first. Then, cautiously, he went on, "But you will have to announce it."

I was taken aback. "I can't do that. They'll kill me!" I said.

No act is considered more abhorrent to a Muslim than leaving the Islamic faith. Unbelievers and infidels are considered lower than animals and are barely tolerated, but a defector is lower still. The Koran is clear in its instructions concerning the treatment of anyone who leaves Islam: they are to be destroyed. I had only considered converting in secret. If a public announcement were required, it would be the duty of every faithful Muslim to kill me.

I pondered for a moment. The priest seemed to be considering the situation, one he had never encountered before.

Finally, he broke the silence. "I'm very sorry, my boy," he said. "Perhaps this book will help." He handed me a small copy of the Gospel of Luke in Arabic. "Come back when you're ready."

I took the book home with me and read it, but I didn't understand the theology. I felt letdown and rejected. The Christian church also disappointed me. I put the book aside, and my questions remained unanswered. Is there a God?

A Historic Election

By the middle of 1994, the double sanctions on our territories had taken a severe toll on the average folk. With the absence of Saddam's tyrannical regime, Jalal Talabani (the general secretary of the PUK) and Massoud Barzani (the president of the region of Kurdistan) faced off in battle in the regional elections. They both promised salvation and democracy and the inclusion of the smaller segments of society.

Suddenly, the atmosphere changed, and it resembled a civil competition for power. Election banners, mottoes, and election lists were raised in the public places of towns and cities. Even those who dwelt in the distant mountains were excited to cast their vote in an election. Schoolchildren sang nationalistic songs. The national anthem echoed during morning hours as children lined up in school courtyards shouting:

> *Behold, all you who are watching,*
> *Survivors are those who spoke the Mead language.*
> *The canon of time cannot stop her endurance.*
> *No one dare to say: "The Kurds are no more."*
> *Kurds are alive and well.*
> *Alive is our flag, she shall never bow.*
> *For, we are the sons of Cyrus and that of Xeroxes.*

For the first time in the history of our country and the Middle East (except for Israel), a free election was going to determine who would rule. Saddam's departure had left a governmental gap. The Kurds thought it was necessary to self-govern. A dozen political parties and prominent dignitaries put themselves on the ballots. Talabani, the general secretary of the PUK, and Barzani, the president of the KDP, were the favorites.

On a hazy day, the people in my town of Slemani cast their votes to elect the Kurdish parliament. Optimism and a positive outlook overwhelmed the inhabitants with no exception. However, it was a rather bitter competition. Leaders accused each other of cheating in the ballot counts and disputed the final count. The official results were that the KDP won 51 percent of the votes and the PUK won 49 percent with other political parties obtaining insignificant percentages. Behind closed doors, Barzani and Talabani threatened civil war, if one of them was to be deprived of power.

Selfishness and greed blinded these men of power. The same men who at one point in time took to the mountains for sanctuary while fighting against consecutive Iraqi regimes dressed in baggy traditional pants and possessing only a rifle. Men whom generations of Kurds looked up to as heroes were now spoiled with the lure of money and luxury. As the saying goes, "Power corrupts and absolute power corrupts absolutely."

The concepts of freedom and self-government took a backseat to the quest for political power. Unable to resolve the dispute reasonably, a moronic solution was reached: the KDP and PUK officials split the parliamentary seats in a fifty-fifty system. This system proved dysfunctional, however, for members' partisan loyalties trumped that of the public interest. This solution hampered the making of every major decision concerning the welfare of the commoners.

Eventually, disaster struck in the form of all-out civil war between the PUK and KDP. The first democratically-elected regional Kurdish government was unsuccessful. The civil war caused a different type of pandemonium: Now the KDP controlled the northern part of the region, where merchandise was exchanged with Turkey. They then blocked trade between our area and the Turks, causing a trilateral sanction. Now we were under the sanctions from the UN, Saddam, and the KDP. Luckily, both parties halted military actions against each other and yet another division within a division imposed itself upon us. Now the Iraqi region of Kurdistan was divided into the northern part controlled by KDP under Barzani and the southern part controlled by Talabani and the PUK. And the whole region was divided with the central government of Iraq controlled by Saddam Hussein.

Harsh and bleak, life continued. My work at the TV station was a solace for me. My job was diversified, and I had built myself a large vocabulary of English words and phrases. The very first documentary I translated was taken from BBC TV. It was about World War II. The second one was about the first nuclear bomb dropped over Japan, and the third, which was the most interesting one thus far, was about the pyramids of Egypt. Then I did documentaries on the history of the Cheyenne tribe during Custer's time, dinosaurs, sharks, and Jack the Ripper, to name a few more.

My dream was to translate an entire movie into Kurdish via dubbing rather than subtitles. Due to the high rate of illiteracy, dubbing would work more efficiently. In fact, all my translated documentaries were dubbed.

To alleviate people's anxiety and stress, I prepared a surprise for our audience and planned to release it for 1995's New Year's celebrations. I had translated a few pop videos and subtitled them, something that had never been done before. Michael Jackson's "You Remember the Time," in which Eddie Murphy has a cameo as the Pharaoh was one of them. Jackson had a huge fan base in the Middle East. Kurdish subtitles for Bryan Adam's "(Everything I Do) I Do It for You," from the *Robin Hood: Prince of Thieves* soundtrack, were also a big hit. Many people stopped me on the streets and thanked me. I felt like a celebrity, although no one took my picture or asked for an autograph.

While things went flawlessly in my professional life and my finances, my spiritual life did not fare as well.

My spiritual life was empty. My questions were not being answered by Islamic scholars, existentialist, or Darwinist readings;

and the Christian church wasn't much help either. None of them offered me any comfort.

That May, and since I already had a bachelor's of science degree from the University of Baghdad in Agriculture, I applied for a job and was hired by the Department of Agriculture in Slemani for a salary of 255 dinars a month. Not a big chunk, but it helped. This was my second job, and the best thing about it was that it required only a three-day workweek. Ironically, my title was agronomist, the complete opposite of my major in college which was food science. I had no clue how the soil and plants behaved.

In June of 1995, I began what I considered the biggest accomplishment of my career as translator: dubbing and translating the movie *The Beast of War*. During the course of the work on this movie, I developed a fine friendship with the editors, two young brothers by the name of Dahna and Hawar. The latter was the younger of the two. In time, he and I developed a more serious friendship.

On a rainy September morning, while we worked on the third floor of the building, dubbing the final stages of the movie, Abbas, the manager, called us all to his office. His face noticeably pale, he cleared his throat and said, "Today, a little boy found a Katyosha like rocket directed precisely at the studio you were working in." He then paused a few moments. "Thank God the timer did not go off because the rain had pushed dirt into the trigger. We miraculously averted a disaster. The rocket is in our possession now."

"Oh my god!" said one of the actors. "Who would do such a thing? Do they have any arrests or suspects?"

"No, the little boy came in and alerted us," responded Abbas. "He found the rocket lying in the soccer field across from our building."

"It's either the KDP or the Islamic party!" shouted Hawar. "Those sons of dogs!" He pumped his fist in anger.

Mr. Hama, the senior audio editor, stood up and cracked a smile. With a gentle voice, he said, "One of you is loved by God. He is watching over you."

God again? Do I ever escape Him? My inner thoughts were then interrupted.

"Well, let's get back to work," said Dahna in his nasal voice.

The dubbed movie debuted on New Year's Day, 1996. A movie dubbed in Kurdish was such an historic event that Mrs. Heroh, Jalal Talabani's wife, asked the TV station's general manager Mr. Abbas to send her a copy for an advanced screening. The crew and I were ecstatic to comply. She liked the work so much that later she sent us an envelope with a note saying, "A job well done," and a gift of one thousand dinars for each of us. She also invited us to her house in Qualchwalan, forty miles north of Slemani. Sadly, I could not make that appointment because of my second job at the Department of Agriculture.

On New Year's Day, the movie was released to the public on our TV station. The response was overwhelming. My coworkers at the D. O. A. congratulated me for this historic accomplishment. Mr. Ali, my boss at the D. O. A., called me into his office and congratulated me. He admired my translation ability and asked me to take over a new position for the D. O. A.

"I would love it if you would become our coordinator with the United Nations office," he said enthusiastically. "They are located on the west side of the city." He paused shortly, and then he walked to the teakettle and poured himself a cup of black tea. "It is a waste that you don't have a job with one of these NGOs. They pay a handsome salary."

Before he finished his sentence, I looked up. "Do you think you can help me get in?" I asked.

"Maybe," he responded as if he knew something but would not tell me. "I have a few friends at high levels. I will see what I can do." He paused and rubbed his fingers on his chin. "But wait," he blurted out. "That means we will lose you here, and the TV station will lose you also."

"Oh no," I responded, trying to reassure him. "They will be fine. I will work both jobs, just please help me with this."

Working for NGOs was truly the only way out of poverty. In the past, all my attempts to work for NGOs were unsuccessful simply because I did not know anyone who was associated with them and could recommend me. NGOs paid salaries in dollars, which would have tremendously enhanced my financial situation. For the past three years, I had watched people who worked for NGOs acquire homes and cars, something that was impossible to achieve with my two salaries at the station and the D. O. A.

In early May of 1996, Mr. Ali summoned me to his office again. The weather had warmed up. I wore a blue T-shirt.

"Ah, welcome," he said as he stood up and stepped toward me to shake my hand. "I hope you have polished your English even more by now because I have recommended you to an NGO, and they want to talk to you."

"Are you serious?" I smiled broadly "Which one?"

"ACS," he responded. "They are Italian. Their specialty is agriculture and food production, and they need a cheese maker. Qualchwalan is the site of a brand-new cheese factory. New equipment is being brought in from Italy. You know how to make cheese, right? You are the man for the job." He looked at me with his eyebrows crunched, and his salt-and-pepper mustache puckered up.

I laughed. "Oh yes, indeed. I know how to make cheese. When do I need to be there?"

"Tuesday," he said. "I will write a letter of recommendation to take with you." He bowed his head and jotted down the address on a piece of paper.

"Kaahk Ali, thank you so much," I said in a low voice. "I will never forget this favor."

"Nah," he said as he still looked down at his desk. Then he raised his head and looked into my eyes kindly. "You deserve it."

Teary-eyed, I stood up, shook his hand, and thanked him again.

The Interview

The next Tuesday, I stood before the office of the ACS, located in the Rizgary quarters. A Kurdish man guarded the building. He wore the traditional garments and carried an AK-47 automatic weapon. He asked for my name and what business brought me there. In response, I gave him the letter from Mr. Ali. He lazily turned around and sauntered into the building. In a few minutes, he was back.

I summoned my thoughts and imagined myself already working in the cheese factory.

The guard accompanied me indoors. He pointed to a room and said, "Wait here until Allesandro comes in."

The ordinary room had been converted into an office. It contained a couch, a coffee table, a desk, and two desktop computers, one at either end of the room.

Moments later, an Italian man walked into the room. He was about my height, six foot two, and had a blue-eyed friendly face. Although he appeared to be thirty, most of his hair had already grayed.

With a thick Italian accent, he said, "Hallo, I am Allesandro."

I stood up, shook his hand, and gave him my name.

"Come on back," he said as he waved his hand. His office was a bedroom that had also been converted into a small office with a desk and a sofa across the room but no computer.

Allesandro asked me the basics of cheese making. I responded, keeping my answer brief and direct.

"Europeans are not chatty," I recalled Mr. Ali's advice. "Be straight and to the point."

In the conversation, Allesandro indicated that earlier that day, another candidate had interviewed for the same position. "We will call Mr. Ali," he said in his heavily accented voice, "maybe in two days."

"Before I leave," I asked him, "could you please tell me what ACS stands for?"

"Associazione della Cooperazione allo Sviluppo,"[27] he said in Italian.

I did not have to wait two days. The next morning my boss gave me the happy news that the ACS had hired me.

"They want to see you Saturday," said Mr. Ali. "You have to fill out some papers." He smiled from under his bushy mustache, and his thin face widened.

This was one of the best breakthroughs of my life. My mind raced eagerly as I contemplated the possibilities. I could purchase a home, eat chicken more often, and, more importantly, get a car. However, a conflict followed: I was no longer a prisoner of my dire financial situation, yet it was bittersweet because now I had to compromise my work at the TV station, which I loved.

On Saturday, Alessandro and I went out to the work site, along with his coworker, a man named Oresto. ACS had rented a few Toyota Land Cruisers with their drivers, which is how they moved around in the area. Oresto, an extremely talkative person, shattered the belief that I held regarding Europeans and their chatting habits. He never stopped chatting until we arrived at Qualchwalan. That day I learned that Italians are talkative people.

The building looked more like a house than a cheese factory. Allesandro, Oresto, and the driver, who later told me his name was Aaram, waited a few minutes until the dust settled from the parked car. A large blue metal door led into a small room with a concrete

---

27   The association for development and cooperation

floor. Poorly installed in the wall were two glassless windows, one looked westward and one to the south. A small milk vat, a pasteurization machine, and a separator were the only items that occupied the bare room.

"I wanted to show you this place," said Allesandro, "and inform you of what to expect."

"This is a prototype," said Oresto, "for a larger cheese factory. A bigger project depends on the success of this one."

"We want to establish a relationship with the farmers of the area," explained Allesandro. "We plan to buy milk from them and make cheese. Other dairy products will be produced, if this one is a success."

"This is great! Hopefully, it will stimulate the local economy," I commented.

"Yeah, yeah," said Allesandro. "That is our purpose." He moved a few buckets, held up the water hose, and began rinsing the floor.

"That's a noble idea," I said. "I would love to be part of it."

"So you think you could connect with the farmers and build trust with them?" asked Allesandro.

"Sure," I replied. "I am from the area after all."

"Now let us make some cheese," said Oresto, laughing.

Their idea was to find a mix of local cheese and Italian varieties. I suppose they aimed to make a new kind of cheese, or maybe they were still in the experimental stage. I was not yet certain.

I learned that in the past few months they had attempted to make cheese with buffalo milk.

Cow milk yields about 10 percent cheese per kilo, but buffalo averages a bit higher since it contains higher amounts of casein, one of the two main proteins in milk.

Allesandro continued rinsing. By now, he had moved on to the pasteurization machine. He leaned his head down. "Maybe we can find a hybrid," he said.

"You mean something like a Kurtalian cheese?" I jokingly asked.

"Yeah, yeah." Oresto nodded his head. "I like that name. What was it, Kurdalian?"

"No, Kurtalian," I explained.

"Ha, ha." Allesandro laughed. "I will tell that to my boss."

A teenage boy walked in unannounced. He nodded his head to the two Italian men and shook hands with the driver.

"This is Kawa." Allesandro pointed at him. "He is the guard, or maybe I should say one of the guard families. They live behind the cheese factory, and they are responsible for keeping it safe."

The boy seemed shy, but bright.

Allesandro and I then went to the back of the building, where he showed me the storage unit. It was a tiny room with a metal door and a small window. An air-conditioning unit stuffed the small window.

"This is to keep the room cool," Allesandro said, pointing to the AC unit.

I nodded my head in agreement.

"And now you've seen the operation. So if you want this position, then we will head back to the office and finish some paperwork," Allesandro said.

The four of us jumped back into the Land Cruiser and headed back to ACS headquarters. ACS had rented two houses. They used one as their business headquarters and used the other as a residence. Only four Italians worked here: Allesandro, Oresto, Andrea, and Vincenzo Brunelli. The latter was the big boss, as they called him. The head office was located in Padua, (or as they pronounced it, Padova) Italy.

A Kurd by the name of Faraydoon had also come along with them. He had lived in Italy and had obtained Italian citizenship. Faraydoon was the coordinator. He worked with them and the Kurdish regional government. I met him briefly that day. It seemed that he took an instant disliking to me for no apparent reason.

"We help refugees," claimed Faraydoon in a Kurdish language but heavily influenced with Kirkuk dialect, "and displaced people. We help build and rebuild agricultural projects. After the Kurdistan mission is over, we will be moving to Mozambique. Funding for our projects here in Kurdistan comes from donors in Italy and USAID,[28] which is an American NGO."

---

[28] United States Agency for International Development

Allesandro gestured me to follow him. "Your salary will be $100 a month," he said. "We will pay you in dinars at the exchange rate for that day. Depends on how much the dinar is worth."

I secretly gasped at that number—a salary I never dreamed to have. Financially, I was about to take a quantum leap. *Ten times more,* I thought.

That evening, I went back to the TV station to talk to Mr. Abbas. "I cannot work full time anymore," I explained. I offered to come in the evenings and help with translations.

Abbas was disappointed, but he expressed his support for my decision.

I left Abbas's office and went upstairs to say hello to Hawar. He was congratulatory when I let him know about my new job and suggested that we should rent a house together. He had just gotten married a year ago and had a baby girl. His proprietor had kicked him out of his rented home because he could not pay the rent on time. I agreed to his proposal, and we sought a place to rent.

A large spacious duplex located two blocks west of the TV station captured our attention. Within a week, we had moved into the new house. The house was a bit expensive, but it was in a great location, a few blocks away from the TV station and also on the way to Qualchwalan, where the cheese factory was located.

I occupied the larger side and paid 60 percent of the rent, which was set at one thousand dinars, a far cry from the fifty dinars I used to pay for the horrible garage where I had lived for a while. Hawar and his family occupied the smaller side.

ACS provided me with some milk the first few days on the job, but Allesandro asked me to find new sources to obtain milk needed for cheese making. I found a few sources of milk, mostly sheep's milk. The average price of a liter ran at five to six dinars, about five cents. This meant that we had to sell the kilo of cheese for about fifty dinars to break even. At an average of 10 percent yield, that was the best result possible.

The first day, I bought three hundred liters of milk in milk cans, only to find out the Land Cruiser could not hold all the cans.

It could hold five cans, at fifty liters each, maximum, and I had purchased six. I had to leave behind fifty liters of milk.

To my surprise, this milk yielded only 7 percent. Something was not right.

"Someone cheated and added water to their milk," I told Allesandro.

"I must order a device from Italy," he responded. "It will help you find water in the milk."

"I am not sure right now what to do to perfectly control the yield so we don't fall below 10 percent," I told him.

"People cheat," said Allesandro. "Even in Italy, people cheat."

While I awaited the arrival of the hydrometer, my work continued with the farmers and milk sellers. At the end of every day, Sarkawt, the ACS money manager, gave me money for the next day's purchase. A second cousin to Faraydoon, Sarkawt occupied the position of accountant without any educational qualifications. The man had no clue how to count money or even hold it properly.

Besides me, ACS had hired many Kurds who worked on different projects. Kamal, a middle-aged man, worked on a turkey farm and a nursery. Another man ran the task of rebuilding three villages in the Qualchwalan area.

Feed the Orphans was a third active project by ACS. Allesandro and Oresto took one hundred kilos of cheese and donated it to the orphans. It was a satisfying feeling to know that I was contributing to the relief efforts for the orphans of murdered Kurds, a worthy cause that encouraged me to work even harder.

The Visitor from Padova

The rental property worked out perfectly for me. The driver from ACS stopped by in the morning, picked me up, picked up the milk cans, and drove to the cheese factory. He would wait for me until I was finished making and storing the cheese. Then he and the teen boy helped with cleanup. Every evening, I strolled down the sidewalk to the TV station, which was only five minutes away.

I found my life to be fulfilling and on track. Everything worked and worked well. The finances improved, and for the first time, I saved money. I bought brand-new furniture, and the quality of the groceries improved. I even went shopping for a used car.

Halfway through the month of June 1996, a woman by the name of Francesca came to visit. I noticed her at times walking around the second house. I learned that she was a kindergarten teacher who volunteered her summer vacation and worked with refugees. One day, I met her face-to-face as she walked out of the house. She smiled, gingerly walked toward me, and extended her hand.

"Hallo," she said. "You must be the cheese man. I have heard so much about you. I am Francesca."

She wore a long blue skirt and a denim jacket and tied her light brown hair in a ponytail. Her eyes were light blue, and her skin was fair. She did not have a hint of makeup on her face.

I extended my hand to shake hers, and immediately she took my arm and held it.

"Ah, I love this color," she said as she rubbed her fingers over my arm. "I want to be as dark as you."

Her aggressiveness shocked me. I had never dealt with women who behaved in such a way. Women in the Middle East are encouraged to be shy and to avoid any sort of external expression that might draw attention to them, just as Nasreen was.

"Hmm, well, I want to be as white as you." I laughed in response. "I guess we all want what we don't have, right?"

"It is true." She smiled, and her Italian accent was exceedingly distinct.

Allesandro walked up and joined us, but Francesca ignored him and kept chatting with me.

"I am going to ask Vincenzo to let me come along with you one day," she said while looking at Allesandro, as if tacitly asking for his support. A moment of silence followed. Then she asked me, "Would you like a drink? We have hard liquor and beer."

I had no idea what she meant by *hard liquor*, but I knew what beer was. I had never been a drinker, especially in the past few years. We could hardly find bread to eat, let alone alcohol to drink. Besides, it is *haram*, "forbidden," in Islam. However, I courteously accepted a can of beer from her and secretly dumped half of it.

Francesca and I clicked from the moment we met. She grew friendlier with me as we spoke with each other that evening. One afternoon, later in the week, she came to visit me at the TV station. I showed her around. She walked tightly near me, her body occasionally rubbed against me. I did not know what to make of her attention and interest in me.

She invited me to go along with her on one of her "help the orphans" trips, but Faraydoon declined me permission. She was extremely upset with Faraydoon for refusing to let me go with her.

Nevertheless, they gave her permission to come to the cheese factory. Part of the concern was safety: the management did not want to put any of the Europeans into harm's way. They did not want any kidnappings or accidents.

Allesandro, Oresto, Francesca, and I took a car ride to Qualchwalan the next week. The three yakked in Italian all the way from Slemani to the cheese factory.

Just prior to getting out of the Land Cruiser, I asked, "So what did you guys talk about?"

"Oh, we talked about everything," responded Oresto. "All of life's details, you know."

We sprang out of the automobile, and I offered my hand to help Francesca out, but she refused.

"Why do you want to help me?" she said. "Is it because I am a woman?"

I blushed from embarrassment and said, "No, I just wanted to be a gentleman." My intentions were not impertinent, but chivalrous. Obviously, that did not impress her.

However, the improvements I made to the factory did. She liked the tiny cheese factory. She told me that she would recommend me to Vincenzo Brunelli since she was related to him. Her piercing blue eyes gazed at me a bit longer than normal.

Once we were back at the Slemani office, she asked me to take a walk with her. She spoke in a soft voice. "What are your plans for your future?" she asked. "Do you think you will ever come to Europe?"

"That would be impossible," I said in a low voice. "Impossible."

"Why would you say that?" she asked as she tapped on my arm in a flirty manner. "Anything could happen."

"How can I? There is no way I can reach Europe or the US. I once dreamt of that possibility and even attempted it, but it did not work out well."

We walked back to the office. Francesca flung the drawer open, pulled out a piece of paper and jotted down something. She handed the piece of paper to me and said, "Here, this is my name, phone number, and address in Padova. Just in case you come to Europe, come and say hi."

I was flustered as she handed me the slip and came closer. Her body was so close I could feel the heat of her skin. I couldn't glance at the paper she handed me for her slim body stood between my arms. She gazed into my eyes, I began to sweat. I didn't know how to behave or what to do next. She, however, didn't mind my inhibition. Her hair touched my lower lips. I could smell her shampoo, a sweet smell of lavender, almost intoxicating. She slipped her hand over my back and gently pulled me toward her. My heart was beating like a drum. Her face came closer and her lips slightly parted. She planted a gentle kiss on my lips. I felt like my heart was going to stop. My knees weakened.

The outside door flung open, and someone walked in, interrupting the silent intimacy. She immediately pulled back and fixed her shirt. I turned away and pretended to read the piece of paper that was just handed to me.

"Okay, ehm." I cleared my throat. In disbelief of what just happened, I gazed at the paper. "I'm telling you, you might have to wait for a long time," I responded to her about Europe.

It was Allesandro who had entered.

"Chao," he greeted Francesca and began speaking to her in Italian as if I was not even in the room. He pulled her arm and took her outside. What did they talk about? I had no way to tell.

From that point on, she and I frequently spent time together. I learned a few facts about her: she was single, twenty-six, did not want to get married yet, and was a nonpracticing Catholic.

By the end of the week, the ACS staff was scheduled to meet with Brunelli. My initial reaction after meeting him was, "Oh, wow, he looks a lot like Federico Fellini."

Brunelli chuckled as Faraydoon translated what I had just said. That was the first and the last time I met Brunelli. He was here to battle accusations brought up against ACS for allegedly embezzling funds allocated to the turkey farm. However, he gave me his blessing to continue the work on the cheese factory.

On July 15, 1996, Francesca left the country without saying good-bye. However, the letter she left behind would change my life dramatically.

Civil War, Round One

Meanwhile, tension brewed among the Kurdish political parties. It had reached its peak in May of 1996, when Jalal Talabani, leader of the PUK, allowed Iranian troops to come into the PUK-controlled areas and bomb another Kurdish political party that was a rival to the Iranian government. This enraged the KDP and Massoud Barzani, who had granted refuge to the Iranian Kurdish militia. Civil war broke out between the PUK and the KDP. PUK Peshmarga forces were able to defeat the KDP and oust them from Erbil (Hawler), the capital of Iraqi Kurdistan.

The CIA, on the other hand, was working with the Iraqi opposition, the Iraqi National Congress, under the leadership of Ahmad Chalabi, a secular Shiia leader and an ally of the US, on a plot to overthrow Saddam. Somehow, Saddam discovered this plan, and he was ready for it. I, personally, hypothesized that the KDP leadership informed Saddam Hussein of the plot. In return, the latter lent his troops to help Barzani defeat Talabani.

As someone who worked for the PUK media, I was closer to the news, but not the details. Although my job was in the newsroom, I never edited the news, only translated it. I found out that editors sometimes partially changed details and twisted some facts. They lied about some things and told the truth about others.

One of the manipulated pieces of news was the fact that the Iranian attack had been orchestrated by the political party that employed me. By the end of July, our TV station had reported scrim-mages between PUK and KDP fighters. We always claimed that they (KDP) were the aggressors and the initiators of mischief. It had become clear that we were on the brink of civil war on a large scale.

Magically, NGOs from the US and Europe, including ACS, decided to go back to their countries for summer vacation. By the first day of August, all foreign NGOs had left Iraqi Kurdistan.

August rolled in slowly, hot and sweltering as it normally was this time of year.

I had saved ten thousand dinars so far, which could have been more, but I enjoyed spending money lavishly. I did not hesitate to purchase fancy dinners that cost a teacher's salary for a month, private cabs, and high-end groceries. It felt comfortable not to push and shove bodies at bus stations and rent a cab instead. I also liked to eat a delicate cut of lamb, chicken, wild-caught fish—things I never would have been able to purchase had it not been for this job. A fridge full of food was also reassuring. My life was quite secure and comfortable.

Yet, occasionally, I wondered what Francesca was doing and how my life would change if I lived in the West. I pondered the difference between her and Nasreen.

On the political front, the dragging of Iranian troops into Kurdistan by the PUK leadership infuriated KDP's leadership and they felt betrayed. Massoud Barzani accused Jalal Talabani of being a traitor. Talabani responded with the same allegations.

The focal point of power now shifted toward the occupancy of the capital, Erbil. Up to this point, the PUK had control of the city. KDP forces, however, were not that far away. Their troops were staged only a few miles outside of the city. In a TV interview, Talabani poked fun at the KDP and Barzani by saying, "They (the KDP) can only watch Erbil through their binoculars." This was a provocative statement from a man known for being a bit impulsive in his judgments. Barzani, on the other hand, had a plot of his own and was determined to prove Talabani wrong, no matter what the cost.

On August 25 and in the midst of this political tension, my oldest sister Huda; her husband Sirwan; their daughter Suha; and her three boys Nihad, Adnan, and Ayad surprised me with a visit from their home in Kirkuk.

Huda always thought I was the funniest little brother anyone could have, although I did not think my jokes were funny. However, this night she was distressed, grim looking. I had to leave them at the house, for my job at the TV station started in the evening. That night, after I came home from work, we had a family dinner and Hawar's (the next door neighbor) family joined us.

Sirwan, my brother-in-law, who also happened to be my cousin, behaved badly. His jokes provoked my friend and me and charged the atmosphere with tension.

By default, and because we worked for a TV station owned by the PUK, Hawar and I were supporters of Talabani; but Sirwan made derogatory remarks about him and his administration. He ended his remarks with an ominous warning.

"Everything that you have here will be taken away," he proclaimed. "The Iraqis are coming back. Mr. President Saddam Hussein is coming back."

Hawar and I ignored his words, and we labeled them as mad ranting.

Then Huda confirmed what he said. "Yes, he is right," she said. "Kirkuk[29] is loaded with Iraqi troops. Rumors have it that Massoud Barzani asked Saddam's help to take Erbil back."

"I am telling you," repeated Sirwan, "Saddam is lending tanks and soldiers to fight on behalf of the KDP and take Erbil back from Talabani."

Hawar and I sat silent in disbelief.

Sirwan continued, "Barzani is paying every Iraqi soldier one thousand dinars to fight for him."

Apparently, Barzani sought revenge and he would stop at nothing to get it.

"Hawar, let's go," I dragged him out. "Let's see what the update at the station is."

We quickly made our way back to the TV station.

---

[29] Kirkuk is only seventy miles west of Sulaimani.

"The news is over with," shouted the guard stationed at the front gate. "Did you guys forget something?"

"Yeah," I responded. "I have a few videos up in my room I need to double-check."

We sprang onto the stairs like harried madmen. On the way up, we ran into Addel, one of the news announcers.

"Addel!" exclaimed Hawar as he panted. "Just the person we are looking for."

"Yes?" Addel responded quietly with his deep voice. "What's the matter?"

"Is it true?" I asked. "Is the KDP launching an all-out attack with Saddam's troops behind them?"

"I heard of that," Addel responded calmly. "It's a rumor. I don't think he (Barzani) has the balls to do that. They are, however, eyeing Hawler."

Reassured, Hawar and I returned home.

Suha, my sister's only daughter, was close to me, and I was her favorite uncle. She had just turned six last May. Her dad and brothers oppressed her. They demanded she do housework and never go to school. Her dad, abusive and negligent, made matters worse. She saw in me a father figure and confided in me about some of her dad's abusive ways of dealing with her mom.

Sirwan, who was my only first cousin (first cousins may marry each other in Muslim countries), had fallen in love with my sister Huda when they were teenagers. He was nineteen, and she was seventeen. He had come over to our house often, obviously interested in her. Huda returned his admiration, and according to my other sisters, they used to sneak out of the house and hang out by the train station.

One afternoon, Sirwan and his parents (my uncle and aunt) came by and asked for Huda's hand in marriage. My parents accepted, and the rest is history. They had their first child, my nephew Nihad, then Suha, and the other two were born a few years later.

The next day I went to the TV station to work on some news reports. It had been a few days since I last spoke or saw my friend Sallam. My busy schedule working three jobs did not spare me time to go visit him. I rose from my desk and took the stairs down to Mr. Abbas' room.

Knock, knock. I gently tapped on the door.

"Come in," he replied. His voice shuttered a bit. "Ah, my handsome translator is here. If you are going to ask me for a raise, I don't have any funds for that purpose, turn back and leave."

"No. If I want a raise, I would take your job," I playfully replied. I sat on the couch placed across from his gray desk.

"Would you like a glass of tea?" he politely asked.

"No, thank you. May you live longer," I replied back in the terms of our culture.

"I am wondering about Sallam. Have you heard anything about him? Is he ill or something of that sort?"

Abbas didn't immediately reply. He looked away, then stooped down below his desk as if he was about to pick up something off the floor. He pretended that he didn't hear me, but I awaited his response patiently.

About a minute later, he shook his head and blew a gust of air out of his mouth. "Sa-l-l-a-m." He elongated the word so that it may have taken him close to ten seconds to finish uttering the word. "Well, how well do you know him?" he asked me testily.

"I have known him since high school. He and I are very close," I replied with a wary tone. "I feel like something isn't right. Did he do something wrong?"

"Well,"—Abbas organized a stack of papers on his desk—"he is a traitor." His reply was somber.

"No, seriously, what did he do?"

"I am telling you. He is a traitor," he replied with vexation.

I knew Abbas was serious in his allegation. He did not wait for me to follow up in my questioning.

"We caught him with evidence that he was working for the enemy," he proclaimed.

"Which enemy?" I asked. "Saddam?"

"No, he was working for the KDP."

"What? He hated the KPD. There must be a mistake."

"No, there is no mistake," said Abbas. "We caught him with his KDP identification card, and the moron carried it with him even when he came to work here."

I was flabbergasted from receiving this news. Could my friend that I knew for so long be a traitor? Was he capable of hurting me in particular?

Am I destined to have close people betray me? First my brother and now my close friend Sallam made my heart ache. My soul wrestled with the betrayal, and my mind was disturbed.

Civil War, Round Two

August 29, 1996, was a normal hot summer day. The sun scorched the pavement even though it was early in the morning. The haze hung over the horizon as I left my home at 8:00 a.m. to meet the driver from ACS. Instead of taking me directly to the factory in Qualchwalan, he had to go to the office. The night before, for the first time, Sarkawt, the accountant, had not dispensed cash to me to buy milk. The driver told me that this day would be an exception.

The regular staffs were late arriving. Sarkawt had not arrived yet either. I awaited him so he could authorize the money to buy milk. Half an hour later, he arrived. I sprang upstairs to request cash.

"I am sorry," he replied. "I have orders not to dispense cash."

"What?" I exclaimed. "Is this intended for me alone or for everyone?"

"Faraydoon called from Italy and asked me to stop every cash transaction," Sarkawt responded. "Not only your project, but everyone else's."

His latter comment was a relief, for I thought I was the only one excluded from funds.

"Is there a reason?" I asked. "Are we out of money?"

Sarkawt displayed a bit of discomfort and did not seem to be willing to answer that direct question. Either he did not know the answer, or he did not want to share it. Without cash available, it was impossible for me to continue work that day for I needed a fresh supply of milk daily. Otherwise, it would spoil.

With no work to do, I stopped over at an acquaintance of mine, Aras, who owned a tailor shop. Groups of friends often gathered there to chat. Today was no exception. I lost track of time, and before I knew it, I noticed it was almost the afternoon.

"Time to go to the TV station."

I left my friends and rented a cab to go to the station. Upon my arrival, I noticed a large truck and a few men loading it with technical equipment. Jamal, one of the news announcers, personally supervised this transaction. He stood next to the truck and gave directions to the movers.

With apprehension, I approached and said, "Greetings, *Kaahk* Jamal."

"Hello, mister," he responded with a smile.

"Are we moving or something?" I inquired.

Without making eye contact, he replied, "No, this is old equipment that needs to be replaced."

His answer did not convince me. I did not think we needed upgrades. Something did not seem right. ACS was out of cash, or refused to dispense it, and now PUK TV is moving machinery out.

Just then I could see Hawar's large black head, in comparison to his stature, coming toward us from a distance. He waved his hand in salutation and began speaking before he reached me. I could not understand what he said.

"What?" I shouted.

"Where were you?" he asked. "I waited for you at home. I thought you would bring the milk."

I briefly explained what had been said in my exchange with Sarkawt.

Mr. Abbas, the director and general manager, abruptly stepped out of his office and announced an emergency meeting. Whoever was nearby gathered in his office, each taking the closest seat. When the seats filled, some remained standing.

Mr. Abbas opened the meeting with praises for Jalal Talabani, the secretary general of the PUK, the provider of our jobs and livelihood. Then he went on to curse the traitors, the KDP, and finally, he dropped the bomb we all were waiting for.

"KDP leadership has betrayed the nation and allied with Saddam's regime!" he shouted in anger. "They hired thousands of Iraqi mercenaries to fight for them. The city of Erbil is already overtaken." He paused. "Our gallant and heroic PUK Peshmarga is fighting them to the death. However, Saddam's heavy artillery, armored vehicles, and tanks are not easy to fight with AK-47s and Kalashnikovs. Mr. Talabani moved from Koysanjak to Qualchwalan in preparation for fierce fighting with the KDP and Iraqi troops."

The air in the room stopped still. Men's breathes grew heavier and silence dominated the environment. Perhaps each one of us thought about the consequences of this move. Perhaps each one hatched a plan to escape with our lives. I looked at Hawar and him at me. I gestured him, and we excused ourselves out of the room and immediately headed home.

As soon as we arrived home, Hawar and I each went to our quarters. I quickly began packing a few things in a duffel bag along with ten thousand dinars in cash. Then, underneath some papers in my nightstand, there it was, the letter from Francesca. I folded it up and stuck it in my back pocket.

My sister stood by helplessly. She wept, along with her daughter Suha.

After a quick discussion, most of us agreed to head out of the city and escape. Another mass exodus was imminent, except on a smaller scale this time. Only those who worked with NGOs and the PUK felt the need to leave the city.

"I am not going anywhere," declared Sirwan, my brother-in-law and my first cousin. "I have nothing to fear. I would rather surrender to Iraqi troops than walk in the mountains. You all go. I am staying back."

This stubborn attitude forced my sister to reconsider leaving town. She was not going to leave without him no matter what kind of a jerk he was. Sirwan took the three boys and left my house. He had claimed to my sister that he had a place to stay the night. Huda and my niece Suha stayed behind in the house with me while I frantically ran my errands. Their decision was to go with me. Hawar and his wife Rokhosh and their baby daughter Oskar were packed and ready to move out.

Ideas were being exchanged about what escape route to take when suddenly Hawar's brother Dahna burst in.

"You people," he exclaimed, "we need to get going! They are fast approaching."

"How fast?" I asked.

"Only forty kilometers away," Dahna responded. "So do the math. I reckon they could be here tonight."

This new development jolted our efforts and made them more urgent. Sounds of hurried labor, pacing feet, and heavy breathing filled the air.

Into the depth of night's darkness, seven people set out walking: Hawar, his wife Rokhosh, his daughter Oskar, his brother Dahna, my sister Huda, my niece Suha, and I.

It had been a little over five years before when I first crossed over the 60 Meter highway and climbed Mount Goyzha. Now, once more, I was leading a fellowship of soon-to-be refugees.

Automobile headlights shone over the paved highway as some residents attempted to get out of town prior to the arrival of enemy troops and KDP guerrillas. The women lagged behind, especially when Oskar cried out for her mom's breast milk.

I should have purchased that car I was eyeing, I thought to myself with regret. *It would have been a lifesaver for a day such as this.*

Oskar clung to her mom's breast, frantically sucking. The scene on the highway was reminiscent of the first mass exodus in April of 1991. Long lines of jammed autos attempting to escape brightened the darkness of the moonless night.

Although not everyone evacuated the town as they did the first time, the numbers overwhelmed the flow of traffic. In addition to escapees on wheels, many had no choice but to walk their way to safety. I had a feeling that this was going to be much harder than the first exodus.

Just as I finished my thought, I heard weeping in the back. It was my sister.

"What is wrong?" I asked.

"My hip," said sister. "It hurts."

I gave her a hug and said, "Listen, a new journey has just begun, and it is far from over. Take your daughter and go back to my house. Here is the key. Tomorrow go back to your husband. It will be much safer."

She did not respond; instead, she continued weeping. After a short pause, my sister agreed. She raised her hand and said, "I don't feel good about this. Suha and I will go back."

Hawar and his wife nodded in agreement.

This time I will find a way out, I thought to myself. *This time I have cash, which will help me find a smuggler to smuggle me into Europe. I will obtain asylum status and leave the country.*

As I entertained these thoughts, Suha blurted, "I am not going back, Mother. I want to go with Uncle."

My sister's response shocked me.

"Yes," she agreed. "Go with Ari. I think that is your better option."

"Are you mad?" I shouted at my sister. "You want me to bring a kid with me on a perilous journey where only God knows what might happen?"

"It's better than staying with her abusive dad," answered Huda. "What hope does she have here? To get married at a young age and have the cycle of abuse continue with her too? I would rather have her go with you. Take her to Europe with you. She will have a better life and future."

"Look, it's the ultimate flattery that you trust me with your daughter more than her own dad," I remarked. "But I think she should stay with you."

I loved my niece very much and did not want her to endure her dad's abusive ways. However, taking a six-year-old girl along with me held risks for both of us, both logically and logistically. After some consideration, I caved in and agreed to take her with me.

I broke down and wept with a heart full of anguish.

Into the Mountains Yet Again

The group now numbered only six continued onward at a faster pace. The night grew rougher as the path toward the mountain became steeper.

Suddenly, we found ourselves all alone, engulfed in the darkness of the night. Only the sound of crickets chirping occasionally broke the silence. The large dark shadow of the mountain loomed in the distance. The headlights of a vehicle approaching from behind us illuminated the steep gravelly road, but it seemed to be quite far away.

"Oh, good," said Rokhosh hopefully. "Maybe we can get a ride."

"Yes, at least, up this steep hill," Hawar added.

"I think we should get off the road until it passes us!" I shouted. I felt instantly wary of the vehicle.

The group quickly climbed down into a narrow gorge that ran parallel to the road.

By now the vehicle was a few hundred feet away, and within seconds, it reached us. Several large silhouettes occupied the back of what seemed to be a pickup truck with a black object mounted on top of the front cabin. The pebbles on the road crackled under the pickup's tires as it drew ever closer.

A machine gun—that is what it was. The menacing black object was a machine gun mounted on top of the truck. I had no way of telling whether these armed men were allies or not.

"Stay down," I whispered to warn the others.

Time went by slowly as the driver of the pickup patrolled our spot. He and his partner seemed suspicious that someone or something was there. Although I did not understand their speech, I could hear a distinct accent as they spoke to each other. Were they friends or foes? I could not tell.

Just then, Oskar awoke and began whining for milk. Her mother quickly began to nurse her, realizing the risk of being discovered. Oskar sucked contentedly, and we held our breath. The men lingered for what felt like an eternity. At last, they moved on.

We now realized that we had to proceed quickly and to stay off the main roads. From this point on, we followed a different path. We walked on and on, deep into the night. Sleepless and exhausted, our legs grew weary, and our spirits dampened.

Rokhosh and Suha were the first to complain about the night. Hawar's wife hurled insults and vengeful prayers at the KDP, Saddam, and the Americans.

"Why would you blame the Americans?" I inquired.

"Well, if they had had the balls to take Saddam out the first time," she responded in her fast-paced way of speaking, "we would not have to deal with all of this now, would we?"

"They had their own reason not to get rid of him," I calmly responded.

"They screw up every place they go, those Americans," said Dahna.

The talk was disturbing to me, but I was not interested in a political debate at that moment. My concern was for the safety of my niece Suha and baby Oskar, the two youngest among us. My previous experience with travels of this kind had me wondering how we were going to manage.

We marched into the deepening shadow of the immortal Goyzha lest we be discovered by evil men. Echoes of birds calling out in flight resonated against the broken walls of the gorges and ravines of this uninhabited land.

At last the night drew away, and dawn twinkled on the horizon. It brought with it the hope of being found by friendly fighters. Our spirits lifted, and we increased our pace a little.

Our goal was to reach Qualchwalan, the small town where Jalal Talabani had built his encampment. Talabani, his wife, and a formidable force of PUK Peshmarga had barricaded themselves there. I determined that if we were near him, we would have the most protection. After all, a leader will not abandon his post. Moreover, being near him would alert us to the latest developments.

The sun rose early, wiping the gloomy night away inch by inch. Nevertheless, the air smelled like war, reminiscent of my last exodus. I could have sworn that the scent of gunpowder filled the air as it did that cloudy day of April, 1991.

Hot and sunny, the last day of August came upon us, and the light helped us find our way back to safety once more. It turned out that we were not that far away from Highway 5. It stretched from Slemani to Qualchwalan, ripping through the western peaks of Goyzha, and some traffic appeared in the distance. Commuting to the cheese factory, I took this very same route every day.

The prevalence of traffic encouraged us to walk toward the highway in hopes of catching a free ride to Qualchwalan.

Suddenly, we heard the noisy engine of a truck as it pulled over to the curb. A man stuck his head out of the passenger side and yelled, "Hawar, is that you? Come on, hop in the back, all of you."

The six of us rushed toward the back of the truck. One by one, we scrambled our way in. I looked back as the day grew lighter. We had already climbed a few hundred feet above the sleepy city.

"I can't believe this man recognized you from behind!" I said to Hawar. "It must be the large head," I jokingly whispered to Rokhosh. Although the back of the truck was already occupied with a dozen of people, there was plenty of space still available.

About forty minutes later, the truck prepared to stop. I craned my neck to check out the scene. Now we were just outside Qualchwalan. A multitude of people had already camped overnight, and more poured in from all four directions.

However, this flight was quite different from the one five years ago in that more people drove their own cars. There were as many cars as people in and around the old castle of Qualchwalan, an ancient fortress built by the Babbani Dynasty circa two hundred years before. The line of men and automobiles stretched in all directions. Many families had learned a lesson from the past and avoided a journey on foot.

Large hosts of armed men watched over the Talabani headquarters. Scattered among the people and the vehicles were tents stretching into the distance. Folks camped here and waited on the news. If fighting stopped, then most of them would return home. However, if it continued and headed in this direction, then most would flee farther away, perhaps as far as the border. The majority, however, were reluctant to go back into Iran after the unpleasant experience of the first mass exodus.

The other men and I hurried to the driver and thanked him for the ride. Then the six of us walked toward the municipal building of the town. Hundreds of parked vehicles and their occupants stood around, awaiting definite news of the civil war. The owner of a German-made BMW did not mind us pitching our backpacks near his car.

I could not locate the cheese factory from where I was standing, for it was several miles farther north. However, I wondered what would happen to it in my absence. Looters might uproot the machinery and sell it on the border to Iranian merchants.

Hawar and I decided to walk up the hill one more mile to see if we could locate the factory. As I turned around, I saw Dahna having a conversation with the man who owned the BMW. Hawar and I did not get a good glimpse of the factory, so we decided to head back. Once we got closer to him, Hawar recognized the man. They hugged and kissed on the cheek and exchanged greetings. Hawar and Dahna introduced him as Ahmad, their second cousin who lived in Germany.

Ahmad's four-door BMW had a German license plate. He had driven his car all the way from Germany back to Kurdistan. He explained that after the Kurdish takeover, many estranged Kurds who lived and worked abroad felt it was safe to come back and visit their families. He chose to drive his BMW for the 3,800 kilometers (approximately 2,248 miles) from Germany, through Turkey, to visit his family. Now, however, he was stuck here because of the civil war. He was afraid to go back through the territories on the Turkish border, which was a KDP-controlled area.

Lately, a trend of buying foreign cars was spreading among the influential men of politics and the fast-growing segment of private sector merchants. Ahmad's car would bring him a large sum of money if he chose to sell it. Perhaps it would be worth more on the Iranian border than in Slemani. The Islamic Republic's import restrictions caused an unusual craving for foreign cars, so Ahmad was thinking of selling his car and flying back to Germany from Tehran. In one way, his car was a blessing, and in another it was a liability, an attention-grabber to thieves and robbers.

The sun rose to the middle of the sky and the temperatures soared. Ahmad and Hawar drove the car around, searching for potential buyers or perhaps smugglers.

Meanwhile, Qualchwalan and the ancient ruins of the Babbani castle turned into a waiting room. Thousands were in danger of becoming refugees if the war continued and a cease-fire agreement was not reached by the end of the day. The latest news brought a bad omen, claiming that the front lines of enemy troops had already entered the west side of Slemani. If Slemani fell, we would be next. The news reports caused a cloud of fear to hover over the vast valley of the old castle.

We discussed our options. Ahmad volunteered his car. He suggested that he transport the women—Rokhosh, Suha, and young Oskar—in case the enemy line advanced upon us. In addition to the women and himself, he had room for one more passenger. One of us men could go with him, but the remaining two would have to continue on foot.

"Take the women and children and get them to the border as fast as possible," I said to Ahmad.

He nodded in agreement.

I pulled Suha aside and asked her to keep the duffel bag with the money in it.

"Guard it with your life and never let it out of your sight," I commanded her.

"I will," she assured me. "But does this mean you are not going to be in the car with us?"

"Yes," I responded. "I have a feeling that I should be the one to go on foot. After all, I have done it before."

Suha began to cry. "No! I don't want to go alone with them. I don't know them!" she objected.

"You either go with them, or you and I will have to go it alone and on foot. I would rather have you not suffer that. Trust me, you will not like it," I gently explained.

I expected myself to be one of the two that would be continuing on foot. Secretly, I hoped Hawar would come along with me and not Dahna. I did not care much for him.

Not half an hour later, I noticed a large mass of people, perhaps hundreds, rushing toward us in a panic. Suddenly, someone shouted at the top of his lungs, "They are coming!"

And that is all it took.

Chaos set in. Crowds hurried to collect their belongings, and some jumped in their cars and instantly drove away. Ahmad prepared to load his vehicle as we had planned. Immediately, I volunteered to stay behind, in spite of Suha's tears. Rokhosh reassured her that she would be okay and promised to watch over her.

Hawar decided to stay back and take the hike on foot along with me. "Where should we catch up with you?" he asked Ahmad.

"Penjwen," responded Ahmad decisively. "Meet us in Penjwen. I will drive them there, and maybe by tomorrow morning you two will get there."

I took one thousand dinars out of the bag and gave Suha the rest to keep under her watch. After a hurried good-bye, they jumped in the car and drove away. I did not pay close attention as to which direction they went.

Hawar and I stood there for a few moments in awe of the situation. Thousands poured out of the valley in all directions, as if they were being chased by a beast.

"Come on," I said to Hawar. "Let's go."

We started out walking eastward. We had not gone far when a truck driver intercepted us.

"Penjwen, fifty dinars!" shouted the driver.

"Perfect!" said Hawar. "It's our lucky day. I guess we will see them sooner than later."

"I suppose it is better than walking. Come on, let's get on," I told Hawar.

We ran after the truck, and on board we swiftly flung ourselves. Although I never saw Ahmad's BMW drive toward Penjwen, I was certain we would see them within the next twenty-four hours.

The drive to Penjwen was long and bumpy. It took us well into the night, during which we made friends with another young man by the name of Ashti. Ashti also had been separated from his wife and baby daughter, so the common goal united us in conversation. Suddenly, there were three of us. I joked about it and called it the League of the Three Musketeers, just to lighten the mood.

The truck arrived in Penjwen just when dawn was around the corner. The light of the easterly sun emboldened the gigantic shadows of the border mountains that separate Kurdistan from Iran.

Perhaps it was five in the morning, or earlier, I could not tell. Sleep deprived, we found a closed tea shop and used its seats to doze off for a short while.

Penjwen was a peaceful hamlet nestled between mountains and the valley of Bashmaq. Her long, snowy winters kept the town from growing any larger than her current size.

Long had it been since any government authorities ruled this region. During the days of the Kurdish insurrection, the Peshmarga hid among the surrounding hills and ravines and used them as springboards to launch guerrilla attacks against Saddam's troops. The absence of a government body also encouraged trafficking of custom-free goods back and forth between Iran and Iraq, or as the locals called it *Qachagh*.

We awoke, uncertain as to how long we might have been napping. Nevertheless, we did not waste any more time before we jumped up and the search for our loved ones began.

Ashti walked beside us. He seemed to be a pleasant man. He worked as a nurse in the Slemani General Hospital and was a member of the PUK. Thus, he felt threatened staying in town.

Ashti searched among the crowds for his wife and daughter. Certainly, he had the more daunting task. Finding a woman and baby amid thousands of people would be more difficult than locating a green BMW in a remote area such as this. Hawar and I rubbernecked through the small village trying to spot the BMW. How hard could it be? It was an unusual car.

I scanned all the vehicles in the area, but saw no sign of a BMW anywhere. However, new refugees poured in from every direction.

"Oh well," said Hawar uneasily. "Maybe they are not here yet."

Not until we found our missing families could we think of any further action or decide whether to cross over to Iran or stay within the borders of Iraqi Kurdistan. Ahmad and his BMW were nowhere to be seen. Hawar and I quizzed a second tea shop owner who was just about to open his shop for business. We asked him if he had seen a nice car with foreign letters on the license plate. He replied negatively. However, this rugged old man suggested we go to the Bashmaq crossing point.

"Large number of cars are headed that direction," he proposed.

Excited by the probability of finding them there, I asked, "What is the fastest way to get there?"

"Oh, by Allah, there are Land Rovers available. For a small fee they will take you there in half an hour," he responded.

"Thank you." I shook his hand.

We immediately headed out to where he pointed. Land Rovers were one of the few vehicles that operated well in this rugged landscape.

"Good luck," the old man shouted from behind us. "Allah is with you."

The two of us simultaneously turned around and waved goodbye to him. I thought about how different things were compared to the first exodus. This time if a ride were provided for a small price, I would not hesitate to take it.

Within a few minutes, we were on the other side of the hamlet. Life was still normal here. The inhabitants did not expect enemy troops to invade their tiny village, for it was so remote that strategically there would be no advantage in doing so.

A few 1970s Land Rovers parked out in the middle of a wide open area took turns picking up passengers. One of the drivers yelled out, "Bashmaq, Bashmaq!" He had two passengers already in the back of his Land Rover.

"Come on!" I called out to the other two. "Let us get in."

"What is the fee?" Ashti asked the driver.

"Twenty-five dinars," the driver replied.

Ashti's face fell in disappointment.

"What is it?" I asked him.

"I don't have the money to pay for this ride. You two go on," he suggested. "I will walk my way up there."

I felt a gentle pat on my arm. I turned around, and it was Hawar. He acted as if he were a little boy asking his daddy for a favor. He placed his hand over his mouth and lowered his large head.

"I, I don't have the money either," he admitted.

"Oh, great," I replied. "Come on, you guys. What am I going to do? You expect me to go it alone? I cannot do that. Get in. I will pay for both of you."

"Really! Thank you, thank you!" shouted Ashti. "I promise I will pay you back once we are home."

"Yes, me too," said Hawar.

"Don't worry about it, guys. Now let's go," I said, handing the driver seventy-five dinars.

Soon we were on our way to Bashmaq.

In my eagerness to find my niece, I did not mind spending every penny I have saved thus far.

The sun had climbed even higher by now, and there was a morning chills in the air, despite the fact that it was the first day of September.

On the way to Bashmaq, we saw dispersed flocks of new refugees, men, women and children, making their way to the border. The unpaved and rugged roadways in this area would not allow cars to go any faster than perhaps ten miles an hour.

"You don't think they would cross over without us, do you?" I asked Hawar as we were being rocked back and forth from the bumpy ride. "How well do you know your cousin?" I continued before he had a chance to respond to my first question.

"No, I don't think they will. Even if my cousin would, my wife and brother would not follow him."

By the time we arrived at our destination, Ashti looked nauseous from the excessive rocking of the Land Rover.

"Thank God, we are here," he said with relief.

Instantly, we jumped out of our seats and spread out in search of our family members. With every moment that passed without finding them, I grew more anxious.

"Maybe it was a bad idea to let Suha go alone," I debated with myself. "My sister...how am I going to ever face her again, if something happened to her daughter? She trusted me with her life." Some dark thoughts stormed through my mind.

"Well, it looks like they are not here," said Ashti disappointedly.

"Damn it!" swore Hawar as he swung his arm in the air. "Where did he take them?" he cried, referring to his cousin.

"A man told me that there is a second crossing point," said Ashti. "It is called Bardah Rash."

"The Black Stone. Hmm, I hope it won't be any blacker than this day," I commented.

"I think we should try there," said Ashti.

Without any other choice in hand, we did not oppose his suggestion.

"Wait," I said. I walked back to the driver who had just delivered us. I asked him how much it would cost to go on to Bardah Rash.

"Thirty dinars." He waved his fingers.

"That's fine," I told him, counting out the money. "Drive us there, please."

Bardah Rash is located at the upper tip of the nose-shaped part of the border between Iraq and Iran. Geographically, it is perhaps the farthest point.

It was midday by now. Feelings of hunger and tiredness crept over us, but the drive to find the missing ones overrode them. The Land Rover hummed and roared, dipped and swung over the rocky roads of Bashmaq Mountains. I thanked God for this ride, rough as it was. Walking would have taken us time that we could not afford to lose. We grew more anxious for the women with every moment. I could not stop thinking of my niece. The enemy was closing in, and she was all alone with people whom she hardly knew.

The old man drove his Land Rover like a pro and got us there in short order despite the natural obstacles. I was deep in my thoughts when Hawar tapped my shoulder, signaling me that we had arrived.

Bardah Rash did not live up to its name. I did not notice any black rocks as we closed in toward the border area. What I did see, however, were more people. Some had set up camp already, and some walked around as if they had some errands to run.

"I want you to find your families soon, *Inshallah* (Allah willing)," said the driver as we stepped out of his Rover. Then he began directing swear words and avenging prayers against Saddam. "Allah, take revenge on Saddam for what he has done to our people!" he shouted as he sped off.

"Amen," said Ashti.

Bardah Rash felt grim and bleak. I had a hunch that we were not going to find the women here. Nonetheless, we spread out once more in an attempt to cover more ground searching for them.

People were waiting for the Iranian authorities to open the border and accept refugees. As of yet, the border remained shut. To us, that was good news because we could be certain that they had not crossed over to the other side.

A light-green car came into view in the distance.

"Hawar!" I shouted. I pointed at the car as I ran toward it.

Soon, Hawar followed me. However, to our disappointment it was a green Italian-made Fiat closely resembling the BMW.

After an exhausting search, it was obvious that our women were not here. Upon inquiring of several people, I was told that there was a third crossing point a few miles to the west of Bardah Rash. This one was named Kahni Sureh, "Red Creek."

Amazingly, we still had plenty of time to make another trip to yet another border point. The sun had hit the middle of the sky, and with it, the temperature had also risen. We were thirsty and hungry. We each had our fill of water, and Ashti found a small stand that sold biscuits and crackers, where we picked up a few for our next leg of the journey.

We strode purposefully toward our next stop. The two-hour walk to Kahni Sureh did not feel too long, but every minute was filled with anxiety We could not afford to lose any time. The Iranians might open the border at any moment. If our family members crossed over, finding them would be a much harder task, if not impossible.

"Hurry up, guys," I urged repeatedly.

Ashti seemed to be tired. Hawar, on the other hand, was quite quick and walked as if it was his first hour.

At last, a large crowd appeared in the distance. Hoods and windshields of cars gleamed against the light of the sun. As we approached, I recognized one of our TV crew, *Mam* Salih (Uncle Salih). He was the music director for the *Children's Hour.* He was a tall, thin man, in his mid-fifties, with a distinct tuft of white hair that hung over onto his forehead. It was easy to spot him among the thousands who patiently awaited the Iranians' green light to enter their country.

"Boy, am I glad to see you, Mam Salih!" I said as I shook his hand. "Tell me some good news." In the meantime, I scanned the surroundings, looking for the green BMW.

"What can I tell you?" He sighed. "So far they are winning. The KDP has taken over Slemani and our TV station. The Iranians are not willing to open the border yet, so I don't really have much good news, my boy." He used to call me my boy often, since he was a very distant relative of my mother's.

"None of that is good news," I agreed ruefully, but I was looking for different news at the moment. "Have you seen Dahna or a green BMW?"

He glanced around quickly as if he was trying to locate them also.

"I haven't seen Dahna since yesterday afternoon," he responded.

Hawar and Ashti scanned and surveyed the area while I conversed with Mam Salih. They too came back without success.

"Uncle Salih, do you know where the next crossing point is?" I asked.

He blew some air out of his nostrils and went into a deep thought. "Oh, what can I say, probably Raniyah? But that is a good two-day walk, if you go it on foot."

I turned around in disappointment and began walking away.

"Talabani is there, if that helps any!" Mam Salih called out from behind us.

I solemnly walked away and huddled with Ashti and Hawar to discuss our next step. We had a decision to make, wait here for the border to open, cross into Iran, and then look for the others inside Iran, or hit the road and hope that we would make it to Raniyah prior to the opening of the border.

The other two wanted to remain where we were, cross over into Iran, and then look for them inside the refugee camps of Iran. I completely disagreed. I was ready to take the risk of going on for two more days, catching up with them in Raniyah and reuniting with them there.

"But what if we miss them? What if Iran opens the borders as soon as we leave here? They will cross over, and we will have to go look for them in Iran after all," Hawar argued.

Ashti agreed with him.

"Listen, if we go into Iran, it will be impossible to leave the refugee camps and roam around the country looking for them. Iranians will not allow us to just simply leave the refugee camps, no matter what the reason might be," I explained. "If you two are not coming, I will take the risk and go to Raniyah alone."

They did not seem to favor continuing the journey. Ashti was exhausted, partly, perhaps, because he was a bit on the chubby side. Another hindrance might have been the heat. It was extremely hot, so hot that the skin on my nose and forehead was peeling like a snake stripping off his old skin.

"We are young, we can walk fast, and maybe we will get lucky and hitch a ride or something," I said, trying to convince them, but to no avail.

It was about three in the afternoon when I decided to leave them and resume the journey by myself.

September first was cruel. The sun beat down relentlessly, and the air was parched and dry. Luckily, the valleys and the broken walls of the surrounding mountains provided me with some shade.

After an hour into my lonely journey, I reached a deep valley where the trees looked eerie. Their branches were twisted and turned like evil beings from stories of the old folks. The rocks were large and irregular, broken as if they had been hewn into weird shapes by ancient men who then ran out of time or some catastrophe came upon them, preventing them from finishing the work. It was dead quiet. Not even the chirping of birds could be heard. The air grew chillier, as if the place was haunted by an evil spirit.

Suddenly, I heard the breaking of branches. Something, or someone, was there. I could not determine who or what, but I felt as though I were being watched. Whatever the thing was, it was closing in on me quickly.

I thought of hiding among the broken rocks. I slipped my slender body between the gap that was hewn in a large boulder and lay still. Something approached. Its steps were audible and coming ever closer. Its breathing was strong and horrible. I crouched, preparing to attack. The thing came closer and closer.

"Uhhh!" I screamed and jumped out of my hiding place to face the menace.

"Oh!" shouted a voice as "the thing" fell backward.

It was Ashti, and Hawar was right behind him.

"Whew!" Ashti breathed as he placed his hand over his heart. "You scared the hell out of me!"

Hawar broke into loud laughter, and soon I followed suit.

"I'm so sorry," I apologized when I finally caught my breath. "I didn't know it was you guys. I thought it was a beast following me, or something."

"Yeah, sure," Ashti said sarcastically. "As if I look like a beast or breathe like a beast, huh."

"What are you doing here?" I asked. "I thought you two were staying behind in Kahni Sureh."

"Nah, we thought we should not leave you alone," Hawar responded. "You might need us."

"Not if you do this to me, though," commented Ashti, laughing ruefully.

I grabbed his arm and helped him to stand up. He dusted himself off, and the three of us set out again, eager to get out of that haunted place.

A narrow trail led out of the rocky area and onto an open grassy knoll. As soon as we walked out of that place, I felt as if a heavy weight had been lifted off my legs, and my stride felt normal again. The sun beat down upon us until Ashti's and Hawar's skin turned pinkish red. A small creek lay ahead where the gradient began descending. Ashti requested we stop for a short period. He needed to use nature's restroom. He went behind the pair of trees that had grown by the side of the creek.

Ashti disappeared behind the trees just as the roaring of an engine approached from the east. A black, topless Jeep gleamed from afar with a lone driver in it. Where this man came from, I could not tell. What I could tell was that we had an opportunity to get a lift.

"Ashti! Ashti!" Hawar and I both hollered, calling him back.

He did not immediately respond.

By then the driver of the Jeep had come even closer. We began waving our arms at the driver in an effort to get him to stop, and he did.

"Where are you going?" the driver asked.

"We want to reach Raniyah. Can you please take us with you?" I asked.

"I am not going that far," he responded, "but I can drop you off at a village. It's a couple of hours away." The man apologized and encouraged us to climb in as quickly as possible. He abruptly seemed to be in a hurry.

"Oh yes," I said. "No problem."

Hawar and I jumped in, but there was no sign of Ashti yet.

"Ashti!" we shouted frantically.

Then, there he was, the poor guy trying to pull his pants up and retie his belt as he ran toward the parked Jeep.

"God have mercy on you two!" he shouted. "As the saying goes, the hunter waits for hours, and then when he takes a dump the deer come around."

We laughed lightheartedly at his predicament. Ashti jumped in the back of the Jeep as we joked about his "mission unaccomplished."

Strangely, the driver never asked us who we were or what we were doing in the middle of the mountains.

Almost two hours later, he said, "Here it is, the village of Harzinah." He pointed toward the eastern hill. "I have to let you go here."

We thanked him deeply for the service, and when I tried to pay him, he refused the money.

We followed the dirt road and headed toward the village. The serene village of Harzinah looked welcoming and safe, and we were extremely tired and burned out from the day.

Shepherds were driving sheep back to the small village, which was situated on a hillside. The unwitting inhabitants were winding down from a busy day working in the fields. This place was the epitome of the simple life once enjoyed by the ancient Kurds who had lived and worked in this region for thousands of years.

Dusk was creeping in now, and the tiny village of Harzinah prepared for evening prayers. We approached the village mosque, which was the only logical place where we could stay the night. The three of us walked into the mosque with all eyes focused on us. We were obviously strangers. Our clothes and demeanor gave away the fact that we were city boys.

Men washed their faces and hands in the tradition of ablution, which precedes Islamic prayer as an act of purification. As I leaned down by the water faucet to wash my hands and face, a teenage boy approached me.

"Greetings," he said warily.

"You are upon my eyes, greetings to you too," I responded.

Hawar and Ashti drew nearer in anticipation of having to defend me.

"You are from the city," said the teenage boy. "Come and spend the night at our house."

"Gladly, thank you!" With relief, I accepted his invitation for myself and on behalf of Hawar and Ashti.

"That's good," said the boy. "But would you please wait until I finish my prayer?"

The Imam of the mosque finished his call for prayer, and the men knelt on their knees and bowed their heads in prayer to Allah. We three did not participate.

After the prayers, we followed the boy to his home, which was a small mud house. His mother received us with the traditional local welcoming attitude. She immediately threw down a few rugs and had us sit in the courtyard located in the middle of the house.

She then brewed a pot of black tea and served us freshly made yogurt, homemade bread, and tea. The yogurt was the best-tasting cup of yogurt I had ever eaten. The combination of the freshly made bread and raw milk yogurt was as good as dining in a five-star restaurant.

The teenage boy, we learned, was called Azhad. He was curious about us. He asked a few questions about the war, and off we went. I made a brief introduction of each one of us.

"I am on a TV staff and worked for an international NGO. Hawar was also on a TV staff, and Ashti worked as a nurse, but is a member of the PUK."

Azhad reassured us that his village and its mayor supported the PUK and they loved Jalal Talabani.

Dodging the Enemy

D arkness fell, and the woman brought out a lantern. She lit it and placed it at the center of the courtyard. We sat around the light, conversed about various topics, and made merry. For a brief time, I forgot about the war, the destruction, and the fact that I was a refugee for the second time in my life, with a family left behind and a lost niece. I shook my head, snapped out of the deep thoughts and reached out to my cup of sweet tea.

We were laughing and having a good time when we suddenly heard the sound of roaring engines, many engines. Then, from between the tree branches, automobile headlights appeared. Azhad stood up to check out what was happening.

"Stay down, you guys. Don't come out under any circumstances," he warned us.

Moments later the engines went idle, as if the vehicles had parked.

A muffled voice yelled, "Let the mayor of the village come forward!"

Then silence followed for a few ticks.

The voice continued, "Have any of the Talabani followers taken refuge in your village?"

I could not hear whoever answered these questions, but by now Azhad was outside the house and down by the vehicles. Soon he

207

raced back to us and said, panting, "Oh Allah, have mercy! That's the KDP search patrol!"

His mother panicked when she heard the news. She wailed and wept in a hysterical way, begging us to hide elsewhere. We froze, not knowing what to do. The headlights lingered, not moving. I was afraid that they would begin sweeping the homes in search of refugees like us to arrest. The son attempted to calm down his nervous mother as she rocked wildly, striking her face with her fingers.

Rattled and shaken, Hawar, Ashti, and I crawled our way into the dark muddy room that overlooked the middle courtyard, attempting to hide. We sat silently against the clay wall in anticipation, straining to listen carefully.

About fifteen minutes later, Azhad came in. "They are gone," he said. "Back to where they came from."

The three of us looked at each other. This was a dangerous situation. We knew that they were so close that if we did not move out immediately, they would detain us on the way to Raniyah the next day.

Without hesitation, I said to the woman and her son, "May god bless your home. We will go now."

Into the darkness of the night, we disappeared.

Without a handheld light, we relied on the faint light of the waning moon. After we had walked for an unknown number of hours, the three of us—hungry, tired, and sluggish—sat under a tree by the side of the trail. I placed my hands behind my head, closed my eyes, and lay back on the ground.

I opened my heart and prayed to the true God for help once more. Sleep must have crept over me for a short interval because I had a dream of a white dove flying over my head in circles. The sun cast its light on my left cheek, its warmth tickled my skin. I lazily opened my eyes, and to my surprise, I lay under a pear tree, a lonely pear tree with ripe fruit hanging on its branches.

"Guys, guys," I whispered.

"What?" Hawar's drowsy voice was the first to respond.

"Look," I said as I pointed my index finger at the tree above us.

"Bingo!" cried Hawar.

We ran around simultaneously collecting the fallen fruit and eating it. With every bite, juice burst out of the ripe pears like little fountains gushing water from the ground. Each one of us loaded our pockets with pears for future provision.

"Okay, enough. We must move out," I commanded the other two, who seemed to enjoy eating pears as much as they did last night's homemade yogurt.

We followed the dirt road ahead as the sun rose higher behind us. A few hours later, we came to a river that flowed with brownish, almost-dirty water. Refugee families and individuals had already camped at the riverbank. Then a godsend: a pickup truck drove toward us from the east. As the driver slowly went by, I jogged next to him and asked where he was headed.

"Raniyah," he said.

Without asking his permission, I jumped in the back, and when Hawar and Ashti saw this, they too jumped in.

The truck roared its way through the unpaved trails. Along the road, lines of people walked slowly and silently westward. Inwardly, I hoped and prayed that the border had not been opened yet.

At least three hours passed before the snowy peaks of Mount Qandil loomed in the distance. The driver finally stopped his truck and hopped out.

"I am not driving any farther," he announced. "I only have half a tank of gas, and I need to preserve it."

The familiar scene of scattered refugees had repeated itself throughout the ride, and there were even more of them where we got off. I had grown to be desensitized.

We continued on foot up over a hill, tiredly plodding our way to the top. A woman ran toward us. Ashti recognized her. He collected his strength and ran to meet her. They embraced, but he did not kiss her in front of us. Hawar and I concluded that this was his wife and the rest of his family was near. We never knew her name, since introducing women is not a normal thing in this culture.

Ashti, who had been a stranger when we met three days ago, had become a companion and faithful friend in this brief time. Now we were ready to leave him behind and say our good-byes.

"I am happy for you, my brother," I said as I gave him a hug and shook his hand, as did Hawar.

Ashti waved good-bye as he held his newborn baby and embraced his wife. They walked back to where the rest of his family camped. I envied him.

Hawar and I reached a green meadow where a large crowd in excess of a thousand people was encamped. I scanned as far as the eye could see looking for the green BMW, but none appeared. However, the current crowd meant one thing: they had not crossed over into Iran.

We inquired of those who were refugees about many things. Some said the border would open that day. Some did not know when. Someone said that this was the last congregation of refugees, and if we were to go any farther north, we would run into enemy troops.

Uncertainty, fear, and hopelessness crept in as I scanned the area as hard as my eyes could. Still, I saw no sign of the BMW. Different scenarios went through my mind. *How was I going to cope with losing my niece? How was I going to face my sister? What was I going to tell her—if I ever did see her again?* These thoughts drained me of energy. I leaned against the boulder near me. Emotions overwhelmed me as I sank to the ground, tears rolling down my cheeks, and I wept. Hawar was not near me. He had continued his search. Legs pulled to my chest, head between my hands, alone I wept.

Through my tears, I heard my name. Hawar was yelling my name as loudly as he could. He was running toward me, waving his hands in the air.

"I found them. I found them!" he screamed. He was about two hundred feet away.

"What a liar," I mumbled to myself, inconsolable in my despair. "Yeah, right. He must be bluffing."

When he reached me, he pulled on my arm. "Come on, I found them!" He attempted to pull me up.

"You are joking, right?" I asked him, certain that he was tricking me. "Really, this is not a good time to joke."

"I am not joking, damn it," he claimed. "Come on, get off your butt, and stop crying. I am telling you. I found them."

As I looked into his face, I knew that he was sincere. Overwhelmed, I bowed my head and thanked God for this miracle.

I jumped up and followed Hawar as he led the way back to where he had spotted them. There they were, with the BMW, sitting behind a mound of dirt that completely blocked them from sight. That was why I could not see them at first glance. My niece's face, when she first saw me, showed the utmost relief.

"Thank God, you are alive!" I said as I hugged her and kissed her on the cheek.

What an ordeal this had been. We had walked three days, and well over two hundred miles, and finally found them at the last stop.

It turned out that Ahmad, Hawar's cousin and the owner of the BMW, had changed his course at the last minute after he learned that Jalal Talabani was headed to Raniyah. He wanted to follow him. Since we had not been able to communicate, we had no way of knowing this. We had unsuspectingly gone to Penjwen while they drove to Raniyah, one hundred eighty degrees in the opposite direction of each other. They had arrived here two days ago.

We exchanged stories about the past two days and shared the details of our own adventures. I learned that the rest of the money had been safe with Suha. She had never let the duffel bag out of her hands.

A clamor of shouts arose around us.

"The border has opened," a loud voice announced.

Miraculously, this announcement came only a few hours after we had found our family members.

Jalal Talabani and his motorcade entered Iran first. Apparently, he had also camped near the border. The Talabani motorcade took well over an hour. After that, they let us, the commoners, in.

Authorities allowed refugees to drive privately-owned vehicles into the country, but not until they filled out a lot of paperwork. Since Ahmad owned the BMW, it would take him much longer to enter. Therefore, we decided to leave him behind.

For the second time, I got in line to enter Iran as a refugee. The form of identification that was used to enter Iran at this point was our work ID. Mine was my PUK television station ID that clearly identified me as TV staff and listed my name, birthday, and position.

We were placed a mere stone's throw away from the border of Iraq, in a makeshift refugee camp known as Qasima Rush. Iranian authorities sent all of us "commoners" into this one camp. Jalal Talabani, however, kept his pride by requesting that the government of Iran place him on the border of Iraqi Kurdistan. He and his entourage went back over into a stronghold village barely inside the Iraqi Kurdistan border. Thus, the refugee camp was split in two: one part housed us ordinary people while in the other camped Talabani, his wife Heroh, and his Peshmarga.

The light of the sun had already disappeared beyond the horizon and the mountains that surrounded Qasima Rush were quickly enveloped in darkness when Mrs. Talabani paid a visit to our side. She came to Qasima Rush on behalf of Jalal Talabani.

Heroh was thinly built, perhaps in her fifties, soft-spoken, humble, and friendly, with gentle manners. She was well respected among the Peshmarga. She played a leadership role during the days when the Peshmarga fought the regime from the mountains of Kurdistan.

Heroh held a lantern while she checked on families and children who took the rocky ground as their temporary home for the night. Two Peshmarga walked along with her as her bodyguard. As soon as she approached us, she immediately recognized the two brothers, Hawar and Dahna.

"Aha," she said. "You were the ones who dubbed that movie *The Beast of War*."

"Great memory!" said Hawar. "Please come join us, Heroh khan." Hawar pointed at me. "This man was the translator of the movie. I am not sure whether you have met him, Heroh khan."

Heroh extended her hand and shook mine, slowly and gently, while she praised the work we did.

After years of mountain struggle, Heroh and her husband had lived a relatively luxurious life, but now, once again they resorted to the mountains to protect them from the enemy. As the Kurds say, "The only friends of Kurds are the mountains."

Heroh visited and conversed with us for a short while, and then she moved on to check on others.

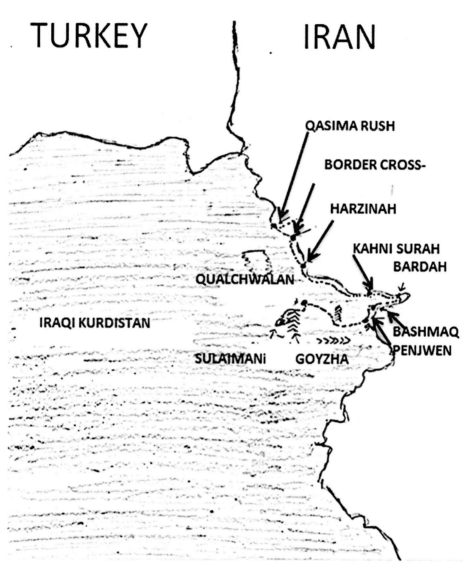

TURKEY   IRAN

QASIMA RUSH

BORDER CROSS-

HARZINAH

KAHNI SURAH
BARDAH

QUALCHWALAN

IRAQI KURDISTAN

BASHMAQ
PENJWEN

SULAIMANI   GOYZHA

Figure 8. Into the mountains yet again, my second journey

Qasima Rush had been an exchange center for the past few years. Merchants would meet here and exchange their goods. Both Iranians and Kurds alike made a living smuggling goods and services across the border during the eight-year war between Iraq and Iran.

However, this area is extremely rugged. Tall mountains surrounded a small valley, and a river ran through the middle, splitting it into two halves. A single, unpaved road led here from the town of Sardasht, a town of twenty thousand people located approximately thirty miles east of us. That was the only and the nearest city to us.

The next day we were awakened by the clamor of Iranian soldiers. The Iranians had just sent a team of twenty guards to watch us. Up to this point, the international community had no awareness of our situation; thus, no UN personnel or refugee agencies attended to our needs. We were on our own. Therefore, the next day, Talabani paid each of us a two-month salary to keep us going. Where did he get the money? I could not tell. This meant that somehow we had to purchase our food and necessities.

The first three days at Qasima Rush were arduous. Iranian authorities had not prepared basic accommodations because this place was not a refugee camp to begin with. A dozen abandoned doorless, windowless structures were carved along the side of the mountain. To the observer, they looked like homes from the time of cave dwellers. With only one dozen of those, the rest of us had to sleep on the ground at night without pads, pillows, or any kind of protection. The ground was our bed and the sky our blanket. Thankfully, after three days, our group—Hawar, his wife and daughter, his brother, Suha and I—were able to occupy one of those abandoned structures.

September was still a tolerable month to sleep outdoors, but by October and beyond, this place would become a refrigerator in the wild. After the first week, the UNHCR sent its first team to this makeshift camp. Quickly, they installed a number of small tents. They gave shelter to families first. Whatever was left over was distributed among the singles.

Two weeks after we left home, the partnership force of the Iraqi and KDP alliance offered an amnesty. Anyone who was willing to return to areas occupied by the KDP and surrender would be allowed to work and live in peace. To me, that would have been a great idea. I could have taken my niece back and returned her to her mother, unharmed. However, in doing so, I also would have compromised my loyalty to my political party, the PUK, my colleagues, and my goal of permanently leaving Iraq.

Meanwhile, Talabani had threatened and promised to launch a counterattack to regain every meter he had lost to the KDP. Over the next several weeks, the PUK Peshmarga, with the help of the Iranian government, prepared for a massive counterattack. I saw truckloads of ammunition and weapons being delivered by the Iranians to the PUK Peshmarga forces that had stationed themselves on the Iraqi side of the border under Talabani's leadership.

High-ranking personnel from the Iranian government visited Talabani a few times. They came in helicopters and motorcades, along with scores of Secret Service people. Rumors had it that the US had pitched several warnings and threats of its own against both Barzani and Talabani. The US demanded that both of them *get their act together* and stop the domestic fighting. This type of pressure favored Talabani, since he and his forces had lost the battle thus far. Barzani and Talabani were both scolded for cooperating with Iraq and Iran discreetly and indiscriminately.

After we had been living in the camp for three weeks, the amnesty grew more attractive and luring for Suha. She complained frequently and was extremely uncomfortable. Then the brilliant idea of using her as my messenger popped into my mind. Women and children abandoned the refugee camp for the life of the city on a daily basis. If I sent her back to Slemani, she would not be going it alone. There would be a number of other females who would travel the distance with her.

"Suha belongs with her mom. You are doing a wise thing by sending her back," said Rokhosh as I discussed my decision with the others.

Hawar also agreed with the plan. A six-year-old girl did not belong in a refugee camp, especially without her parents. Life was tough here—no electricity and no running water made it impossible to practice routine daily hygiene.

On September 22, 1996, I put Suha in the company of four women who were on their way back to Slemani.

"Go and bring your mom back with you," I gave her instructions.

In the Kurdish culture, there is something called *amana*, a binding word, or promise, by someone to keep an item or person in their possession until a certain purpose is fulfilled. For example, if I would ask these women to keep Suha in their *amana* until she reached Slemani, they would do whatever they could to keep her safe until the *amana* was fulfilled. Amana could apply to anything—cash, a secret, a house—anything. It is comparable to a bank safety deposit. I was confident that Suha would make it safely to Slemani.

The UNHCR erected new tents over the course of the next several days. They also installed a large plastic water tank that held back water flowing from the mountain spring for drinking purposes. Slowly, but surely, everyone moved into the newly built tent village. Hawar and I were the primary collectors of wood for burning and cooking. The neighboring mountains provided an endless supply of fallen branches and twigs.

On the first day of October, a Dutch man, who represented a refugee aid agency, drove through our camp. He made frequent stops, chatted with random folks, especially those who spoke any English. I walked up to him and started a conversation with him. He introduced himself as Manfred. He told me that he represented the UN. Then, Manfred said something that shocked me to the core. The US government was airlifting those individuals, and their families, who had worked for American agencies or had worked for agencies funded by USAID. It was Manfred's job to announce this news to the prospects.

Now I was uncertain about ACS's affiliation with USAID. I needed to find out if my NGO was included in this program. The only certain way to do so was to call Francesca. She would provide me with accurate answers.

My heart grew anxious, and my thoughts raced frantically. To have a chance of being airlifted to the USA would be a dream come true. Yet I was wedged into a refugee camp in Iran, without the freedom to move about and find the information I needed. Considering the impossibility of the odds, negativity and thoughts of self-defeat crept in, until I slipped my hand into my pocket and found Francesca's letter, which included her home phone number.

If only there was a way for me to call her, I thought to myself. I diligently asked camp inhabitants for a way to reach the nearest city. There were always those who ventured away from the camp and found ways to sneak out undetected. Finally, I spoke to a young man by the name of Hyder, who said that if I woke up early enough, before dawn, I could walk out of the camp by going around the entrance checkpoint.

"Then follow the trail for about half an hour. You will find a tiny hillside village where you can ride a minibus to the town of Sardasht," said Hyder.

Although Sardasht was a small town, it had international telephone bureaus, where, for a small charge per minute, one could call anywhere throughout the world, except Israel.

The night had not faded away yet, and the cock had not crowed when I sprang out of my uncomfortable bed. I sneaked behind the front gate checkpoint easily and then followed the dirt trail until the point Hyder recommended. There I stood waiting. As the eastern sky brightened right before sunrise, a minibus came. I took a seat at the very back of the bus and waited for other passengers to fill it up. One by one, villagers came in and each took a seat until the bus was half full. Then the driver turned on the engine, and away he drove. If memory does not betray me, I believe the fee was either twenty or thirty toman.

The driver picked up a few scattered passengers along the thirty-mile road to Sardasht. The countryside views made the slower-than-average ride easier to tolerate. Colors of fall displayed an astounding mix of orange, red, and gold on the trees. The scattered little hamlets on the mountainsides of Iranian Kurdistan looked like a painting from the classical era.

This nation had inhabited this region for thousands of years. The Bible mentions a few accounts about the Meads and Persians coming down from this region and freeing the Hebrews from enslavement under Nebuchadnezzar, the ruler of Babylon.

The vast majority of the Sardasht population is of Kurdish descent, which made communication with the native people relatively easy once I arrived in town. The locals informed me of several phone bureaus on main street that were open for business. In spite of their imposing name, a small shop, an attendant, and a telephone booth were all that constituted these so-called telephone bureaus.

The first shop I walked into was just opening for business. I greeted the young man sweeping the concrete floor in Kurdish. He responded courteously and welcomed me to his shop.

"Do you think I could make a phone call to Italy?" I asked.

"*Albetta* (of course)," he responded. "You must be from across the border." He could discern my origins because of the way I was dressed. A local could always tell who was from out of town and who was not.

"Yes, I am from Slemani," I responded.

"Ah, no problem," he said. "We are all brothers, welcome." Then he promptly ordered me a cup of black tea from the neighboring tea shop.

"Oh, you don't have to get my tea," I apologetically remarked. "I only need to make a phone call."

"No, no problem." Then he politely reminded me, "Isn't it a tad early to call Italy?"

I looked at the clock that hung on the opposing wall. It was 7:30 a.m., which meant 5:30 a.m. Italian time.

"You know what, you are right," I said. "I am early."

In my anxiety and excitement, I had totally forgotten about the time difference. The shop owner suggested I go eat breakfast and come back within a couple of hours. I thanked him for his kindness, and right before I left his shop, I asked, "How much would you charge for such a phone call?"

"It is forty toman a minute," he answered.

Before I thought about having breakfast, I remembered the wonderful public bathhouses available for a small fee. After asking for directions, I was led to a public bathhouse, and before I knew it I was feeling the warm water on my skin, inconceivably good after over a month of going without. I felt light as a feather afterward and was ready to tolerate the refugee camp for another month. Breakfast had an entirely different taste with a clean body compared to a filthy one.

It was about nine thirty when I began walking back toward the phone shop once more. I handed the man two hundred toman in advance and dialed the numbers. First, I dialed Italy's area code, then Padova, and then Francesca.

With every ring, my heart raced a bit faster and faster until I heard a click, then "*Pronto.*" A female voice responded, rendering me speechless and in a trance-like state. I did not know what to say. All this happened within a second, but it felt like an eternity.

"Francesca?" I inquired.

"*Si, come posso aiutarla?*" she responded.

"It is me, Ari."

"Ah, Madonna, I can't believe it!" she shouted in her heavy Italian accent. "Where are you calling from?"

"Long story," I said. "But I am in Iran right now. I heard that the US is airlifting people to America. Is it true?"

"Yes, yes, it is true. Brunelli asked Faraydoon for a list of names. Is your name included?" she inquired.

"No, I am in Iran stuck in a refugee camp," I explained. "Can you do me a favor? Register me?"

"Absolutely, of course," she said. "I will do that. Spell me your name and anyone else with you, please?"

I gave Francesca the spelling of my name.

She informed me that the US government airlifted only the individual who was employed and his or her immediate family. She needed to leave because she was about to head out to work.

Ecstatic with the news, I thought the refugee camp seemed much less intimidating. After all, I was only going to be there for a short time.

However, the journey back to the camp was not a cakewalk in any sense. First, finding a bus back to the village took a large portion of the day. No one knew if such a route was available, and I did not know the name of the village near the camp. I was having no luck until I scrupulously described the location to an elderly person who directed me to a tiny garage.

Half a dozen minibuses journeyed to the boonies, areas that one cannot locate even on a local map. Only two minibuses traveled to the proximity of Qasima Rush. One took off at eleven in the morning, and the second one at four in the afternoon. The second bus was my only choice since I had bummed around town for a little longer than I planned. The bus filled up with passengers rather quickly. We took off soon after some of the passengers recited the Muslim prayers of travel.

Several miles from the outskirts of town lay a few soldiers in wait. They set up a military checkpoint—something I had not accounted for or expected. The driver obeyed their signals ordering him to stop.

A stout plainclothes man climbed up into the minibus and began asking for IDs. I had nothing on me except my PUK television staff ID that I presented to him.

He took a glance at it, then looked at me and said, "You are an Iraqi Kurd, huh?"

I did not verbally respond to his inquiry.

The man paused for several seconds and then said, "I will let you go back this time, but if I ever see you here again, I will arrest you."

I kept my head down and did not stare at his eyes. The plainclothes man brushed his thick mustache and got off the minibus. He gave the hood a pat and waved his hand to the driver to let him know that he was free to go.

The westward sun reflected on the autumn's golden leaves, making the three-dimensional scenery even more spectacular than it was earlier that morning. By the time the minibus arrived at the neighboring village, only I and another passenger remained onboard. Everyone else had been dropped off at one of the farming communities scattered along this ancient highway.

The Iranians had already built a barbed wire gate to the makeshift refugee camp. The two sentinels guarding it let me in without asking a single question. Going back inside was easy. It was walking out that caused interrogations and stoppages, unless, of course, one bypassed them as I had that morning.

The camp was a contrast between hurried labor and the lack of it. Women and children congregated near the river. Some washed dishes. Some did laundry, and others partially bathed their kids. Men, on the other hand, came and went aimlessly, not knowing how to kill the abundance of time.

Hawar came sprinting toward me.

"Where did you go?" he asked. "Wow, you look clean and... wait, did you go to town." He crunched his lips, and before I could say anything, he gently punched my shoulder. "You bastard, why didn't you say something. I would have loved to go with you."

I stated to him that I went to the city for personal reasons. I did not tell him the details. From within, I was burning to convey to everyone that I might be flying to the USA, but sharing this information might have caused a backlash. First, I was on Iranian soil. Had they heard such a claim, they would have grown suspicious of me. They might have accused me of being a spy or an agent. I had not forgotten the pressure Etellat had put on me back in 1991. It was easy to get in trouble in a totalitarian country such as the Islamic Republic; moreover, there was slim chance of being acquitted. Secondly, my friends and coworkers would have begged me to take them with me or add their name to the list. I clearly recalled that Francesca said only the person and his immediate family would be helped.

Other than me, none of my siblings had left their homes this time around. Since I was the one who had worked for an NGO and the TV station, I had no choice but to escape. Iraqi troops had assisted the KDP Peshmarga to overcome the PUK, but they did not actually occupy the cities. Saddam was restricted under the no-fly zone mandates; therefore, Iraqi soldiers had not invaded Kurdish territories, only KDP Peshmarga did.

At the time, I did not know this. We on the move were driven by propaganda and false reports. The PUK media machine put out news that Iraqi mercenaries were killing Kurds at will; thus, intimidating everyone who was remotely associated with the NGOs and/or the PUK. Saddam would have risked an airstrike from the coalition forces for violating the no-fly zone established five years earlier by the coalition. All of this meant that the city of Slemani was still a bustling metropolis with business as usual, so to speak. Approximately thirty thousand to fifty thousand had left their homes. Compared with the mass exodus of 1991, this one was not noticed by the world media.

Outwardly, the civil war appeared to be over, establishing the KDP as the power in charge. However, secretly, the PUK leadership, with the help of Iran, was preparing its Peshmarga for an all-out assault to regain control over the territories they had lost to the KDP in the first round. Both parties betrayed their nation. The KDP associated itself with Saddam, an archenemy of the Kurds, and the PUK with Iran, which was not any better than Saddam when it came to its own political issues. Folks in the city assumed that the PUK had a massive meltdown, and that it was gone for good. Certainly, Talabani made it appear that way in a maneuver to surprise the KDP with a massive assault.

The days crawled by. Fall was approaching quickly and with it crisp, cool air. The dark, tall westward mountains blocked the sun earlier than its normal setting hour. Golden leaves twirled on the rugged dry ground of Qasima Rush, and the few thousand inhabitants hurried back to the warmth of their tents. The women fetched water from upstream and from the plastic tank that the UNHCR had installed on the south side. The men stood by the entrance of their tents conversing with their peers.

One such day, Hawar approached me with a solemn face. He asked if he could talk to me privately. As we walked some distance away from everyone else, I felt a gut-wrenching sensation, as if what he was about to say could not be good.

"You know I have hung with you so far," he said. "You are my friend, and even like a brother to me." His voice was strained, and his facial expression hinted of something foreboding.

"You are scaring me. What is it? Tell me, please," I anxiously pleaded.

"I don't know. I cannot be sure. But there is news of an accident..." He trailed off, as if he did not want to finish.

"Okay," I said, encouraging him. "Please go on."

"Okay, well." He paused, clearing his throat. "It was up the road, near the KDP checkpoint."

"Ah…but what does this have to do with me?" I asked.

"Well, they said the driver had two passengers, a woman and a child. The car was heading toward Qasima Rush. It was hit by a rocket. The bodies inside were charred and burned."

"And you are thinking what?" I asked him again, uncomprehendingly.

"We think it might have been your sister and her daughter."

His final words fell on my ears like stone on soft ground.

It did not sink in immediately. I stood numbly, trying to take in his words. Then I realized what he had said. My sister and niece were dead. I would never see them again.

I could not breathe. Involuntary tears sprang to my eyes. I asked no more questions. Instead, I fell apart, weeping uncontrollably. He held me, put his hands on my arms, and tried to hold me straight.

"That is why I haven't heard from them. They are dead."

Hawar placed his arms around my shoulders. "I'm sorry. I didn't want to tell you. We can't be certain. It could be someone else," he said as he tried to console me.

At that moment, an insane idea crept into my head. "I have to make sure," I said. "I am going back to Slemani. I need to know for certain. I have to."

Hawar did not try to object. He knew that when I made up my mind to do something, I was going to do it.

The Search

That night I mechanically packed a leather bag, wrapping up the cash in some clothing. With churning emotions, I set out walking early in the morning the next day. I was determined to find out the truth, although the ramifications of taking such a step were very serious for me. It would cost me my reputation as a faithful PUK member. The only way I could go back to Slemani was by surrendering to the KDP.

With anguished heart, I told myself that perhaps it was all a mistake, a case of resemblance. Many Kurds look alike. I could not bear to think that my sister and her daughter were dead.

On my way, I passed a few Peshmarga. They jeered at me and made sarcastic comments.

"What? Are you are going to surrender?" one of them shouted from behind me.

"The accommodations are not to your standards?" said another. "You are a coward!"

His last remark slashed a wound in my heart, I am not a coward. Love is my motive. War is not my goal. I chose to ignore the remarks. At this point, I did not care what anyone thought.

A narrow rocky trail led upward. The mountain was to my right, and a deep gorge carved by an unknown river nestled in its foothills. Only a few hundred feet from the KDP-controlled checkpoint, I saw it. The burned Land Cruiser had tipped sideways over and into the

224

gorge. I did not have the heart to take a second look. Instead, I chose to look ahead.

I arrived at the checkpoint at around sunrise. Torn between my loyalty to my party and my family, I had to make a decisive move. I could either continue forward or turn around and go back to the camp. I felt like a traitor and a martyr at the same time.

The KDP Peshmarga welcomed me back, and they were extremely polite. However, I understood this to be a mind game. Even though I was not a Peshmarga, they welcomed men to leave Talabani's camp. After all, that meant fewer men to fight against in case of a counterattack. Thankfully, these men cannot read my mind because I did not intend to stay in Slemani. My return to the camp was inevitable. I only needed to go to the city for a few hours, or perhaps a day. I certainly wasn't going to let them know that. I pretended to be someone who wanted to take advantage of the amnesty.

A tall, stout man had me sit on the floor, and then he did the same. He jotted down my name.

"So why did you escape from Slemani in the first place?" he asked.

"Because I worked for an NGO," I answered briefly and to the point.

"I see," he said. "Which NGO?"

"It is called ACS. They were from Italy," I answered.

"Okay, who did they represent?" he asked.

"I do not know. They were Italian," I responded.

"I understand," he continued. "But who brought them in? Which party invited them? Did the PUK or the KDP invite them?"

I had not realized that the NGO had to be invited by either party.

"I honestly don't know," I responded.

"All right, that's fine." He sprang up and walked back into a small concrete room. He came back with a piece of paper.

"This is a pass, and you can present it at the upcoming checkpoints. They will let you go without trouble. After all this is a no-questions-asked type of amnesty."

I took the paper, which contained my name and address. I left him, and proceeded down the hill and away from the checkpoint.

A few Toyota Coasters were parked along the road. The drivers intermittently yelled, "Raniyah! Raniyah!" advertising the destination to which they drove.

To the left, the fields of Raniyah stretched as far as the eye could see. Mount Qandil stood proudly to my right, her peak covered with white gleaming snow-like crystal. Another three hours separated me from Slemani, the city of my birth. I somehow got into a vehicle and began the first leg of my journey. My emotions felt like wood. My mind shuffled scattered thoughts. I wondered about my sister and my niece, Francesca hopped in between, the thought of embarking an airplane and flying to America intercepted. Daydreaming saved me from counting hours and minutes until the car reached its destination.

By noon, the Toyota arrived Raniyah. Here I would find larger buses to take me back to Slemani.

I dared not take time to eat lunch. The daylight was relatively shorter during autumn. I had to continue my travel as quickly as possible. I must have looked awful. My beard was long, for I had not shaved in over two months. My hair lay freely on my shoulders, curly and black. My face looked dingy and unwashed. People instantly recognized that I had not been in a town for some time. They stared and whispered to each other.

I decided not to wait for a bus. Instead, I hired a private cab for fifty dinars. By three thirty in the afternoon, we were on the outskirts of Slemani. The city looked peaceful, and the traffic flowed relatively easily. Except for the presence of KDP Peshmarga pickup trucks, one could not tell that there had been a civil war at all. The cab driver dropped me off at my old house.

My neighbor came out to greet me.

"Have you seen my sister and my niece?" I asked.

"I took them to Penjwen," he replied.

Relief washed over me, and I suddenly felt weak.

"You mean to tell me they are alive?"

"Yes, why wouldn't they be?" He looked at me with a puzzled expression.

Although Penjwen was the farthest point from me, it didn't faze me. I would gladly travel a thousand miles to reunite with them. They were alive!

"Okay. Well then, I must be on my way to Penjwen right now," I told him.

"At this instant?" he questioned me. He stared at me as if I were insane. "Why don't you stay the night, or at least eat some food?"

"Thank you, no. I don't have time. I must go now," I insisted.

"Well then, I will go with you." He walked back into the house, and within minutes, he was ready.

"No, please, you really don't have to come with me." I put up my hand to stop him.

"Don't be silly. I took them there. I am responsible for them as well," he replied with confidence.

I rented a private cab straight to Penjwen. The two-hour drive was an opportunity for me to take a welcome nap, for I was exhausted with exertion and relief. My neighbor and the driver chatted the entire way.

The sun had slipped behind the western sky when we pulled into Penjwen. I was once again back at the same little village where I had begun. The private cab driver requested one hundred dinars for his services, a well-earned fee.

The mosques had just finished the call for evening prayer, and scores of folks were leaving the mosques to go back to their homes. The tiny village did not have electricity, so the inhabitants enjoyed each other's company under flickering lanterns.

All day I had not eaten, and hunger began to creep into my consciousness. I realized that I needed to grab a bite. A local baker was about to close his shop when I caught up with him. The man gave us two pieces of freshly baked *naan (tandoori bread)* for one dinar. The traditional flat bread had never tasted more delicious.

The village did not have a hotel or a hostel. The only place that one could lay his head would have been the local mosque. We entered the main hall of the nearest mosque and asked the caretaker to let us spend the night. He promptly welcomed us and lit the wood heater to warm up the room. Typically, mosque floors are carpeted, as was this one, which allowed me to lie on my back and rest a little. Every now and then, a new guest walked in, and in a few short hours, the mosque was full of weary travelers.

A young newcomer walked in and took a seat next to me. We struck up a polite conversation. We exchanged facts about ourselves. I understood that he was in the Slemani police force and that he was here because he was fleeing the country.

"Do you know how far away the camp is?" I asked him, my curiosity peaked.

"Not too far," he replied. "I heard its right across the border. Before you can cross over, one must obtain a permit from the KDP security office here in Penjwen."

"Is it in exchange for money, or is it free?" I quizzed him.

"I don't know," he responded. "We will find out tomorrow. However, let us hope that they won't close the border."

"Who would close the border?" I asked in alarm. "The Iranians or the KDP?"

"The KDP." He lowered his voice and quietly whispered, as if he did not want anyone to hear him.

"Why would they?" I whispered in reply.

"Because they will suspend the amnesty," he said softly. "But they have kept it secret. We could get in trouble, if the amnesty is suspended. When will it be suspended? It could be any minute."

If the amnesty was suspended that would mean the KDP would not allow me to go across the border. I believed the KDP was expecting a major counterassault. Perhaps that was why they planned to suspend the amnesty and disallow traffic between the PUK refugees and the border towns of Iraqi Kurdistan. I knew that my sister and my niece were right across the border from me at that moment. Somehow, I had to reunite with them.

Dawn came early, and the sun seemed closer to the mountain from where I stood. Hungry and exhausted from traveling, I headed out to the *chaykhana*, the local tea shop, to have breakfast. My neighbor had already awakened. He was used to waking up early. He sat at the chaykhana, sipped his glass of tea, and struck up conversations with the rugged old men of the east. With my hair all shaggy, my beard long and thick, I walked up to him.

"*Bayani bash,*" I greeted him with the conventional morning greeting.

He responded with the same.

Figure 9. *Chaykhana,* serving tea at the tea shop

"Welcome," said the shop tender. "What can I get you?"

"Thank you, may you live long," I responded. "I would like a plate of cream of milk (*qaymach*) and sweet black tea and a piece of *tandoori* bread, please."

"Upon my eyes," said the shop tender. He turned away to fetch my order.

"Here is what I learned," said my neighbor as he slipped to the seat next to me.

"One needs a written permit from the KDP to cross the border. I do not want you to go inside their headquarters. I will do it. I will go in and get you a permit."

"How is that going to work?" I asked.

"I shall give them a fake name and pretend the permit is for me," he responded. "If you go in and ask for a permit, I don't believe they will give you one."

"Ah, I see, and then I could use the name on the permit as if it belongs to me," I concluded.

"Exactly, they are not going to double-check names. How could they? But I will not use your real name," he said. "Someone might recognize your name and cause you trouble."

The waiter brought me my order, and I enjoyed fresh-baked bread, sweet tea, and organic cream of milk.[30] When I was about to pay him for the food, I was shocked to find in my wallet my staff ID card from the PUK television station. I should have left it behind with Hawar.

I can't walk around carrying this damaging evidence with me. The ID card exposed me as a PUK member in an area dominated by the KDP.

Although I never considered the KDP to be my personal enemy, they, however, would have considered me an enemy of theirs.

It was true that at that time the KDP had offered an amnesty. However, the civil war was not over yet, and no peace treaties had been signed by the two parties. Moreover, the amnesty was shaky and subject to the whims and caprices of whomever one had to deal with.

Hamaali, my neighbor, left the tea shop to go to the KDP security office to obtain a permit for me. I waited for him at the tea shop. Across from me sat a young man sipping his sweet tea from a *glass finjan*. When I scrutinized him, I saw that he was the same man who had sat next to me in the mosque last night. I walked across the room and said to him, "Greetings, do you remember me?"

He looked up and smiled. "Farhad is my name," he said as he shook my hand. "Yes, I know you. I know who employs you. Your brother is my neighbor. I have seen you at their house from time to time. By the way, I loved some of your work, the pyramids, and the movie *The Beast of War*. Excellent work!"

---

[30]   Qaymach: an ancient dairy product made from risen cream of milk with a consistency of paste

"Thank you," I said as I shook his hand. "I am who you say I am."

Farhad and I struck up a conversation while sipping our sweet tea flavored with a pinch of cardamom. We both had the same goal and that was to cross the border into Iran.

Farhad took leave to go purchase a border permit. As soon as he left, Hamaali came back to the tea shop, his face pale, his hand shaking.

"What happened? Are you all right?" I asked.

"No," he said. "They wanted to arrest me. One of the men at the security office was from Slemani, and he recognized me. He accused me of lying and threatened to arrest me if I did not leave immediately.

You can figure out a way for yourself. You are a smart man. Be careful!" Scared and rattled, he hopped into a taxi and went back to the city.

Disappointed and desperate, I sat at the tea shop not knowing what to do. It was approaching noon, and Farhad had not come back yet. A young waiter, a different one, came to take my order once more. He asked if I needed anything besides tea.

"Yeah, a permit," I said as I stared at the floor beneath my feet.

"Psst," he whispered. "I can get one for twenty dinars."

"Here," I said without hesitation as I took the money out of my wallet and handed it to him. "Get me one, please."

At this point, I had no other alternative. He was either going to help me or hand me over to the KDP. The young man folded the money and put it in his pocket, turned around, and walked away.

Meanwhile, Farhad came back with a border permit of his own. His fake name was Umed Abdullah.

"How did you get this?" I asked.

"I bought it," he responded.

The young waiter came back with a piece of paper. He handed it to me.

"The name is Saeed Ahmad. Sorry, that is all I could manage," he said apologetically.

"Honestly," I replied, "I don't look like a Saeed, but at this point I don't care. Thank you very much for your help."

After paying the server for the tea, I quickly got up and Farhad and I headed out to look for a way to reach the border now that we were armed with permits. A few Polish-made minivans ran passengers between the little hamlets for a small fee. Farhad and I, all smiles, boarded one of them to go to the border.

Nearly a mile before the border post, the KDP Peshmarga had set up a checkpoint. Between that point and the border post, stretched a no-man's zone, it separated the KDP Peshmarga from the PUK. Beyond the border post was the entrance to the refugee camp that housed those who had fled their homes because of the civil war. All of this was connected by a narrow trail of unpaved road. An ancient highway, it was once used by mule riders and smugglers and later expanded by the Iraqi army to serve as the logistical line during the eight-year war against Iran, then the Anfal operations against the Kurds.

The worn-down Polish minivan arrived at the checkpoint about noon. The sun had climbed high in the sky already. KDP Peshmarga guards ordered the minivan to halt for a routine inspection procedure. I counted no less than twenty armed men with AK-47s at this station.

Their leader, a thin short man with a long mustache across his face, commanded the passengers to get out. Everyone cooperated, and we all came out of the minivan. He scanned the passengers, quickly recognizing from the way we were dressed that Farhad and I were the only nonlocal passengers. My tall, sturdy stature drew his attention, and he walked straight to me. He stood before me for a few seconds, staring at me and shaking his head.

"So," he began and then paused for a second or two, "why do you want to go to Iran?"

I was prepared for this question and had a clever answer ready.

"I am going to bring my family back," I replied politely. "They need to understand that it is safe to go home."

"Hmm," he murmured. He lowered his head and with his foot kicked the sand in front of him. He raised his head, looked me in the eye, swung his right arm, and struck me on my face as hard as he could. He burst into a violent rant, hurling profanities at me and everyone else.

"You are not leaving this country." he shouted. "Go back to where you came from. No one will pass beyond this point today by the orders of Massoud Barzani himself." He then yelled to the driver, "Your minivan, turn it around and take them back from where they came. Now!"

I was humiliated and outraged. I wanted to jump on his throat and strike him until he bled from his mouth. However, I knew I could not take on twenty men with machine guns. Broken and defeated, I turned around and climbed back into the minivan.

Farhad and I were dropped off in the middle of the local bazaar of Penjwen. It was the afternoon by now, and the marketplace hustled with business. With no place to go, we went back to the tea shop.

Business in the chaykhana had not slowed down either. Men ate lunch and drank tea. The young waiter hurried back and forth between the kitchen and wooden couches the guests sat on. He saw us from the distance and came up to us as soon as we sat down.

"What happened?" he asked.

I gave him the short version of the unpleasant encounter with the KDP official who slapped me on the face. Rumors went around that the KDP had decided to shut down the border based on new orders from their leadership.

Suddenly, things looked gloomy. Now it was illegal to go beyond the KDP final checkpoint. The no-man zone was empty of traffic, as the alert level was elevated by the KDP in anticipation of a PUK counterattack. That meant that I could not get back legally. I had to do it illegally. How? I had no way of answering that question.

A heavy man walked into the tea shop. In his late twenties or so, he wore a white buttoned shirt and charcoal-colored traditional baggy trousers. He looked around for a bit and then walked toward us as we sat on the wooden bench.

"Greetings," he said. "The server told me about your dilemma. I can help you. I know a way, a different route. We can bypass the KDP checkpoint."

"Where does that road lead us to?" asked Farhad.

"I will take you to northeast of the official border," he replied, "in the middle of the mountains. There you can go across easily. There is no one around for miles. It is totally safe."

"What do you ask for this service?" I asked.

He looked to his right, then to his left, then whispered, "Two hundred a person. I am doing this because I love Jalal Talabani. It costs me gas and wear and tear driving in the mountains. It is a rugged area."

Despite some skepticism on my part, we agreed to ride with him. The day was winding down, and we had no time to lose. Although occupied by the KDP Peshmarga now, historically, this area had been PUK sympathizers. That, we reasoned, brought some comfort that this man would not double-cross us. Moreover, if he had wanted to, he could have done it here in town, and he would have no need to drive us elsewhere.

"Farhad, I have to go," I said. "You don't have to come with me."

Farhad insisted that his situation also required him to leave the country and that he was going along with me wherever this man was going to take us. The Toyota Land Cruiser was parked half a block from the tea shop.

"It is a reliable car," said the man as he checked the oil level. "It doesn't need extensive maintenance either."

The sun had less than two hours to set by the time we took off. It slowly decreased westward.

Doves Don't Fly in Mountains

With the duffel bag that I purchased at the *bazaar* earlier; my wallet; and Farhad, my new friend, I headed into the mountains. The road was unmarked and unpaved. Our driver went slowly because of the steepness of the drop to the left. Carefully and skillfully, he drove deep into the mountains. An hour into the journey, the sun had already slipped behind the horizon. The gray dusk covered the sky above us. Farhad did most of the talking with the driver. I was not in the mood for small talk.

I slipped back into daydreaming again. This time my thoughts were intentional. I saw myself driving on American highways and speaking English to my future American friends. Oh, and I had an American girlfriend.

Cognitive dissonant slammed me when I beheld the scenery: I am still in Kurdistan. The harsh reality set in, but not without struggle.

Only a fragment over an hour had gone by when the driver made it known that we were approaching our mark. He pointed out a bend in the mountain and said, "You glimpse that bend? That is where we are going."

The surrounding mountains gave the place an eerie appearance. Sharp rocks dangled, and large boulders loomed ahead. Trees looked sickly and twisted, with bark dry and wrinkly.

The car slowly rounded a bend so close that it was almost touchable. As soon as we cleared it, the cocking of machine guns inter-

ARI BARZANJI

rupted the creepily quiet atmosphere. At least ten men with guns drawn rushed toward our car and shouted orders to stop. Bewildered, the driver shifted his car to park and raised his hands.

The men yelled for us to get out of the car. Because of the way they were dressed, they looked like KDP Peshmarga, although there was no way of telling. My heart trembled with fear. I could not imagine what awaited us next. Two of the armed men opened the passenger door and forced Farhad and me out of our seats. The driver got out voluntarily.

The militia leader, a vicious short, chubby man with a limp in his left leg, began hollering insults at me. He struck me with a wooden rod that he held in his left hand.

"You son of a pimp," he shouted. "Son of a whore." Then he commanded two men to take Farhad and me away. "Take the son of a dog to the back."

Never have I been as certain of dying as I was at that moment.

Once more, I was captured and beaten. I followed the two militiamen to the back of a recently constructed clay room. One of the men snatched my duffel bag out of my hand and ordered me to sit on the ground. Quickly, he unzipped it and looked through the contents. He found a towel, a toothbrush, items of clothing, and eight thousand dinar in cash.

I thought even if they didn't kill me they would take the cash and I could do nothing about it. The worst-case scenario was that they would kill me, take the cash, and dump my body in the middle of nowhere. No one would find me. No one would ever know what happened to me. All these thoughts bolted through my mind and made my heart tremble as I sat on the ground completely helpless, or so I thought.

To whom do I scream for help? Where does my help come from? There were no villages nearby, not even a shepherd was close. Then I remembered the hidden weapon I had used before. Five years ago on Mount Goyzha, I prayed to God—the True God, whoever He was. I asked for help, for protection, and He responded. Now I needed His help just as desperately. Although I was not a Christian, Jesus was the divine Name I had invoked five years ago and was about to invoke once more.

The militiamen ordered us to show our wallets. I panicked and grew even more frightened because nothing would condemn me like the evidence in my wallet. I carried two different identification forms, one by the name of Saeed Ahmad on a permit I purchased for twenty dinars. The other was my real name on my TV staff ID card that specifically showed me as a member of the PUK.

Unhurriedly, I took my wallet out of my pocket while I intensified my prayers. I asked God for help to save my life. I bowed my head as the gunman went through my wallet. He found my permit. He called me by the name on the permit.

"Kaahk Saeed," said the rugged-looking man. "You are a young, handsome man. Why do you want to be killed?" He paused for a moment. "Even if I let you through, the Iranians will shoot you dead."

Meanwhile, he kept rummaging my wallet. As I watched him from under my lowered eyes, I anticipated him blowing me away once he discovered my identity.

Yet somehow, miraculously, he missed it. He missed the PUK ID card. He did not see it or find it, although it was there. It was in that wallet, in his hands, right before his eyes.

Finally, he gave me my wallet back and said, "I order you to go back to Penjwen. Don't ever come back here again."

What? I could not believe my ears. Still, I expected him to keep my duffel bag with the cash. To the contrary, he returned that to me as well. As I took my wallet and duffel bag from him, I breathed a sigh of relief and raised my head to the sky to thank heaven for this miracle.

I looked up into the dusky blue sky, and there I saw a white dove flying in circles over our heads. The hair stood up on the back of my neck. The sight of a dove was extremely puzzling. These mountains were teeming with hawks and falcons, doves archenemies. For a dove to fly around freely in this area was like a suicide. For years afterward, I have wondered about what happened back there in that rocky, rugged mountain area of Kurdistan. Was it a miracle or not? Only God knows the true answer.

I sprang to my feet, feeling surreal. Everything seemed to slow down around me as if it were a dream or a twilight zone. Feeling almost bedazzled, I picked up my duffel bag and at a snail's pace headed back to the car. What just happened lingered in my thoughts even as I was exiting toward freedom!

They will shoot me from behind, I thought. *Any minute a barrage of bullets will penetrate me.* Step-by-step I approached the car. I opened the door and leaped in.

Farhad was already in the car. Then the driver took his seat. I had not known that the driver also received a beating. They blamed him for soliciting us. The ferocious leader ordered him to turn around and return us to Penjwen.

The driver turned on the engine, shifted into reverse, and backed up a short distance. Next, he turned his car in the opposite direction. Little by little, the bend came within reach. I still awaited a surprise, a change of stance from the gunmen. In an instant, surely they would call us back. All of this felt like a cat-and-mouse game.

Figure 10. A white dove circled over my head.

Finally, we were clear of the occupied area. Immediately, the driver shouted, "By God that was close." The driver went on and on, claiming that this had never happened before and that they must have just established this checkpoint.

I was speechless and motionless. My heart was heavy, and I felt drained. The experience of being ambushed by several armed men in the middle of the mountains made my life flash in front of me, so to speak. My mind kept replaying what had just happened—the interrogation, the inspection of my wallet, the dove flying above...

These thoughts raced through my mind throughout the drive to Penjwen. I paid no attention to how much time had gone by. Darkness had already fallen, and the stars flickered in the heavens. The quiet night was interrupted occasionally by the roar of the car engine as the driver attempted to avoid potholes and rocks on the trail. Long had it been since we left the clay room, or so it felt.

"Ten minutes," said the driver. "We should reach the main road fairly soon."

As soon as he merged onto the main road, headlights of another car flashed from the distance. In concert, both automobile operators flicked their headlights at each other. I guess it was their way of recognizing one another. As the car approached, our driver lowered his window. They exchanged words for several minutes, and then our guide turned around and said, "Listen, this man is my friend. He will help you to get out. Go with him. I trust him."

I glanced out the window at the second car, which had parked next to ours, and I saw the shadows of two men within. I paid our driver his fee, and we sprang out of this car to embark the second one.

"*Salaam Alykoom.*" I saluted the passengers and the driver. Two older men sat in the middle seats of the second Land Cruiser. They were robed in traditional Kurdish garments, and I assumed that one of them was a mullah, for he wore a turban. Farhad and I squeezed our slender bodies into the rear seat of the minivan.

"May you bring peace," said the mullah in the traditional salutation.

"Thank you. May God keep you hale and hearty," we responded simultaneously.

The second man and the driver conversed with the mullah in a respectable manner. They asked him religious questions, and he responded meticulously, giving answers that I personally had much experience with in my teenage days when I had studied Islam extensively. I contemplated the time when I practiced my faith with fervor and then the day my mother died before my eyes. I recalled the fateful day when my friend Zardasht furnished me with Darwin's book, *The Theory of Evolution*. I had lost my faith in religion in general. "Religion, it is nothing but opium for the masses." My friends and I had repeated these atheistic words of the philosopher Karl Marx.

Nonetheless, I was interested in a deeper connection with the Divine, a meaningful rapport, an intimacy with God. I had not found that connection in Islam, or perhaps a better way of saying it is that Islam had failed to reveal it to me. However, at that moment I sought to block anything religious from my mind. My haughty heart desired to deny that what happened few hours earlier was the work of a God, or the God.

And if it was, I considered it a metaphysical interference, entirely different from religion. I reminded myself that religion is not God. God is personal; religion is rituals.

Abruptly, the car came to a screeching halt. Another KDP night patrol blocked the road.

Not again, I thought.

"Shush, keep quiet," warned the driver.

Farhad and I kept silent in the back seat. A militiaman opened the door and popped his head into the minivan.

"*Salaam Alykoom*," he saluted.

"And peace be upon you as well," the mullah replied.

"*Hazarti*, mullah," said the militiaman. "Do you know the two seated in the rear?" He was referring to us.

"Aw, my boy," said the mullah good-naturedly, "it is late at night. Let them go. They are harmless."

We sat in silence, motionless but fretting inwardly. The seconds ticked away slowly. I waited, holding my breath. What this armed man should decide would shape my future. I was either in or out for good. I discerned that this third inspection by a KDP patrol would make a damaging case against me.

Instead, he closed the door tightly, tapped on the hood of the car, and motioned with his hand to the driver to move out. Just then, I realized that it was at this checkpoint that the man had struck me in the face earlier today. Miraculously, they let us go this time, and we entered the no-man zone, the line that separated the PUK and the KDP. Miracle after marvel had come my way all day today. Someone was watching over me.

Several minutes later, our guide pulled over to the dusty curb.

"Go now," he said.

Farhad and I stepped out of the car and into the bleak dark night of the east.

"Glance to your left," the driver requested. "Do you see that lantern shining its light out of the window? Go to that house, knock on the door, and tell them that I, Abdurrahman, sent you. They will know what to do."

Like blind men, we probed our way through the unkempt landscape until we reached the wooden door of the house.

Clunk, clunk! I knocked with an ancient metal handle that had hung on this door for the past few decades. The undersized mud house looked more like a hobbit home than a regular dwelling. Wooden beams protruded from the side of the roof, as did yellow hay mixed with mud.

A man opened the door. He wore traditional clothing, as did all inhabitants of this area. After I greeted him, I passed on the message from Abdurrahman. He at once offered us a warm welcome and invited us into his house.

Immediately, he called upon his wife to serve us dinner. The woman quickly warmed up some bulghur and served it in a comely ceramic dish. The *sawar* (bulghur) and vegetable stew tasted out of this world; after all, neither of us had had anything to eat in the past twelve hours. We ate our fill and replied to our host's questions.

"I only need to go to the refugee camp on the Iranian side," I explained. "So does this man." I pointed at Farhad.

Our host confirmed his sympathy for the PUK. He advised us to wake early in the morning. His brother would smuggle us behind the enemy lines before the sun rose.

The visit with these local folks lasted a few hours, and we had discussed various topics. Now it was time to disperse. The host apologized for the lack of room in his house. He suggested we sleep in the stable for the night.

The stable was a small mud hut filled mostly with fodder for the animals. Farhad and I headed out to the stable. We each found a spot to rest our heads for a bit.

"Good night," said Farhad. "Think five-star hotel." He laughed lightly.

"I am glad," I said. "We should have laughter after the erratic day we have had."

Farhad agreed with that statement.

Sleep did not visit me smoothly that night. I lay awake thinking. Time crawled by, and I was forced to pay attention to every creak and groan the livestock produced. I tossed and turned.

Before dawn had cracked the thickness of the night, the young man who was supposed to spirit us out of the country walked into the stable. None of us exchanged many words. Instead we simply jumped up and followed him. Due to the darkness, I did not see much of his facial details, but he seemed to be a younger fellow and of average height. He too wore the traditional clothing. A donkey and a dog accompanied him.

He led the way through the ravines. About a mile into our journey, he forced his dog to go back by hurling rocks at him. He did not speak unless spoken to. I assumed he needed us to be quiet for fear of enemy patrols. I, personally, had no idea where we were, except that it was a rugged landscape, something familiar to me now. After all, I had strolled through rougher ones.

Daylight broke in the east. The sun was shining, and its warm golden rays sneaked between the crevasses of the surrounding mountains. Approximately four hours had gone by when our young guide pointed out a watchtower ahead of us. He began whistling and waving his hands to the man who stood on the tower.

"*Xomanaya, Xomanaya!*" he yelled. "They are on our side."

We had bypassed the no-man's zone and arrived at the territory controlled by the PUK. The green flag of the party fluttered atop the building next to the tower. Suddenly, our worry lessened now that we no longer were subjected to KDP authorities. Joyously Farhad waved his hand at the men who guarded the watchtower. What village was this? I did not ask. I paid my young guide twenty-five dinars to his joy and gratitude.

"No," I said to him. "I am the one who is grateful to you. You saved my life."

The guide, whose name I did not learn, and we parted ways. From where I stood, the fence that separated the two countries was detectable. Guarded by two uniformed Iranian sentinels, the gate to Iran was only a stone's throw away. The sentinels were from the *Passej* force, common volunteers. They watched over two short wooden poles and a barbed entrance. One of them spoke Turkmen.

"*Gun Ayden, Nasselsen agha,*" I greeted him.

He replied politely.

"We want to go to the refugee camp," I said as I pointed ahead.

"Go right ahead," said the Passej sentinel.

A narrow gravelly trail stretched ahead for the next half mile to where several tents could be seen. Farhad and I stepped into the country of Iran legally and unopposed. The Passej did not even frisk us.

This is my third time and, hopefully, the last, I thought. From afar, I saw a crowd of people assembling around a large beige tent. Out of the center of the crowd, a child emerged and began playing in the dirt.

"Interesting," I said to Farhad. "That little girl is wearing a coat similar to the one my niece had."

As I walked closer and closer, it became clear to me that it was her.

"Oh God, that is my niece!" I shouted.

I ran toward her as fast as my weary legs could carry me. I swooshed her up in my arms and lifted her in the air. I turned her around and indeed it was my niece. Tears ran down my face. My emotions overwhelmed me and a consciousness of love engulfed me, rendering me heedless of my surroundings.

Suha looked at me in surprise. It took her a moment to recognize me. Then her small, short arms wrapped themselves around my neck. She embraced me as tightly as her tiny arms could and kissed my face with her dusty lips. She wept tears of joy, as I did! I had missed her a great deal, and at one time I thought she and her mother were dead. Our embrace lasted a long time. Her dark eyes shone like the moon.

The large mountains dropped their slopes right into the camp and provided a stunning background for this reunion scene. I was too occupied with my niece to notice that Farhad had disappeared.

Then I realized someone else was missing. Where was Suha's mother? Why would she let her daughter play in the dirt unsupervised? I lifted my head and looked around. To my surprise, we were surrounded by as many as fifty people gawking at the emotional sight. Some wiped their own tears, and others smiled joyfully. Then there was a roar of applause. A theater-like reception was what they gave us. Hands patted my shoulders, and words of congratulations comforted me.

Nevertheless, my sister had not yet appeared.

A dreadful sense came upon me that something was not right. When I asked about my sister, no one dared to share details with me.

A woman waved at me from inside her tent. She gestured for me to come in. I observed a solemn look on her face. An elder man also joined us in the tent.

"It was a tragic accident," said the old man. "She and some women were caught in between friendly gunfire near the river. They were fetching water from the river during daylight. Nevertheless, the Peshmarga began firing at what was thought to be enemy scouts. The women dispersed in an attempt to save their lives. Unfortunately, your sister did not make it."

"May your heart be comforted," said the woman sadly.

A moment ago, I had wept with joy. Now I cried out with grief. I was saved from certain death more than once, but now another person was plucked out of my life. Nothing comes without a price. Who knows what the ultimate purpose of life is? Who could predict the future and plan their lives accordingly? Had I known this was going to happen, I would not have sent a message with Suha to fetch them. Sadness, anger, and joy mixed in a single moment, like a candy dish covered with poison.

"Where is the body?" I choked, submerged in a pool of conflicting emotions. "Did they retrieve her?"

"A message was sent to her husband yesterday," explained the old man. "They temporarily buried the body on the Iraqi side of Kurdistan. You might have passed it on your way here."

"Your niece was well taken care of by Muzhda khan and me," said the woman.

Then a red-haired, freckle-faced young woman stepped into the tent. She saluted every one and took a seat on the rug that lay on the floor, as if she heard her name called out.

The woman sad, "This is Muzhda."

Muzhda expressed her grief and thanked God for my arrival to the camp safely.

"I am very sorry about her mother," she said, referring to my niece. "May God forgive the dead and give them access to Paradise, and may God grant us patience."

I found out that Muzhda was the sister of Nawzad, my former boss at the TV station. The solidarity of the people and the support my niece received amazed me and humbled me.

I took my leave to step out of the tent and breathe some fresh air, trying to clear my head. Farhad was nowhere to be spotted.

I wonder where he went, I thought numbly.

The refugee camp was comparatively small with limited room for privacy. Little Suha came running to me when she saw me standing by the tent. Her small hand slipped into mine, and we went for a walk. I stroked her hair and wondered what was next for us.

A group of people congregated at the clearing between the tents. I learned that they were awaiting a bus ride to Qasima Rush. Interestingly, the Iranian government provided transportation between Penjwen camp and Qasima Rush. Instantly, I registered my name for the next ride available. They informed me that one would be leaving at four in the afternoon.

Suha and I lingered around the tiny camp for the next few hours while we awaited the bus. Never again did I see Farhad or know anything about his whereabouts, and when I described him to people to learn if they had seen him around the area, no one had any idea what I was talking about. Who was the strange man who had spent an entire day with me traveling through perils? I would never know, for he had disappeared just the way he had appeared in my life.

The minibus was already full and ready to take off when we slipped into our seats. The four-hour drive to Qasima Rush stretched to six because of security precautions. We had to stop every now and then for an inspection and head count. Nevertheless, the landscape of the western parts of Iran provided a distraction. Most of the way the bus cruised on paved roads except for the last leg of the trip, which was when we veered off to the gravelly portion of the journey. I knew then that we were closing in on Qasima Rush.

We arrived at our destination about ten o'clock that night. I spent that night with Hawar and his wife and their tent.

The next day, the UNHCR quickly allocated me a private tent, food, burning oil, a heater to cook with, a plastic bottle for water, and a few blankets to use.

The rest of my friends welcomed Suha and me back with open arms. For the next few days, I received condolences from nearly everyone who knew me or knew of me.

Coming to America

In mid-October of 1996, the PUK Peshmarga launched a furtive all-out attack on the KDP positions, from the gray mountains of Penjwen all through the black boulders of Qasima Rush. Jalal Talabani did not stay behind; instead, he moved along with the foraying troops. Without the help of Saddam Hussein, the followers of Massoud Barzani abandoned their ramparts and fled. Within a week's time, PUK Peshmarga recaptured the majority of the territories they had lost to the KDP a month and a half earlier. The city of Hawler (Erbil), the capital of southern Kurdistan, was spared. The boys of the green flag roamed the craggy terrains unreservedly.

Hawar came storming into my tent one day to give me news about the man who had struck me in the face.

"Justice is served." He smiled widely. "He hit you on the face, did he not? Well, he will never be able to raise his hands again," he declared as he pumped his fist. "They killed him in the battle."

Surreptitiously, the US State Department had issued warnings to both Barzani and Talabani to cut it out and get their act together. Despite Talabani's request for help from Iran, the Americans gave him the green light to launch the stealthy attack. Slemani was taken back within a few days. Now we were free to go back. Droves of refugees left Qasima Rush and went home.

In another matter, Saddam survived a coup attempt organized by the Americans in tandem with the Iraqi opposition groups, mainly the Iraqi National Congress. The US State Department issued a public safety law that granted political asylum to all those who participated directly or indirectly in the conspiracy to overthrow Saddam. The US Congress also approved a $10 million rescue operation for those who had worked with American and European NGOs.

I saw the need to speak to Francesca once more before I went back to Slemani. I seized an opportunity to make the dreaded journey back to Sardasht to call her from the phone service bureau. Francesca clued me in about the procedure to gain asylum. She said to meet the American delegation at the Turkish border. From there they would airlift me to an unknown destination.

"The border town of *Ibrahim Khalil*," said Francesca. "That is where you need to go."

The little town of Ibrahim Khalil is the gateway between Iraq and Turkey. However, that place teemed with KDP Peshmarga forces. A man in my position would have to be extremely stealthy to escape detection by them, especially since the two parties had not arrived at a mutual agreement to end the civil war.

Meanwhile, in a speech aired on the radio, Talabani invited all refugees to come home. The once-heaving camp of Qasima Rush emptied its residents by the end of October. I was one of the very few who stayed behind, only to give in eventually and move back to Slemani.

Back in Slemani, Muzhda, Hawar, and his family were a great help with babysitting Suha while I tried to take care of matters. I reckoned that to travel through a KDP-controlled area, the stealthiest ways would be necessary in order to escape in a hurry. Francesca had told me that Faraydoon, the coordinator, would be in Ibrahim Khalil, the small border village that separates Iraqi Kurdistan from the country of Turkey between December 8 and 15.

To prevent fraud, the Americans required all NGO managers and directors to be present at the time of entry into Turkey. While impatiently waiting for the month of December to arrive, I consistently contemplated my new life in America. *What would it be like? What would I do for a living? Where would I live?* I had countless other questions that I had no way of answering.

I did not see the need to rent a place or hold on to any possessions. I sold every piece of furniture I had, and I lived like nomads, moving from house to house.

December approached and Suha and I were excited to leave the country for good. I used my imagination and devised a sly way to travel from Slemani to Ibrahim Khalil without being detected. On December 8, my niece and I disembarked the private cab I rented in the city of Zakho, another border town approximately fifteen miles southeast of Ibrahim Khalil, and I rented a hotel room for us.

That night I had a dream. In my dream, Bill Clinton, who had just won a second term as US president a month earlier, came to visit me. I gave him a tour of my town. The next night, I dreamt of Kevin Costner. He sat on my couch and talked about his movie *Dancing with Wolves*. My subconscious mind was preparing me for the journey.

"We are going to America, girl," I said to Suha. "Give me a high five." I was excited and did not quail at the thought of going to America, mostly because I desired a better future for us. It was the "land of opportunity," as the saying goes. Who knew what she would become if she grew up in the USA?

The wind blew the fallen leaves over the sidewalk as we trotted our way to the restaurant next to our hotel room. The sun shone less intensely as autumn waned for the advent of winter. The fighting between the PUK and KDP had already ceased, but no reciprocated agreement had been reached yet. However, the fighting divided Kurdistan into two parts: northern, from Zakho down to Hawler and the lands in between controlled by troops loyal to Barzani, and southern, from Kalar to the outskirts of Hawler controlled by troops loyal to Talabani. Each leader played on people's emotions and promised to be the deliverer. They tossed around political mottoes, promising an independent Kurdistan, a separate country from Saddam's Iraq.

Faraydoon arrived in Zakho from Ibrahim Khalil within two days' time. He stationed himself at the ACS facility located north of the town. I already knew where to find him because of Francesca. She had given me the information during our last phone conversation.

The first cab driver I hired knew exactly where the building was, and he whisked me there in a few minutes. Holding my niece's hand, I walked into the ACS building.

To my surprise, all my coworkers were already there. Faraydoon was on the phone in the main office.

"I have a $600 plane ticket," he shouted into the receiver. "I cannot miss my flight back to Italy."

Khazhal and Bayan, two of my female coworkers, leisurely sipped their cup of tea as they chatted. Bayan raised her head and saw me walk in.

"Hey, handsome," she said. "Come, sit with us."

I walked briskly and took my seat next to them while I held Suha's hand.

"Hush, don't say stuff like that," I said. "We are still in Kurdistan."

"Screw it," she responded. "I don't care anymore because I am going to America. Ha, ha." Pertly, she then blurted out, "Khazhal thinks you have manly shoulders."

"Stop it," Khazhal said, placing her hand on Bayan's mouth as her face blushed with shyness.

"Manly shoulders are better than not having any, I guess," I jokingly responded.

"Faraydoon said that the Americans have a schedule," said Bayan. "It is based on the number of employees. Evacuation is supposed to go on for the next two weeks. Our turn is on Friday. There are a total of three thousand souls to be evacuated. That will take some time."

This meant a few more days in hotel rooms and dining at restaurants. On Tuesday, December 10, 1996, I ate my breakfast and headed out to the ACS office. When I arrived, everyone was at the building except for two male coworkers. Faraydoon had just announced the names on the list. As soon as he saw me walking in, he immediately called me back to his office.

"I need to tell you something," he said. He had a somber look on his face, and his tone sounded ominous.

My heart fretted and twitched. I expected bad news. I swallowed hard.

"Yes, what is it you need to tell me?" I asked.

He held a piece of paper in his hand and looked down at the wooden floor for a short time.

"Is this your name?" He pointed at a name on the paper. "I don't think this is right. Your name is not on the list," he continued hurriedly.

I glanced at the list, and indeed my name was not on it. Heaviness fell upon me, like a thick veil of darkness. Hopelessness, dread, and gloom overtook me.

"Why isn't my name on the list?" I asked. "Francesca jotted them down in the correct spelling."

"I know," he responded. "She gave me the names. I do not know what happened. The FBI agent must have screwed things up."

"What do you mean the FBI agent screwed up?" I exclaimed.

"Well, I had to fly to Washington, DC," he explained. "I met with the FBI because they wanted to make sure the names of the evacuees and their family members were correct. This is the final list. I am sorry, but I cannot change the FBI listing. This means you are not going to America." He sounded cold and uncaring.

"You don't understand," I said as tears ran down my face. "I have to go. I've lost everything. There is nothing left for me in this country. I have lost my family and home. You must help me." I begged him to do something, but he would not budge.

I thought about my niece, who was outside playing with Bayan. I thought about my future in Iraq. There was absolutely nothing left there for me. The NGO had left the country, the TV station had fired me because I had lingered in Iran longer than I should have, and my house had been looted.

Just as I had begun to believe that my life was taking a good turn, this news hit me like a brick. I left Faraydoon's office feeling as if the world had collapsed around me.

Suha received me with a smile. I am a man without a country, and she does not know that. I am without a family and without hope. *God, why are you doing this to me?* I called out in my heart.

We went back to my hotel room. I locked my door and wept the entire afternoon. Suha climbed onto my lap. She lifted my head and said, "It is going to be okay."

I determined not to give up. I quickly changed to street clothes, took Suha with me, and hailed a cab. I asked the driver to take me to a place where I could make an international phone call. Soon I was dialing Francesca's number.

"Pronto," she said.

"Francesca, it is me, Ari, again." I broke down and cried on the phone.

"What is the matter?" she asked in alarm.

Hysterical and panicky, I spoke in a speedy manner. "Francesca, Faraydoon says my name is not on the list. I can't go to the US. I don't know what to do. Please help me."

"Oh, Madonna!" she shouted as she inhaled a deep breath. "That skunk. Before he flew to DC, I gave him your name and your family's. Ugh, he is a dubious man. I never trusted him."

"I don't know what to do," I said. "Please tell Brunelli, call the FBI, and call the US government…anything. Please help me."

Worried, she replied and said, "I promise you I will do everything I can to help you. And I will go to church to pray for you."

We hung up the phone. I was surprised that she said she would pray for me. The dreadful thought of God interfering in my life again did not please me. After all, didn't he allow all this to happen to me?

My morale at its lowest, my spirit dim, and my heart broken. I held back tears, and my throat dried. I sluggishly placed the phone recover back in its place, turned around, and walked out of the building, oblivious to what went on behind my back.

Meanwhile, the very moment she hung up the phone with me, Francesca called Mr. Brunelli. He was in Padova at that time. Brunelli instantly called Faraydoon and yelled at him for his screw up. He ordered Faraydoon to help me and make me his priority.

The next day, as soon as Faraydoon saw me, he once again called me into his office. He was furious with me.

"How dare you? You called Italy. What do you think they will do for you? I am the one who can help you, not them. You should not have called," he fumed.

"Wait, yesterday you told me you could not help me. Now you're telling me you can?" I asked him.

"Oh well," he mumbled. "I will see what I can do."

Brunelli must have threatened him. That was why he was so furious.

"I have to set up a meeting with the American delegate in Ibrahim Khalil," said Faraydoon. "The man in charge has to review your case, and I will plead for you. We will see what happens. I cannot promise you much."

After a slight pause, he seemed to think of something. Suddenly, he spoke in a much calmer tone, as if he was a different person.

"What is today?" he asked.

"Wednesday, December 11," I replied.

"Okay, good," said Faraydoon. "We are scheduled to leave on Friday the thirteenth. I have to ask the Americans to postpone our departure until the fourteenth."

I left ACS headquarters and went back to my hotel feeling less stressed. I held Suha's hand while we slowly climbed the stairs at toddler speed. On my way up, I ran into an older woman.

"I am sorry, my boy," she said in her frail voice. "I noticed you were weeping yesterday. Whatever it is, I shall pray for you." I noticed that she wore a crucifix over her long black garment.

I was astonished. "Okay, whatever," I sarcastically remarked.

"I have been already praying for you, my boy. I have been already." She gently placed her hand on my shoulder and gave me a nudge.

"Don't you need my name to pray for me?" I naively asked.

"God knows your name," she replied. She continued her descent down the stairs.

I shook my head in disbelief and went on to my room. God again. This being doesn't seem to leave me alone.

The next two mornings were cloudy. On and off rain fell from the gray clouds. I hung around in my room and never had the courage to visit ACS.

On the eve of the scheduled departure, I went to speak to Faraydoon and inquire about the latest news.

"Nothing new," he said. "Here is what you need to do." He continued to explain the procedure. "You must come to the border with your niece. There, the Americans will review your case. It is entirely up to them to let you out or reject your case."

With these words, I left his office to spend my last night in Zakho, or perhaps in Iraq.

Saturday, December 14, Suha and I packed our belongings and rented a cab to the ACS house. Three minibuses were booked by ACS to drive its employees from the city of Zakho to the border town of Ibrahim Khalil. There NGO employees were called by name, and they and their families proceeded to the inspection station.

The Turks then received the evacuees and conducted their own inspection, name verification, and interrogation. A picture of each individual was then taken.

The line of people awaiting permission to enter into Turkey stretched a long way. The evacuees stood before a small metal gate to a two-story tan-and-beige building that was safeguarded by a number of armed men.

We arrived sometime near midmorning. A busload of Kurds had just departed and crossed the bridge that linked Iraqi Kurdistan to Turkey. I beheld the bus leaving with its jubilant passengers singing and clapping. For a moment I wished I were on that bus, worry-free and looking forward to my new life in the "land of opportunity."

I noticed that one by one, names of heads of household were being called in. *What went on behind that metal gate?* I wondered.

Faraydoon stood outside the building, and when everyone who was ACS employees had arrived, he called for a short outdoor meeting.

"This is an American humanitarian act," he explained. "Operation Pacific Haven is the name. It includes those who worked for the Iraqi opposition and for NGOs. You will be given a chance to apply for political asylum in the USA. Once approved, you will move on to Turkey, where they will do their own inspection and interrogation.

"Each family and single person then will be escorted to a large bus for a seven-hour drive to Batman Airport. From Batman, airplanes shall take off to Abu Dhabi, refuel, then to Colombo, Sri Lanka, to refuel one last time. From there you will be flown directly to Anderson Air Force Base in Guam. Please be respectful of authorities, do what you are told, and good luck to all of you." He paused for a few second. "I cannot answer your questions. At this point I am just as informed about things as anyone else."

Every single one of my coworkers was lighthearted and carefree. They looked forward to their free trip to America. I, on the other hand, was a nervous wreck. I did not know what to expect or what awaited me behind that metal gate. Would they approve me, or would they tell me to get lost? One would have a promising impact on my life, and the other would be devastating.

The gatekeeper called out the names. With every name called, I grew more anxious. After an hour, the man finally called my name. Right before I raised my hand to show I was present, I noticed another busload of people leaving the building toward Turkey. This time it was full of ACS employees. They happily waved good-bye as the wheels of the bus hit the metal bridge.

I waved my hand in the air. "Present!" I yelled. With every beat, my heart pumped faster. I felt as if the whole world was isolated from me, and I walked with my niece holding my hand. My senses were numb. I could not hear or feel the air surrounding me.

I stepped in beyond that dreaded metal gate and into a small room. A panel of five men sat at a long table. Four Kurds, including Faraydoon, and an American observed me as I entered the room, holding my niece in my arms.

I instantly began pleading my case. "Please believe me, I worked for ACS. Someone made a huge mistake and forgot to put my name on the list."

One of the men told me to go and wait on the second floor. With Suha in my arms, I climbed the stairs that led to a half-empty room furnished with nothing but two chairs and a couch. Half an hour later, a second applicant walked in. This time it was a man, his wife, and two sons. He had worked for NGOs for the past four years, but he left his position only days before the civil war erupted and his manager had omitted his name. However, he believed that he should be included in this free trip. Then a third one came in. This man had both his parents on the list but his little sister was not on it. He pleaded for her to be included.

According to the instructions, only one applicant among the three of us would be allowed to move on to the States. I reckoned that I had the weakest case among them; after all, one man had worked four years and the other only needed the addition of one name to his list.

An hour and a half went by when finally Faraydoon came upstairs.

"I am going in soon to discuss the cases," he said. "Only a single case shall be approved."

Why does everything in my life have to be such a nail-biter?

A group of men went into the room opposite the one we occupied, and they closed the door. The clock on the wall ticked away. The seconds, minutes, went by slowly; and the room seemed as cold as a winter's morning. Every time the door opened, my heart jumped in my throat in mixed anticipation and dread.

Suha sat next to me patiently. My head down, I rubbed my palms together nervously as the clock continued ticking.

Then the door opened and an energetic young man stepped into our room. He stood at the entrance. He looked at the paper he held in his hand.

"Ari and Suha," he read from the paper. He lifted his head, expecting one of us to answer.

"Yes, that's me," I replied.

He spoke a few muffled words quietly and unceremoniously. My heart pounded in my ears. I was not certain I had heard correctly.

"What do you mean?" I anxiously asked.

"You are going to America." His voice cleared up behind the veil of ether.

I was not sure how to react, seconds passed by slow and firm. My heart and mind fluttered simultaneously, like someone shook them. My legs unintentionally thrust my body couple of feet upward. My throat and my eyes struggled to which one will cry from joy.

"Yes!" I screamed in ecstasy. I jumped up and down uncontrollably and repeatedly. I kissed the man on the cheek. Faraydoon came out smiling. He stretched out his hand to shake mine. Instead, I hugged him, and in the Middle Eastern style, I kissed his cheeks.

Tears ran down my face.

"Thank you, thank you very much!"

About the Author

Ari Barzanji was born in the shadows of the mountains of Iraqi Kurdistan, into a culture rife with conflict, war, and inconsistencies. He experienced the wrath of war at an early age when, during the Kurdish insurrection, the government of Baghdad killed his elder brother and sent his lifeless body to his parents. Ari grew up dreaming of a better life because he found no home in his surroundings. He yearned for peace and freedom, concepts as elusive to his culture as the wisp of mist playing on the mountaintops. He graduated from the University of Baghdad with a bachelor's degree in food technology and human nutrition.

In the middle of the nineties, the political circumstances forced him to flee his country and live in a refugee camp in Iran. Afterward, and thanks to Operation Pacific Haven, organized by the US Department of State, he and four thousand Kurdish individuals were airlifted to Guam. While in the states, Ari continued his education and now is a pastor at an American church. He authored several books and does speaking events in his spare time.

Ari and his wife live in the mountains of the West Coast and enjoy several hobbies.

CPSIA information can be obtained
at www.ICGtesting.com
Printed in the USA
VOW07s1549030517
2929LV00002BA/345/P